The United States and the Iranian Nuclear Programme

The United States and the Iranian Nuclear Programme

A Critical History

Steven Hurst

EDINBURGH
University Press

Edinburgh University Press is one of the leading university presses in the UK. We publish academic books and journals in our selected subject areas across the humanities and social sciences, combining cutting-edge scholarship with high editorial and production values to produce academic works of lasting importance. For more information visit our website: edinburghuniversitypress.com

© Steven Hurst, 2018

Edinburgh University Press Ltd
The Tun – Holyrood Road,
12(2f) Jackson's Entry,
Edinburgh EH8 8PJ

Typeset in 11/13 Adobe Sabon by
IDSUK (DataConnection) Ltd, and
printed and bound in Great Britain.

A CIP record for this book is available from the British Library

ISBN 978 0 7486 8263 8 (hardback)
ISBN 978 0 7486 8264 5 (webready PDF)
ISBN 978 0 7486 8266 9 (epub)

The right of Steven Hurst to be identified as the author of this work has been asserted in accordance with the Copyright, Designs and Patents Act 1988, and the Copyright and Related Rights Regulations 2003 (SI No. 2498).

Contents

Acknowledgements

This book has been a long time in its gestation and has gone through various iterations over that period of time. I would like to thank those who have read and commented on those earlier versions, including John Dumbrell, Eddie Ashbee and the participants at numerous conferences, most notably those of the American Politics Group of the Political Studies Association and the US Foreign Policy Working Group of the British International Studies Association.

I would also like to extend my thanks to the British Academy, which generously provided me with funding from its small grants scheme that facilitated the research for the book. Thanks also to those former policy-makers who agreed to be interviewed by me in the course of my research – Bruce Riedel, Allen Keiswetter and Paul Pillar, and to the editorial team at Edinburgh University Press for putting up with my ever-extending deadlines for completion of the manuscript.

Finally, as ever, my greatest debt of gratitude is to my wife, Sam Faulds, who had to put up with more complaining about lack of progress and bouts of despair at the seeming impossibility of ever finishing than she has had to with previous projects. She did so with her usual grace and good humour, for the most part.

Abbreviations

ADA	Atomic Development Authority
AEC	Atomic Energy Commission
AEOI	Atomic Energy Organization of Iran
AIPAC	American Israel Public Affairs Committee
AP	Additional Protocol
BOG	Board of Governors
bpd	barrels per day
CIA	Central Intelligence Agency
CW	chemical weapons
EO	Executive Order
ERDA	Energy Research and Development Administration
EU	European Union
FBR	fast breeder reactor
FDI	foreign direct investment
FY	fiscal year
HEU	highly enriched uranium
HWR	heavy water reactor
IAEA	International Atomic Energy Agency
ILSA	Iran and Libya Sanctions Act of 1996

IRGC	Islamic Revolutionary Guard Corps
IRI	Islamic Republic of Iran
JCPOA	Joint Comprehensive Plan of Action
JPA	Joint Plan of Action
KWU	Kraftwerk Union
LDC	Less Developed Country
LEU	low enriched uranium
LWR	light water reactor
MEK	Mojahedin-e Khalq
MNF	multinational facility
MOIS	Ministry of Intelligence and Security
MW	megawatt
NIC	national identity conception
NIE	National Intelligence Estimate
NMD	National Missile Defense
NNWS	non-nuclear weapons states
NPT	Treaty on the Non-Proliferation of Nuclear Weapons
NSC	National Security Council
NSDD	National Security Decision Directive
NSDM	National Security Decision Memorandum
NSG	Nuclear Suppliers Group
NSSM	National Security Study Memorandum
OIC	Organization of the Islamic Conference
OPEC	Organization of the Petroleum Exporting Countries
PHRC	Physics Research Centre
PNE	peaceful nuclear explosion

SNIE	Special National Intelligence Estimate
SNSC	Supreme National Security Council
START	Strategic Arms Reduction Treaty
SWIFT	Society for Worldwide Interbank Financial Transactions
TRR	Tehran Research Reactor
UN	United Nations
UNAEC	United Nations Atomic Energy Committee
UNSC	United Nations Security Council
UNSCR	United Nations Security Council resolution
WMD	weapons of mass destruction
WTO	World Trade Organization

Introduction

> One definition of insanity is doing the same thing over and over again, getting the same results over and over again, yet expecting a different result every time from the one you got last time. If you accept that as a working definition of insanity then our policy toward Iran has been certifiably insane for nearly three decades.[1]
>
> Again and again, domestic considerations have driven foreign policy stances.[2]
>
> It has been one of the defining features of US–Iranian relations over the past fifty years that Iran's domestic politics have been the most important among a range of forces determining their course.[3]

On 14 July 2015 Iran, the United States and the other members of the P5+1 signed an agreement to resolve the conflict over the Iranian nuclear programme.[4] Two and a half years later President Donald Trump announced that, if that agreement was not substantially rewritten to impose new restrictions on Iran, 'the United States will not again waive sanctions in order to stay in the Iran nuclear deal'.[5]

Trump's declaration conformed to a number of traits which had come to characterise American policy toward the Iranian nuclear programme. In the first place, despite protestations to the contrary, Trump acted unilaterally, failing to consult states who were joint signatories to the Joint Comprehensive Plan of Action (JCPOA) and whose support would be necessary for the effective implementation of any new strategy. Secondly, his decision was strongly influenced by domestic political considerations. Finally, he paid no heed to how his actions were likely to resonate inside Iran. In all three aspects his behaviour mirrored that of his predecessors, with the notable exception of Barack Obama, the president who had been able to reach a nuclear agreement with Iran precisely because he had deviated from the established patterns of US policy. Under Trump, however, the 'insanity' that had characterised America's Iran policy for the previous three decades had returned.

This study examines the history of American policy toward Iran's nuclear programme. The JCPOA represented the culmination of a thirteen-year period in which the nuclear issue was *the* bone of contention between Iran and the United States, and of a much longer period during which it had been a more or less prominent concern. Many aspects of this history remain hotly contested: at a political level, whether the JCPOA represented a victory for the USA (with Iran successfully prevented from developing nuclear weapons) or for Iran (which retained the ability to operate the nuclear fuel cycle and the capacity to 'break out' and develop nuclear weapons) remained a live issue in both countries, as Trump's actions indicated. Amongst scholars there was disagreement as to the deal's merits as well, but also over how to explain it. For some the JCPOA was a product of effective coercion by the US and its allies.[6] For others it resulted precisely from Obama's recognition of the failure of American efforts to force Iran to give up control of the fuel cycle.[7]

Connecting these questions, and accounting in part for the differing answers given to them, is a further question: What exactly was (is) Iran's 'nuclear ambition'? For some analysts Iran's intention to develop nuclear weapons was never really open to question. Unsurprisingly, those in this group tend to overlap with those who regard the JCPOA as a coercive success for American policy, given the distance between Iran's assumed ambitions and what it had settled for.[8] Directly opposed to that perspective are those who claim that Iran never had any intention of developing weapons and was only ever interested in peaceful nuclear power. For such observers American policy has been a travesty of unjust persecution and a disastrous failure. The JCPOA might finally have recognised Iran's right to enrich, but only after years of unnecessary conflict and sanctions.[9] A third line of argument suggests that there never was a definitive 'Iranian' position on the question of nuclear weapons. For some observers there is simply insufficient evidence that there was ever a clear decision one way or the other.[10] Others argue that, while there was consensus in Tehran on securing the fuel cycle, some policy-makers wanted to develop weapons whereas others rejected them in order to secure objectives such as access to global markets, security guarantees and a recognition of Iran's right to a more prominent regional role.[11] From this perspective the question of who gained most from the JCPOA is a much more complex one, since it is not merely a question of whether the 'USA' or 'Iran' won but of which groups within each state 'won'. This argument also brings the efficacy of coercion into question.

This study seeks to provide clearer answers to these and other questions, in the context of an analysis of US policy toward the Iranian nuclear programme between the early 1970s and the signing of the JCPOA in 2015. While the majority of analysis of the nuclear relationship has focused on the period since 2002, and the disputed questions above focus on the eventual outcome of the nuclear stand-off, a fuller understanding and better answers to those questions are gained by placing these issues in a wider historical context.[12] What happened in 2015 was not simply the end point of a dispute that began in 2002, when Iran was revealed to be in violation of its safeguarding agreement with the International Atomic Energy Agency (IAEA). The US–Iranian (nuclear) relationship goes back much further than that, and what happened in the twenty-first century was profoundly shaped by what had happened in previous decades.

The Nuclear Problem

As will be demonstrated, the wider US–Iranian relationship has had an enormous impact on the evolution of the nuclear question. Nevertheless, the nuclear issue also has its own specific dynamics, at the core of which lies a fundamental technological problem:

> The development of atomic energy for peaceful purposes and the development of atomic energy for bombs are in much of their course interchangeable and interdependent. From this it follows that although nations may agree not to use in bombs the atomic energy developed within their borders the only assurance that a conversion to destructive purposes would not be made would be the pledged word and good faith of the nation itself.[13]

As the authors of the Acheson–Lilienthal report thus recognised at the dawn of the atomic age, any state that developed the capacity to produce nuclear energy would also have most of the technical know-how required to build nuclear weapons. In an attempt to manage this inherent problem, the international community has created a non-proliferation regime, built around the IAEA and the Nuclear Non-Proliferation Treaty (NPT). Designed to allow states to develop peaceful nuclear energy whilst simultaneously providing guarantees against weapons development, the regime in practice achieves neither end satisfactorily, while simultaneously creating further tensions.

As with most such regimes, the rules of the non-proliferation regime were written by the dominant states in the international system, which also happened to be the states that already possessed both nuclear energy and nuclear weapons.[14] Consequently, while the regime nominally has three key objectives – to prevent the proliferation of nuclear weapons, to support the development of peaceful nuclear energy, and to facilitate nuclear disarmament – the real emphasis of the regime has always been firmly on the first of these. Progress toward nuclear disarmament has been negligible and support for the development of nuclear energy in non-nuclear weapons states (NNWS) extremely limited, with Washington, in particular, opposing NNWS being given the means to develop the complete nuclear fuel cycle. The non-proliferation regime is thus regarded by many NNWS as embodying a fundamental double standard, in which their right to peaceful nuclear energy is discounted in favour of non-proliferation.[15]

Nevertheless, whilst the bias of the NPT regime is clearly toward the objectives of the nuclear haves, it is far from entirely to their satisfaction. No state was willing to sign up to a regime that would permit the degree of intrusion that would be necessary to ensure beyond doubt that its nuclear programme did not involve any surreptitious weapons-related activities. Consequently, the regimes of reporting and inspections that do exist are quite limited (the IAEA can only inspect declared nuclear facilities) and have failed to provide a watertight guarantee against nuclear proliferation.[16]

Despite the efforts of the international community to resolve the nuclear conundrum, therefore, the issue of nuclear energy and nuclear weapons proliferation remains inherently problematic. The fundamental technical dilemma is irresolvable and the regimes that have been put in place to manage it have failed wholly to satisfy anyone. The NNWS who wish to develop nuclear energy regard the NPT as rigged against them and abused by the nuclear powers to deny them their rights. The nuclear states, for their part, and the USA in particular, remain unsatisfied with the degree of security against proliferation provided by the regime.

US–Iranian Relations

Conflict and distrust between the nuclear haves and the nuclear have-nots is thus built into the non-proliferation regime. As a consequence, and as is demonstrated in Chapter 1, the nuclear issue caused significant tensions between Washington and Tehran even when the two states were allies. Since 1979, however, that inherent problem has been dramatically exacerbated by its embedding in a wider relationship of conflict and hostility.

Chapter 2 provides an overview of how American involvement with Iran has served to produce the mutual demonisation which now characterises US–Iranian relations. On the American side this is, above all, a product of the Iranian Revolution, an event that not only produced a regime which seemingly opposed every American objective and interest in the Middle East, but which did so in the name of an ideology, and in a manner, both of which were profoundly alienating to Americans. The foreignness of a regime which claimed to govern in the name of Islam, the outrage resulting from the Iranian hostage crisis, and a widespread and casual racism all combined to produce a thorough demonisation of the Islamic Republic of Iran (IRI) in the American mind.[17] The incomprehensibility of the regime's ideology and behaviour led all too readily to the conclusion that the IRI was led by irrational religious fanatics who could not be understood or reasoned with, only relentlessly opposed.[18]

The IRI thus became what Ali Ansari has described as the 'quintessential Other' – a state both utterly alien and antithetical to the United States.[19] In its most extreme form this 'othering' led to assertions such as that of Alan Dershowitz, who claimed that Iran was 'the world's first suicide nation – a nation whose leaders have not only expressed but, during the Iran–Iraq war, demonstrated a willingness to sacrifice millions of their own people to an apocalyptic mission of destruction'.[20] This profound antipathy toward the IRI inevitably had consequences for any assessment of its nuclear activities – the assumption that Iran was intent on developing nuclear weapons, for example, was rarely questioned. The conclusion that such an outcome must be prevented at all costs inexorably followed, since the rational logic of nuclear deterrence, which had thus far served to prevent a nuclear conflict, would not apply to religious fanatics.

The history of recent American–Iranian relations is as central to the Iranian perception of the United States as it is to the American view of Iran. In the Iranian case, however, it is the American role in the 1953 coup in Iran, Washington's subsequent support for the Shah's dictatorship, and its backing of Saddam Hussein in the Iran–Iraq War which form the core of the narrative.[21] In this narrative the United States is the 'Great Satan' – the imperial power ruthlessly exploiting and oppressing Iran even as it hypocritically asserts its noble intentions. This United States claims to be the apostle of democracy and an upholder of international law, yet it staged a coup, sustained a dictator and supported the aggressor when Iraq invaded Iran. This United States is an exploiter and an aggressor, and Iran its innocent victim.[22]

Just as the IRI did for the United States, therefore, America became the other against which Iran defined itself. However, whilst direct experience with the USA was the proximate cause of this development, Iranian antagonism toward the United States was fuelled by other aspects of the Iranian worldview, at the heart of which is a powerful Iranian nationalism. Historically, Persia was one of the oldest and greatest civilisations in the world, and modern Iran, whether ruled by the Shah or the IRI, has regarded itself as the rightful successor to the Persian Empire.[23] That sense of Iran's significance has been challenged, however, by modern Iranian history, which is one of successive subjugations by external powers – the Russians in the early nineteenth century, the British in the late nineteenth and early twentieth centuries, and the United

States after World War II.[24] This combination of self-conscious great power status and successive humiliations has generated an extremely powerful nationalist sentiment, an acute sensitivity to any indication of a lack of respect, and an 'almost obsessive pre-occupation with outside interference in Iran's internal affairs'.[25] These characteristics, in turn, have greatly exacerbated the Iranian sense of injustice with regard to American behaviour.

Iranian nationalism has also had important implications for the nuclear relationship. In the first place, the acute status-consciousness translates into an assumption that Iran can and should be a nuclear (energy) power, since mastery of nuclear technology is a requirement and symbol of great power status. According to Iran's Supreme Leader, Ayatollah Ali Khamenei, scientific progress is 'the secret of economic, political and military power'.[26] The nuclear programme was the primary manifestation of Iran's scientific progress and for both the Shah and the IRI, therefore, it was a *sine qua non* of Iran regaining its rightful place in the world. The nuclear programme consequently took on an enormous symbolic significance for Iranians as a manifestation of their country's capabilities.[27] To a greater extent than almost any other country, Iran has developed a powerful 'nuclear myth' in which nuclear progress and the possession of nuclear technology have become measures of national status and a source of national pride.[28] As one Iranian policy-maker put it, Iran's pursuit of its nuclear programme was 'as much about earning respect for Iran as about developing nuclear power'.[29]

Iran's sense of its national rights and its high degree of sensitivity to any perceived slighting of them, moreover, have made Iran a leading critic of the double standards of the non-proliferation regime. The belief that Iran has an absolute right to the fuel cycle under the terms of the NPT, and that the American rejection of that argument is an abuse of the non-proliferation regime and a deliberate attempt to prevent Iranian development, was shared by both the Shah and the leaders of the IRI. While that sense of double standards is widespread, moreover, in the Iranian case nationalist sentiment and the memory of past humiliations have produced an extreme reluctance to accept them. The defiance which has thus resulted has been described by one observer as Iran's 'arrogance of nonsubmission'.[30] In short, Iranian nationalism, and the place that the nuclear programme came to hold within Iran's sense of itself – as a symbol of scientific achievement, independence and national pride – more or less guaranteed that demands that Iran abandon its nuclear ambitions would be met with a fierce and implacable resistance.

Diplomacy and Domestic Politics

Iranian nationalism and the mutual hostility resulting from the recent history of US–Iranian relations thus go some way to explaining the course of the nuclear relationship. The extent of their impact, nevertheless, was also a product of a third crucial factor, namely the way in which they interacted with the domestic political institutions and processes of each country.

No single theoretical lens can capture the course of the US–Iranian nuclear relationship over the decades. Geopolitics provides some insight; Iran's strategic position in the Persian Gulf, the United States' role as the global hegemon, and the centrality of Gulf oil to the global economy all serve to ensure that Washington will take a keen interest in Iran and regard a hostile regime in Tehran as a threat to American interests.[31] Nevertheless, the structure of the international system alone does not account for US–Iranian conflict. Though the Shah sought to make Iran the dominant power in the Gulf, he chose to do so whilst retaining America's friendship. Only when he fell did the United States and Iran become enemies. Ideology and belief systems are also, therefore, of importance. The revolutionary Islamic ideology of the IRI is central to its antipathy toward the USA, while the image of Iran that evolved as a result of the Iranian Revolution ensured the development of an equally ideological dimension in US policy toward Iran.[32] While ideology thus provides a useful lens through which to examine US–Iranian relations, it also has its limitations, however – while hostile ideologies are pervasive in both societies, there is clear variation in the degree to which they have shaped the behaviour of individual policy-makers. Presidents Hassan Rouhani and Barack Obama, for example, manifested the influence of dominant ideologies to a far lesser extent than did Presidents Mahmoud Ahmadinejad and George W. Bush. At key moments, not least in relation to the signing of the JCPOA, the role of the individual has made a difference to the course of events.

Geopolitics, ideology and individuals all play a part in the analysis offered here. The primary theoretical lens employed, however, emphasises a different variable, namely domestic politics. In a seminal article published in 1988, Robert W. Putnam characterised diplomatic negotiations as a 'two-level game'.[33] In this conceptualisation 'level one' is constituted of the relationships between governments while 'level two' refers to the relationships between governments and their domestic constituencies. Putnam's fundamental proposition is that, given that the key priority of any government is to remain in power, international negotiations can only be brought to a successful conclusion if the agreement reached is acceptable not only to the governments in question but also to their domestic constituencies. Agreements which meet both criteria constitute the 'win-set' of a given state. It is a central proposition of this book that throughout the course of the US–Iranian nuclear relationship, domestic politics has had a major influence on the policy positions of both sides and has typically ensured that there has been no overlap between the win-sets of the two states at any given time.

Three sets of factors are crucial to determining the nature of each state's win-set: level two preferences and coalitions, level two institutions, and level one negotiators' strategies. The first of these has, to some extent, already been addressed. As a consequence of events since 1979, the vast majority of Americans hold an overwhelmingly negative view of Iran.[34] Any action that can be seen or represented as making a concession to Tehran thus leaves policy-makers open to attack. In the words of Thomas Pickering, 'anytime we try to communicate directly with Iran, the message has to be written in such a way that the message in the needle could pass through the hole of domestic political considerations'.[35] A Department of State official put it more bluntly, describing Iran as the 'third rail' of American foreign policy politics.[36] On the Iranian side hostility toward the US government is equally prevalent.[37] When combined with Iranians' attachment to the nuclear programme as both a 'right' and a symbol of national pride, this leaves limited room for manoeuvre. Any action perceived as surrendering Iran's 'rights' will face a political backlash. In sum, the pervasiveness of a profoundly hostile perception of the 'other' means that 'a reward structure exists in both countries which encourages severance of relations and punishes those who want to improve the situation'[38]

The extent to which level one negotiators need concern themselves with such perceptions depends, nevertheless, upon the extent to which the institutional structures in a given country compel them to pay attention to the preferences of domestic constituencies. The more democratic a country, Putnam argued, the more policy-makers would be constrained by domestic politics.[39] In some instances this is simply a matter of electoral considerations. Both George H. W. Bush and Barack Obama, for example, were inclined to pursue engagement with Iran on their election but ultimately held back from more meaningful action partly because of their preoccupation with being elected to a second term.

In the case of the United States, however, the key feature of the level two institutional context is Congress – 'the U.S. separation of powers imposes a tighter constraint on the American win-set than is true in many other countries'.[40] While Congress exercises far less power in relation to foreign policy than it does in domestic affairs, several of the policy areas in which it does have the capacity to exercise real influence – trade, sanctions and the ratification of treaties – have been central to US–Iranian relations and to the nuclear problem.[41] The significance of this congressional capacity to shape policy is compounded by the factors motivating its behaviour. The average member of Congress is driven first and foremost by considerations of re-election, and policy matters are typically viewed through that lens.[42] When it comes to foreign policy this approach typically produces one of two standard responses: either ignore the issue entirely because constituents have no interest in the matter, or take a position which does not alienate any of those constituents.[43] Since there are no votes in being nice to Iran, opposition to any policy which might be seen as insufficiently tough on that country is generally guaranteed by such an approach to policy-making.

A further factor reinforcing congressional hostility toward Iran is the openness of Congress to the influence of lobbyists and the formidable organisational and financial capacity of the Israel lobby. As Bruce Riedel expressed it:

> the US–Iranian relationship is a trilateral relationship because, to paraphrase the late Princess of Wales, in this marriage there's always a third party in the bedroom, and that's the Israelis. . . . And their influence is enormous . . . and complicates the bilateral relationship in many, many ways.[44]

Israeli influence on American policy toward Iran operates in two dimensions. Firstly, there are direct government to government relations, in the course of which Israeli policy-makers lobby their American counterparts directly and seek to persuade them of Iran's malign intent. More important, however, is the way in which Israel has exerted influence over the perception of Iran within wider American society and in Congress. Israel and its American allies, such as the American Israel Public Affairs Committee (AIPAC), have worked tirelessly to fuel negative images of Iran in order to limit the room for manoeuvre available to American policy-makers in both Congress and the executive branch.[45] The former, however, are far more susceptible to the effects of this lobbying, and throughout the period under examination we find repeated examples of Congressional intervention constraining the freedom of manoeuvre of the executive branch as a result.

According to Putnam's logic, domestic political considerations ought to have been less of a concern for Iranian policy-makers, given the authoritarian nature of successive Iranian regimes. In practice, however, domestic politics has, if anything, been an even greater influence on Iranian policy than it has been on that of the USA. The reasons for this lie in both the particular nature of the Iranian policy-making process and the centrality of relations with the United States to Iranian foreign policy.

If there is one conclusion that all analysts are agreed on with regard to the nature of the Iranian policy-making process, it is that it is both complex and opaque. According to one group of scholars, 'the large number of institutional and non-institutional actors, family ties, personal relationships, overlapping institutional authority, and mixture of religion and politics all contrive to make it difficult to identify who has a say on what issue'.[46] In the first instance this complexity stems from Iran's institutional arrangements, which involve a mixture of elected bodies – the Majlis (Iran's legislature), the presidency and the Expert Assembly – and unelected religious bodies – the Guardian Council, the Expediency Council and the Supreme Leader. In addition there are institutions which sit outside the formal political structure, such as the Islamic Revolutionary Guard Corps (IRGC), which nevertheless have significant political power.

Broadly speaking, the religious bodies have more power than the elected bodies, and the Supreme Leader has the greatest power of all, with the Constitution of the IRI giving him a supervisory role over all branches of government.[47] Nevertheless, the Constitution also grants formal powers to the other institutions in the same areas as it grants them to the Supreme Leader. Indeed, it typically grants powers to several institutions in the same policy area. The end result is a situation in which 'institutions with similar or competing roles often check or balance out each other's powers [and] perform overlapping functions' and where no single power centre dominates permanently.[48] While the Supreme Leader presides over this competition, he is not typically able to determine its outcome unilaterally. He is not a dictator – a powerful enough coalition of the other institutions could, should they deem it necessary, remove him from power.[49] In practice, therefore, he typically negotiates the competition and seeks to forge coalitions favourable to his objectives or acts as a balancer between factions in order to maintain regime stability.[50] Even Ayatollah Ruhollah Khomeini, who was a far more charismatic and powerful Supreme Leader than his successor, Ayatollah Ali Khamenei, was unable to impose his will on every occasion.[51]

Political competition within Iran is not just, or even primarily, one between institutions, however. Overlying the institutional infrastructure is an equally complicated pattern of political factions. These are not formal political parties so much as 'loose coalitions among like-minded individuals or groups and . . . personal patronage links'.[52] Each faction is, in turn, comprised of smaller groups and loyalty to them is typically weak and often to a particular individual rather than any coherent ideology. Nor is there always a clear distinction between factions on certain issues, with cross-factional alliances being commonplace but also varying from issue to issue. Factions also appear and disappear as well as transforming over time. The result is a fluid and complex form of political competition in which it can be hard confidently to identify the 'party line' of a given faction at any time on a given issue and/or who is a member of that faction. The lack of formal names generates a further problem of accurate and consistent labelling – different accounts indicate the existence of different numbers of factions and employ different terms to describe them.[53]

For all the ambiguity and uncertainty that thus results, the balance of power between different groupings within the institutional structure of the IRI is crucial to determining what policy position prevails. Some attempt to determine what factions exist and when, what their policy positions are, and what degree of influence they hold, is consequently vital to an understanding of Iranian policies.[54]

It is contended here that, by the mid-1990s, there were three reasonably clear, if fluid and evolving, factions of real political significance in Iran. All were committed to the maintenance of the current Islamic regime but diverged in their views of precisely what that meant and how it was to be achieved. The first of these factions was the pragmatic conservatives, whose key representatives in the period under study were Presidents Akbar Hashemi Rafsanjani and Hassan Rouhani. The policy positions of this group have been described by one observer as conforming to the 'Chinese model'.[55] For them regime survival was best achieved by a combination of continued political repression allied to a degree of social and economic liberalisation. The latter measures, by producing economic growth and a greater degree of social freedom (decreased restrictions on dress, music and interaction between the sexes, for example), would, it was felt, be sufficient to keep the majority of Iranian citizens satisfied. In foreign policy terms they favoured a policy of 'détente' with the USA and improved relations with the rest of the world in order both to facilitate better integration into the global economy (and thus economic growth) and to minimise external threats to the regime.[56]

The second important faction was the reformists. This group is a good example of the fluidity and transformation of Iranian factions over time. Many of the reformists, such as Mir Hossein Mousavi, were originally among the most radical and anti-American leaders of the IRI. By the mid-1990s, however, they re-emerged as the most liberal of all the factions. They shared with the pragmatists a commitment to economic and social liberalisation but also argued for a degree of political liberalisation as well. They believed that regime legitimacy could only be maintained by emphasising the democratic rather than the theocratic elements of the Iranian Constitution, as well as improving the Iranian people's standard of living. In foreign policy they also sought to minimise conflict and integrate Iran more fully into the global order so as to enhance economic prosperity and stabilise the regime. The reformists had come to the conclusion that American hegemony was a reality of world politics that it was futile to seek to alter. Some, such as President Mohammad Khatami, were even optimistic that a degree of normalisation between the two countries might be possible.[57]

The third and final faction of note was the hard-line conservatives, with the Supreme Leader and President Mahmoud Ahmadinejad most prominent amongst them. Again, this faction demonstrates the fluidity and complexity of Iranian factional politics. Initially dominated by reactionary clerics, it was later expanded by the emergence of the Ahmadinejad-led Islamic Developers Coalition, or 'Abadgaran' group, in the early 2000s. That development, however, also subsequently complicated matters when the hardliners began to fight each other, as well as the other factions, for power. In policy terms the hardliners can be understood as ideological purists. For them regime legitimacy was best ensured through a commitment to the original values of the Revolution and the theocratic dimensions of the Constitution. Domestically, they opposed both social and political liberalisation. In foreign policy they were committed to the continued export of the Islamic Revolution and confrontation with the imperial powers, led by the USA. Whereas the reformists argued for the need to come to terms with the reality of American hegemony, the hardliners remained committed to the objective of overthrowing it.[58]

These factional divisions, in turn, had important consequences for the nuclear issue. Reformists and pragmatic conservatives, to different degrees, sought to integrate Iran into the global economy and to accommodate it to the realities of American global hegemony in order to secure the regime through reduced international isolation and an improving economic performance. The pragmatists and reformists consequently came to reject the pursuit of nuclear weapons because they understood that the international isolation that would result would undermine their larger objectives. Hard-line conservatives, in contrast, continued to pursue a foreign policy of confrontation and rejection, seeking to sustain regime legitimacy by rekindling the flame of revolutionary ideology. For them isolation held no fear and continued confrontation with the USA only helped to rationalise the need for a nuclear weapons capability. The factional balance of power in Tehran consequently had enormous implications for US policy toward the Iranian nuclear programme.[59]

That fact, in turn, had significant implications for the final factor in Putnam's model – the negotiating strategies of each government. Looked at through the lens of domestic politics, those strategies have the potential to shape the win-set of each government in two ways. They can influence the perceptions and attitudes of each government's own constituencies, but they can also affect the views of the other government's constituencies as well. By and large, in both cases, the behaviour of the American and Iranian governments has tended to narrow the win-sets rather than to expand them.

To a great extent this fact is a product of the demonisation of 'the other' which characterises popular perceptions in both countries. This creates a circular and self-reinforcing process in which rhetoric is honed and policy crafted with more than half an eye on appeasing domestic audiences rather than on effective communication with the other government.[60] By endlessly repeating existing narratives about the other side's inherent wickedness, policy-makers further embed those tropes and contribute to the constraints upon their own room for manoeuvre. In many cases this is a by-product of simple political opportunism, but in others the action is quite deliberate. Hardliners on both sides have had a vested interest in stoking the hostility of their own citizens against the other country in order to undercut the political position of those who would seek to find a resolution to the conflict through compromise.

Such deliberate provocations have also been evident in relation to the effects of each government's actions upon the domestic constituencies of their opponent, an effect Putnam refers to as reverberation. There have, for example, been instances over the years of hardliners in Iran engaging in actions deliberately designed to produce a backlash in the United States in order to undermine diplomatic engagement.[61] For the most part, however, such effects have been a product of ignorance and a lack of consideration, rather than active calculation. Putnam quotes Glen Snyder and Paul Diesing to the effect that, for the most part, governments do not even think to consider the impact of their actions on domestic constituencies beyond their own, and even when they do, they 'generally do not do well in analyzing each other's internal politics in crises'.[62] Such has certainly been the case in the relationship under examination, in which a combination of profound ignorance of the domestic political context inside the other state, a preoccupation with appeasing one's own domestic constituencies, and a lack of concern for how actions reverberate on the other side has characterised actions on both sides. On the American side in particular, we find policy-makers repeatedly pursuing actions which reverberate in the Iranian context in ways which reinforce the position of hardliners and close off the possibility of a resolution to the nuclear dispute.

While domestic politics has thus been a central factor shaping both countries' policies, it was suggested above that it imposed a larger constraint on Iranian policy-makers than those in the United States. In part, it was suggested, this was a product of the particular nature of Iranian factional politics. But it is also, and perhaps primarily, a product of the relative significance of each country in the mindset of the other. Whilst the hostility of the American public toward Iran may be comparable to that of Iranians toward the United States, American policy-makers generally had greater domestic room for manoeuvre simply because Iran was not constantly at the forefront of American thoughts. There were other enemies – the USSR and Iraq – who were of greater concern in the 1980s and 1990s. Iran, while loathed, was not seen as a significant threat by most Americans until the revelations about its nuclear programme in 2002. Consequently, as long as public attention was not focused on Iran, American policy-makers had a degree of latitude (albeit one which should not be overstated) to explore diplomatic initiatives toward Iran.

In contrast, the United States was, along with Saddam Hussein's Iraq, Iran's enemy number one from the early 1980s onwards. Whereas most Americans spent little time thinking about Iran, the USA was a preoccupation for most Iranians and a virtual obsession for the Iranian leadership. Moreover, in addition to their genuine fears about the threat posed by the USA, Iranian hardliners, in particular, were more than happy to exploit that threat and Iran's resistance to it as a means to legitimate the regime and its actions. The inevitable consequence of this preoccupation with the American threat and its exploitation, in combination with Tehran's vicious factional politics, was to create a situation in which any hint of compromise with the 'Great Satan' was all too readily represented as tantamount to treachery. Somewhat counter-intuitively, therefore, the politicians in the democratic state were less constrained by the ramifications of mutual antipathy than those in the authoritarian one.

The United States, Iran and the Bomb

American involvement with the Iranian nuclear programme goes back to 1957, when the two countries first signed a nuclear cooperation agreement. Chapter 1 examines the nuclear relationship from that point until the fall of the Shah. The main focus of the chapter is on the period between 1974, when the Shah's decision to accelerate his country's nuclear programme brought the nuclear issue to the centre of US–Iranian relations, and his fall in 1978. This short period witnessed the emergence of a number of key features of the US–Iranian nuclear relationship: the divergence of perspectives on proliferation and the fuel cycle quickly became clear. Even in a context in which the two were Cold War allies, Iranian nationalism and ambition and American fear of proliferation produced deadlock in their nuclear negotiations. The American refusal to provide Iran with fuel cycle technology was, moreover, strongly influenced by pressure from Congress, which was able to exploit the need for its ratification of any nuclear agreement to great effect. Finally, the chapter reveals a tension between unilateralism and multilateralism that would recur in US policy, as it tried to persuade the other nuclear powers to join it in not transferring sensitive nuclear technology whilst also pursuing its own national interests and accommodating domestic pressures.

Chronologically, Chapter 2 focuses on the 1980s, but the main theme of the chapter is the development of mutual antipathy between Iran and the United States through an examination of their interactions from the 1953 coup to the Iran–Iraq War. The chapter also examines the origins of the IRI's nuclear programme and its connection to the emerging conflict with the USA.

Chapter 3 explores developments under Presidents George H. W. Bush and Bill Clinton. It examines the continued development of the Iranian nuclear programme, US efforts to curtail it, and the broader course of US–Iranian relations. The chapter demonstrates how domestic politics on both sides continued to prevent coherent policy-making and resolution of the conflict. Leaders with an interest in dialogue found their efforts to engage the other government undercut by the actions and opposition of hardliners in both countries. The need to pander to domestic (and Israeli) pressures also undermined the efficacy of US efforts to curtail the Iranian nuclear programme by driving them down a path of unilateral coercion that was completely ineffective. Consequently, the Iranian nuclear programme continued to develop largely unhindered by the United States.

Chapter 4 looks at US policy during the administration of George W. Bush. The revelations that focused international attention on the Iranian nuclear programme in 2002 also exposed divisions within the Iranian elite over the nuclear programme, with the pragmatists and reformists who controlled policy-making until 2005 making repeated efforts to pursue a negotiated solution. Hard-line conservatives in the Bush administration, however, had no interest in compromise with Iran. They were committed to regime change (at best) or compelling Tehran to abandon its pursuit of the fuel cycle (at worst). Once again, however, the policy was incoherent and ineffective. It contained no meaningful incentives for Tehran while the coercive measures employed were ineffectual, with Washington's continued unilateralism undermining its efforts to bring effective pressure to bear. Bush's rejection of the outreach of the Khatami government, moreover, contributed to the discrediting of the latter and to the reassertion of Iranian hardliners. The subsequent election of Ahmadinejad to the Iranian presidency in 2005 guaranteed continued stalemate.

The final chapter examines US policy under Obama and the developments that led to the signing of the JCPOA. Obama introduced significant changes to US policy that brought ambitions more effectively into line with the means available to achieve them. He secured more effective multilateral cooperation from key states, which in turn enabled him to impose more effective coercion. Of equal importance, however, was his abandonment of the demand that Iran give up the fuel cycle. That decision was driven by his recognition that continued enrichment was non-negotiable as far as Tehran was concerned and his fear that the alternative to acknowledging that would be war. That fear also led him to take on the intense domestic opposition to compromise – opposition which was ultimately overcome by a combination of the effects of partisan polarisation and the ineptness of his political opponents. There would have been no JCPOA, however, without parallel changes inside Iran. After eight years of dominance by Iranian hardliners, the 2013 election saw Hassan Rouhani returned to office. Obama's concession on enrichment created the political space for him to pursue a negotiated solution while Iran's economic problems and growing legitimacy crisis persuaded the Supreme Leader to support him in doing so. A nuclear agreement was finally reached as a result of smarter diplomacy on the part of the USA, the exhaustion of coercive options short of war, and domestic political changes on both sides, but especially in Iran.

Notes

1. Blight et al., *Becoming Enemies*, p. 185.
2. Chubin, 'Understanding Iran's nuclear ambitions', p. 54.
3. Pollack, *Persian Puzzle*, p. 303.
4. 'Joint Comprehensive Plan of Action'. The other signatories were Russia, China, France, the UK and Germany.
5. Trump, 'Statement by the President on the Iran nuclear deal'.
6. Debs and Monteiro, *Nuclear Politics*; Rezaei, *Iran's Nuclear Program*; Katzman et al., 'Iran: Interim nuclear agreement', p. 49; Maloney, 'Why "Iran style" sanctions worked against Tehran'.
7. Parsi, *Losing an Enemy*.
8. Debs and Monteiro, *Nuclear Politics*; Rezaei, *Iran's Nuclear Program*; Khan, *Iran and Nuclear Weapons*; Stein, 'Kilowatts or Kilotons?'
9. Porter, *Manufactured Crisis*.
10. Chubin, 'Understanding Iran's nuclear ambitions'.
11. Kamrava, 'Iranian national security debates'; Solingen, *Nuclear Logics*; Kazemzadeh, 'Foreign policy decision making in Iran'.
12. Notable exceptions being Patrikarikos, *Nuclear Iran* and Alvandi, *Nixon, Kissinger and the Shah*.
13. US Department of State, *Report on the International Control of Atomic Energy*.
14. Bechoefer, 'Negotiating the statute of the International Atomic Energy Agency'; Keeley, 'Legitimacy, capability, effectiveness and the future of the NPT', pp. 26–8.
15. Shaker, 'The third NPT review conference', p. 7.
16. As was demonstrated when Iraq was found to have been close to a nuclear weapon after the 1991 Gulf War, despite its nuclear programme having been subject to IAEA inspections.
17. See Little, *American Orientalism*, ch. 1.
18. Ansari, *Confronting Iran*, pp. 94–5, 102–5; Pillar, 'The role of villain'.
19. Ansari, 'Civilizational identity and foreign policy', p. 243.
20. Duss, 'Dershowitz: Iran is suicide nation'.
21. Ansari, *Confronting Iran*, p. 36.
22. On the general process of mutual alienation, see Beeman, 'Great Satan' vs the 'Mad Mullahs'.
23. Axworthy, *Revolutionary Iran*, p. xviii.
24. Ansari, *Modern Iran Since 1921*, pp. 4–5.
25. Ehteshami, 'Foreign policy of Iran', p. 285.

26. Khamenei, 'Leader's address to university professors and elite academics'.
27. Hossein, 'Iran's assertiveness'.
28. Frey, 'Of nuclear myths and nuclear taboos'. Opinion polls have repeatedly demonstrated that overwhelming majorities of Iranians support Iran's 'right' to nuclear power and see nuclear technology as proof of Iran's status as a leading power; see WorldPublicOpinion. org, 'Iranian public opinion on governance, nuclear weapons'; Elson and Nader, *What Do Iranians Think?*
29. Slackman, 'Iran rebuffs US on talks'.
30. Ehteshami, 'Foreign policy of Iran', p. 285.
31. Chubin and Zabih, *Foreign Relations of Iran*; Chubin, 'Iran's strategic predicament'; Parsi, *Treacherous Alliance*; Fuller, *The 'Center of the Universe'*.
32. Hunter, *Iran's Foreign Policy in the Post-Soviet Era*; Adib-Moghaddam, *Iran in World Politics*; Khalaji, 'Apocalyptic politics'.
33. Putnam, 'Diplomacy and domestic politics'.
34. Frank Newport, 'Americans still rate Iran top U.S. enemy', *Gallup*, 20 February 2012, <http://www.gallup.com/poll/152786/Americans-Rate-Iran-Top-Enemy.aspx> (last accessed 7 July 2015).
35. Blight et al., *Becoming Enemies*, p. 252.
36. Parsi, *Single Roll of the Dice*, p. 224.
37. WorldPublicOpinion.org, 'Iranian public on current issues'.
38. Hadiyan, 'Iran–US Cold War'.
39. Putnam, 'Diplomacy and domestic politics', p. 449.
40. Ibid., p. 448.
41. Rudalevige, 'Contemporary presidency'; Peterson, 'President's dominance in foreign policy-making'.
42. Mayhew, *Congress*; Brady and Fiorina, 'Congress in the era of the permanent campaign'; King, 'Vulnerable American politician'.
43. Ornstein and Mann, 'When Congress checks out'; Fisher, *Congressional Abdication*; Weissmann, *Culture of Deference*.
44. Riedel interview.
45. Mearshimer and Walt, *Israel Lobby*; Lieberman, 'Israel lobby'.
46. Byman et al., *Iran's Security Policy*, pp. 21–2.
47. *Constitution of the Islamic Republic of Iran*, Articles 57 and 110; Ganji, 'Latter-day Sultan'.
48. Kamrava, 'Iranian national security debates', p. 85.
49. Kazemzadeh, 'Foreign policy decision making in Iran'.
50. Warnaar, *Iranian Foreign Policy*, pp. 45–6.
51. Keynoush, 'Iran after Ahmadinejad', p. 131.

52. Buchta et al., *Who Rules Iran?*, p. 7.
53. Kamrava, 'Iranian national security debates'; Buchta et al., *Who Rules Iran?*; Ehteshami, 'Foreign policy of Iran', p. 292.
54. On the face of things this emphasis on factions might seem to contradict the argument made above about the hostile worldviews on each side. However, it is important to understand that, while those worldviews are pervasive and influential, images of the 'other' are not identical in the mind of every policy-maker. Nor is there consensus on every policy. Rather, there is on both sides a pervasive and powerful worldview which is widely shared and which imposes significant constraints on those who seek to pursue policies which do not conform with it, but the latter exist and the worldview can be challenged and altered over time.
55. Kazemzadeh, 'Foreign policy decision making in Iran', p. 203.
56. Moslem, *Factional Politics in Post-Khomeini Iran*; Kazemzadeh, 'Foreign policy decision making in Iran'; Kamrava, 'Iranian national security debates', Warnaar, *Iranian Foreign Policy*, pp. 47–53.
57. Behravesh, 'Iran's reform movement'; Mirbagheri, 'Narrowing the gap or camouflaging the divide'; Adib-Moghaddam, 'Pluralistic momentum in Iran'; Moslem, *Factional Politics in Post-Khomeini Iran*; Kazemzadeh, 'Foreign policy decision making in Iran'; Kamrava, 'Iranian national security debates'.
58. Khamenei, 'Supreme Leader's speech to government officials'; Kazemzadeh, 'Ahmadinejad's foreign policy'; Moslem, *Factional Politics in Post-Khomeini Iran*; Kazemzadeh, 'Foreign policy decision making in Iran'; Kamrava, 'Iranian national security debates'; Warnaar, *Iranian Foreign Policy*.
59. This emphasis on the importance of factions in explaining Iranian nuclear policy is strongly influenced by Etel Solingen's argument about the way in which differential attitudes toward 'internationalisation' affect nuclear policy decisions; Solingen, *Nuclear Logics*.
60. Beeman, *'Great Satan' vs the 'Mad Mullahs'*, p. 40.
61. The *Karine-A* incident is one possible example; see Parsi, *Treacherous Alliance*, pp. 419–22.
62. Snyder and Diesing, *Conflict Among Nations*, pp. 516, 522–3.

1 The 1970s: The Nuclear Relationship under the Shah

The United States and Nuclear Proliferation

As was noted in the Introduction, the fear that the knowledge of how to make nuclear weapons would spread dogged American policy-makers from the day the United States successfully tested the first atomic bomb. They quickly recognised that prevention of the dissemination of that knowledge was likely to prove impossible because of the technological overlap between the requirements of peaceful and military nuclear programmes.[1]

In the face of this dilemma the administration of President Harry Truman determined that, rather than make a futile attempt to keep the nuclear secret to itself, the United States should seek to prevent the spread of nuclear weapons by offering the world a deal. The United States would share its knowledge and assist other states in the production of peaceful nuclear energy in return for their acceptance of international controls designed to prevent them from developing weapons. That was the essence of the proposal that the American representative, Bernard Baruch, put to the recently established United Nations Atomic Energy Committee (UNAEC) in June 1946. Baruch proposed the creation of a United Nations (UN) Atomic Development Authority (ADA) which would control all nuclear installations with the ability to produce nuclear weapons-related material and have the right to inspect all other nuclear facilities. Once the authority was operating successfully the USA would then destroy its own nuclear weapons. In order to ensure effective punishment of any state which violated the system he further proposed that on nuclear matters no state should have a veto in the UN Security Council.[2] In the context of the emerging Cold War, however, the Soviet Union was not prepared to surrender its veto and open its facilities to international inspection in return for a promise that the United States would, at some point in the future, surrender its nuclear monopoly. Moscow therefore counter-proposed that the USA destroy its nuclear weapons before negotiations on a suitable system of international control began.[3] With neither side willing to compromise, the first American attempt to control nuclear proliferation failed.

For the remainder of the Truman administration Washington reverted to a policy of nuclear secrecy. By 1953, however, with both the Soviets and the British having developed atom bombs, it was clear that the fears underpinning the Baruch Plan had been justified. The Eisenhower administration therefore initiated a second American effort to develop an international mechanism to halt nuclear proliferation. In an address to the UN in December 1953, President Dwight Eisenhower proposed that the existing nuclear powers supply uranium and fissionable material to a new UN body called the International Atomic Energy Agency (IAEA). The IAEA would use that material to support the development of peaceful nuclear programmes in states which wished to pursue them. In return for such assistance those states would pledge not to develop nuclear weapons and allow their programmes to be inspected by the IAEA.[4]

The ineffectiveness of unilateral American efforts to halt proliferation, and the difficulty of securing agreement on effective multilateral policies, would become a recurrent theme of American counter-proliferation policy. In the case of Eisenhower's 'Atoms for Peace' proposal, as with the Baruch Plan, it was Moscow's refusal to cooperate which neutered it as an effective disarmament proposal. Nevertheless, even without Soviet participation, the administration pushed ahead with the plan, not least because it feared that, were it not to, the USSR would step in to act as the world's nuclear supplier of choice. The IAEA consequently came into existence on 29 July 1957. In accordance with Eisenhower's original proposal, the organisation's two principal objectives were to 'accelerate and enlarge the contribution of atomic energy to peace, health and prosperity' and to 'ensure, as far as it is able, that assistance provided by it or at its request or under its supervision or control is not used in such a way as to further any military purpose'.[5] With this statutory framework in place, for a short time Washington became an enthusiastic promoter of peaceful nuclear development. By the late 1960s the USA had signed nuclear cooperation agreements with over twenty countries, including Iran.[6] In their April 1957 agreement Washington pledged to assist Tehran with the development of civil nuclear power by providing technical assistance, enriched uranium and a five megawatt (MW) light water reactor (LWR) for research purposes. Iran in turn agreed not to develop weapons and to submit its programme to IAEA safeguards.[7]

However, within less than a decade of the founding of the IAEA, American policy-makers were having second thoughts about the wisdom of their chosen course. Successful atomic tests by France (1960) and China (1964) had increased the number of nuclear weapons states to five while the number of proposed new nuclear energy programmes had increased dramatically, and with them the potential for nuclear proliferation.[8] With the USSR now an established (and consequently increasingly status quo oriented) nuclear power, the two superpowers agreed to cooperate to strengthen the non-proliferation regime. The result was the Treaty on the Non-Proliferation of Nuclear Weapons (NPT), signed by sixty-one nations, including Iran, in July 1968 and coming into force in March 1970.

While representing a significant expansion and formalisation of the non-proliferation regime, the NPT was still clearly an extension of the same trade-off which had been central to both the Baruch Plan and Atoms for Peace. On their side, the three nuclear weapons states who signed the NPT (China and France refused to do so) agreed not to transfer nuclear weapons or weapons-related technology to the non-nuclear weapons states (NNWS) while still assisting the latter to develop peaceful nuclear energy. They also pledged eventually to eliminate their own nuclear weapons. The NNWS signatories in return pledged not to develop nuclear weapons.[9] The IAEA, meanwhile, was integrated into the new NPT regime with a greater emphasis on its safeguarding role. The agency was required to carry out on-site inspections of the nuclear activities of NNWS signatories (safeguarding) and to report any violations of the NPT to the UN Security Council.[10]

The United States, Iran and the Cold War

While Iran had a walk-on part in US non-proliferation policy between 1945 and 1970, it was central to American efforts to contain Soviet influence in the Middle East. Iran's geostrategic position between the USSR and the Persian Gulf, and its extensive oil and gas reserves, ensured its significance to US policy-makers, and the 1946 Iranian crisis was one of the first significant clashes of the Cold War.[11] Initially, however, Washington was largely content to let its British ally, long established as the dominant external power in Iran, take the lead in ensuring Tehran remained within the Western camp. That situation changed, however, during and after the events of 1950–3. A growing confrontation between Britain and Iran over the threatened nationalisation of Iranian oil production led the Eisenhower administration, fearing that growing instability threatened to render Iran vulnerable to Soviet influence, to lend its support to a coup against Prime Minister Mohammad Mossadegh.[12]

Having helped to remove Mossadegh, the United States subsequently took on a much more prominent role in seeking to guarantee Iranian political stability and its allegiance to the West, usurping Britain as Tehran's main ally. For the next decade and a half, however, Iran played a largely secondary role in America's Persian Gulf policy. Britain remained the United States' key military ally in the region and Washington urged Iran's autocratic ruler, Mohammad Reza Shah Pahlavi, to devote his attention to securing his regime's future by pursuing social and economic reforms that would legitimise his regime with the Iranian public, rather than trying to make Iran into a regional military and strategic heavyweight, as was his wont.[13]

By the late 1960s, however, the US–Iranian relationship was beginning to change. A more confident Shah, buoyed by Iran's growing economy, apparent political stability and increasing oil wealth, was less and less willing to be constrained by Washington. As he told his adviser Asadollah Alam, 'America must be made to realize that we are an independent sovereign power and will make way for no one.'[14] For its part, meanwhile, Washington's ability to resist his demands was in decline. The Vietnam War had sapped America's economic and military resources and its will to make new overseas military commitments, as was demonstrated by President Richard Nixon's announcement in June 1969 that henceforth America's allies would be expected to deal with conventional military threats themselves, without the assistance of American troops.[15] With the British government having announced its intention to withdraw all of its armed forces from bases east of the Suez Canal two years earlier, the United States found itself without a significant military ally in the Persian Gulf and unable to police the region directly.

The Shah consequently found himself pushing at an open door when he called on the incoming Nixon administration to allow Iran to take on the role of guardian of the Gulf.[16] The new American strategy was formally articulated in National Security Decision Memorandum (NSDM) 92 of November 1970. This stated that US policy was now to promote 'cooperation between Iran and Saudi Arabia as the desirable basis for maintaining stability in the Persian Gulf while recognizing the preponderance of Iranian power'.[17] What this meant was that Saudi sensibilities would be appeased by their being described as one of the 'Twin Pillars' of the new policy while Washington would rely on the Shah to be its new military proxy in the region. The implications of this decision were made clear when Nixon visited Tehran in May 1972. At that meeting Nixon agreed to sell Iran any conventional weapons system that it requested and to exempt it from standard arms sales review procedures. In return he asked the Shah to 'protect me'.[18]

The Iranian Nuclear Programme

Two years after that meeting the Shah decided to relaunch Iran's nuclear programme. Despite having been one of the first countries to sign a nuclear cooperation agreement with the United States, by the early 1970s Iran barely had a programme worthy of the name. Factors of both demand and supply accounted for this lack of progress. On the demand side, Iran had far too little installed electrical capacity to justify nuclear power and no national grid to connect any nuclear power stations to. On the supply side, it lacked the scientists and technicians to support a substantial programme. In addition, rather than being established as a standalone programme, nuclear activities had been subsumed into the Iranian Plan Organization, which was responsible for general economic development, meaning that bureaucrats with no understanding of or interest in the programme were responsible for it.[19]

All of this suddenly changed in March 1974, however. In his annual *Nowruz* message the Shah announced that Iran would build twenty nuclear power stations producing 23,000 MW of electricity by 1994.[20] In order to ensure that this time action was taken, he created the Atomic Energy Organization of Iran (AEOI) and placed its Director, Akbar Etemad, under his own direct supervision, promising him whatever resources he required. Words were rapidly followed by action and in June 1974 Etemad and the Shah visited Paris, where they signed an agreement under which France was to supply Iran with five 1,000 MW reactors, uranium and a nuclear research centre. By the end of the year Iran had signed further agreements with Kraftwerk Union (KWU) of West Germany and the French company Framatome, each for the building of two LWRs.[21] In January 1975 Iran purchased a $1 billion stake in a new uranium enrichment plant at Tricastin in France.[22] From $30.8 million in fiscal year (FY) 1975 the AEOI budget rose to over $1 billion by FY 1976.[23]

The reasons the Shah gave for this dramatic escalation of Iran's nuclear programme were primarily economic in nature. As he put it in his *Nowruz* address, 'the oil we call the noble product will be depleted one day'.[24] His fear was that by the mid-1990s Iran's oil reserves would be running out. If Iran was to be able to supply the energy needs of the advanced industrial economy he intended it to have, he needed to begin putting the infrastructure in place. Prompted by the sudden rise in the price of oil, the Shah reasoned that Iran should now develop nuclear power so that it could both export more oil and diversify Iran's energy infrastructure in preparation for the future. An additional consideration was the fact that Iran had a growing quantity of 'petrodollars' in need of productive investment and Western governments, not least that of the United States, were pressing Iran to recycle them by buying Western industrial goods.[25]

Economic considerations were not the only reason for the Shah's pursuit of nuclear power, however. Although he was not pursuing a nuclear weapons programme (see below), theories of why states seek nuclear weapons can usefully be brought to bear here. Status and prestige, rather than rational calculations of security needs, are the best explanation of why some states (France being an example) develop nuclear weapons, and a similar logic can be seen to apply to some civil nuclear programmes.[26] It is noticeable, for example, that those Less Developed Countries (LDCs) that have pursued nuclear energy, such as Argentina and Brazil, tend to have aspirations to regional, or even global, power status. Such was certainly the case with the Shah, who fully intended to make Iran 'one of the five great non-atomic weapon countries of the world within a single generation'.[27]

Vast amounts of Iran's newfound oil wealth were being ploughed into economic development, building thousands of miles of new roads and railways, dams for hydro-electricity, schools, universities and hospitals.[28] In 1977 the Shah asserted that if development continued at the present rate, 'we shall construct during the next twelve years a solid industrial, agricultural and technological substructure for the country's development and will reach the present level of progress of Western Europe'.[29] Reaching the technological level of Western Europe also meant mastering the technology of nuclear power, as had been made clear during a visit by the Shah to London in 1972. While there he had spoken with Lord Rothschild, head of the Downing Street Central Policy Review Unit. When the latter raised the question of nuclear power with him the Shah 'said he was interested in keeping technologically abreast of the United States and Great Britain'. When Rothschild then suggested that Iran could actually move ahead of those two countries if he pursued fast breeder reactor technology, the Shah reacted enthusiastically and indicated that he would like to have an expert sent to Iran to discuss it.[30] For the Shah, as it would come to be for his successors, possession of nuclear technology was not merely an economic necessity but a measure of Iran's status as a modern great power.

It has been argued that the Shah's nuclear ambitions went beyond energy production to the acquiring of nuclear weapons.[31] Such claims are supported by the Shah's reported statement in 1974 that Iran 'will have nuclear weapons, and sooner than people think', and the diaries of Asadollah Alam, who wrote that the Shah 'has a great vision for this country which, though he denies it, probably includes our manufacturing a nuclear deterrent'.[32] Despite those statements, however, the evidence suggests that the Shah had no immediate plans to develop weapons and that this was not the reason that he accelerated the nuclear programme.

If the Shah had wanted to pursue a nuclear weapons programme then he ought to have chosen to build heavy water reactors, which would produce weapons grade plutonium, rather than LWRs whose spent fuel had to be reprocessed to be usable in weapons. LWRs are the best means to provide reliable energy and the worst method to produce weapons grade material available.[33] A government focused on weapons would also have put a great deal of effort into developing indigenous scientific and technological knowledge. The Shah, in contrast, pursued a 'turnkey' approach in which foreign companies provided the expertise, the technology and the fuel.[34] Nor would a state that sought weapons status have been likely to sign and ratify the NPT, place all of its nuclear facilities under full IAEA safeguards and sponsor initiatives at the UN to make the Middle East a Nuclear-Weapons-Free-Zone (NWFZ).[35] All of the Shah's choices, in short, fit with a focus on achieving nuclear energy as quickly as possible rather than seeking to develop nuclear weapons.

In point of fact the Shah did not see the development of nuclear weapons as being in Iran's interest. In the first place, given the Nixon administration's laissez-faire arms sales policies, Iran was rapidly becoming the dominant conventional military power in the Persian Gulf.[36] Instigating a regional nuclear arms race would only have served to neutralise that advantage. Furthermore, the nature of the Shah's ambitions for his country mitigated against the pursuit of weapons. While the development of nuclear power would incur international status and prestige, the development of nuclear weapons would bring international opprobrium, with Iran potentially subject to diplomatic isolation and economic sanctions.[37] Such an outcome would not have fitted at all well with the Shah's ambitions. He wanted Iran to become a leading player in the established order, not to challenge or undermine it. Above all, he did not want to alienate his superpower patron, as he explained to Etemad when the latter asked him directly whether he wanted to pursue a weapons programme. The Shah said he did not, firstly because Iran had sufficient conventional military power to defend itself but mainly because he feared alienating the USA, which was the ultimate guarantor of Iran's security and of his entire project to modernise Iran and make it a global power.[38]

In his discussion with Etemad the Shah nevertheless added an important caveat to his stated intentions, namely that if another regional state developed nuclear weapons then the situation would have to be reconsidered. As Etemad recalled it,

> the Shah had the idea at the time that he's strong enough in the region and he can defend our interests in the region [and] he didn't want nuclear weapons. But he told me that if this changes 'we have to go for nuclear'. He had that in mind.[39]

Nor was that the only occasion on which the Shah used this formulation. In an interview in September 1975 he said, 'we do not want Iran to procure nuclear weapons just for the sake of having them. But I tell you quite frankly that Iran will have to acquire atomic bombs if every upstart in the region gets them.'[40] Thus, while the Shah had no plans to develop nuclear weapons, he clearly wanted to have that option, should it prove necessary in future. As head of the Iranian nuclear programme, therefore, one of Etemad's objectives was 'to ensure that if Iran ever decided to build a bomb, it would be able to do so'.[41]

The American Response to the Shah's Plans

The initial response of the Nixon administration to the Shah's announcement was enthusiastic. Just over two weeks later the Department of State cabled the US embassy in Tehran to say that the administration viewed civil nuclear energy as an area in which the United States should collaborate with Iran, and that the chairman of the US Atomic Energy Commission (AEC), Dr Dixy Lee Ray, was ready to lead a team to Tehran to discuss it.[42] That visit duly took place in May and a provisional agreement was reached for American companies to build two LWRs and supply the fuel for them.[43]

Washington's positive response to the Shah's plans reflected a variety of considerations: in the first place, given the objective of engaging Iran 'so intimately as to assure an enduring relationship under this or successor regimes', this was a golden opportunity to develop long-term cooperation in an area of vital interest to the Iranian government. Moreover, the administration did not want the American nuclear industry to lose out in the competition for what promised to be extremely lucrative contracts. Finally, it represented an important opportunity 'to influence Iran on oil supply, oil pricing, and financial management of oil revenues to the benefit of broader world interests'.[44] In the wake of the 1973–4 oil crisis Secretary of State Henry Kissinger, in particular, wanted to find ways to break the power of the oil producing states. On the basis that their leverage came from vast uninvested sums of foreign exchange which allowed them to cut off oil supplies at no harm to themselves, his plan was to reduce those cash reserves by encouraging their investment in the purchase of Western goods and services, investments which would also give them a growing stake in the health of the Western economies.[45]

However, the same month that Dr Ray went to Tehran to negotiate a new nuclear agreement, India conducted a peaceful nuclear explosion (PNE). Given that India's nuclear programme had been safeguarded by the IAEA, this development destroyed any optimism that had developed about the efficacy of the nuclear non-proliferation regime. Not only did the Indian PNE appear to discredit the NPT, moreover, it also demonstrated that another aspect of the American approach to non-proliferation was not working. For two decades Washington had sought to control proliferation in part by maintaining America's position as the dominant supplier of nuclear technology and material and imposing bilateral safeguards on any country with which it signed a nuclear agreement.[46] The Indian PNE, however, was based on plutonium extracted from a reactor supplied by Canada, reflecting the fact that by the mid-1970s the American share of the nuclear export market was in decline.[47] After the 1973–4 oil crisis many states were seeking to develop alternative energy sources and had settled upon nuclear power as the best available option. Japan, West Germany, France, the UK, Brazil and South Korea all had ambitious plans. To make those plans financially viable they would need to export their nuclear expertise and technology. With the resulting excess of supply over demand in the nuclear market-place, there was a real risk that suppliers would be insufficiently concerned about what they sold to whom and what the latter planned to do with it. [48] Five days after the Indian PNE, Nixon ordered a review of US non-proliferation policy with a remit to 'consider the full range of issues posed by the changed circumstances affecting our posture toward non-proliferation and the NPT and present options for future U.S. policy'.[49]

A further reason to initiate such a review was the reaction to the Indian PNE in the US Congress, which was highly alarmed and increasingly hostile to further sales of nuclear technology and material.[50] In September 1974 the head of the Center for Defense Information, Rear Admiral Gene R. La Rocque, claimed in congressional testimony that Iran was 'one of the early contenders now for nuclear weapons', while Senator Stuart Symington stated that, with the reactors France was contracted to build, Iran would have enough material for 'a minimum of 200 Hiroshima bombs a year'.[51] With the Nixon administration proposing to sign nuclear cooperation agreements with Israel and Egypt as well, Congress moved to impose strict controls on what the US could transfer abroad. In the proposed Export Reorganization Act of 1975 any country accepting nuclear assistance from the US would have to adopt safeguards that were 'at least substantially comparable' to those applied in the US and an independent body, the Nuclear Regulatory Commission, would be given responsibility for determining if they were.[52] Though that bill failed to become law, it was clear that Congress was determined to ensure effective control of nuclear exports. Given that any expansion of the existing US nuclear relationship with Iran would require formalisation in a new nuclear cooperation agreement ratified by Congress, this was a reality the administration could not ignore.

An August 1974 Special National Intelligence Estimate (SNIE) on the proliferation problem concluded that by the 1980s nuclear weapons production would be 'within the technological and economic capabilities of many countries' as the technological and cost barriers came down. It went on to outline the two routes by which states might seek weapons. The most likely, it argued, was the plutonium reprocessing route. Spent reactor fuel contains a mixture of uranium and plutonium and by reprocessing that spent fuel (chemically separating its elements) states can recover uranium which can then be fabricated into new fuel rods for their reactors. The same process, however, produces plutonium which can be used in nuclear weapons. The other path to the bomb is through the uranium enrichment route. Natural uranium constitutes of two isotopes of uranium, being 99.3 per cent U-238 and 0.7 per cent U-235. Since it is the latter which is used in the nuclear fission process, it is necessary to increase the proportion of U-235 to 3–5 per cent to produce uranium suitable for use as reactor fuel. This is a much more complex and costly process than reprocessing, involving transforming natural uranium into uranium hexafluoride gas and then enriching the gas by putting it through either a gaseous diffusion or centrifuge process. Nevertheless, were a state to develop the capacity to enrich fuel to 5 per cent then there would be no technological barrier to it enriching to 90 per cent, which is the level required for use in nuclear weapons. The problem identified by the Department of State in 1946 – that the processes central to civilian nuclear programmes were in large part identical to those used in weapons programmes – thus continued to plague American non-proliferation policy.

The SNIE also considered the likely trajectory of various countries' nuclear programmes. In the case of Iran it concluded that there was no doubting

> the Shah's ambition to make Iran a power to be reckoned with. If he is alive in the mid 1980s, if Iran has a full-fledged nuclear power industry and all the facilities necessary for nuclear weapons, and if other countries have proceeded with weapons development, we have no doubt that Iran will follow suit.[53]

Even before the administration's review of proliferation policy was completed, the impact of the Indian PNE on American policy was evident. In early June 1974 Nixon issued NSDM 255. This document stated that any national reprocessing and/or enrichment programme should now be regarded as a proliferation threat and advocated that they be replaced by multinational facilities.[54] At an international level, the Nixon administration took the lead in establishing what became known as the Nuclear Suppliers Group (NSG), comprising fifteen of the major nuclear suppliers. The administration sought to make it a vehicle for agreeing new multilateral guidelines for nuclear exports.[55] Meanwhile, the State Department informed the embassy in Tehran that because there had been strong congressional and media criticism of similar nuclear cooperation agreements with Egypt and Israel, and because of the impact of the Indian PNE, the US would only be going ahead with contracts for two reactors at this point. Furthermore, these contracts would contain 'additional bilateral controls' beyond the standard IAEA safeguards, including a US 'veto over availability, disposition, and storage of the plutonium generated by the reactors'.[56]

When the proliferation review, National Security Study Memorandum (NSSM) 202, was completed in December 1974 it confirmed that 'the proliferation problem is at a crucial juncture' and that the US needed to put in place an 'intensified program' to prevent further proliferation. Specifically, it argued that the United States should seek the cooperation of the other nuclear suppliers to tighten safeguards on exports of nuclear materials and technology with the objective of restricting the spread of national uranium enrichment and reprocessing capacity. It further recommended that the US impose special conditions on nuclear exports to countries in sensitive regions (such as the Middle East), including 'requiring that reprocessing, storage and fabrication of plutonium . . . take place in mutually-agreed facilities outside the country or region in question'.[57] By preventing the export of enrichment and reprocessing technology, and by denying states the right to reprocess spent fuel, the report aimed to cut off the path from a peaceful nuclear programme to the bomb.

The administration's difficulty was that in implementing this approach it had to strike a balance between a number of competing considerations. If it imposed conditions of sale that were too strict, it risked potential customers taking their business to nuclear exporters who were less scrupulous, thus doing nothing to prevent proliferation while hurting the US nuclear industry. However, if it did not impose sufficiently strict controls, there was a real danger that Congress would refuse to ratify the nuclear agreements reached, resulting in the same outcome. The most desirable solution from the administration's point of view was therefore the creation of a multilateral regime imposing effective constraints on the transfer of enrichment and reprocessing technology. This would negate the ability of states seeking nuclear technology to play the nuclear suppliers off against each other and allow the US to continue to be a supplier of nuclear material.[58] If it was to achieve that outcome, however, the administration would have to take a tough enough line with Iran both to ensure congressional approval of any proposed nuclear agreement and to persuade the other nuclear suppliers that Washington was ready to abide by the same rules it was asking them to apply to their exports.

Two days after the delivery of NSSM 202, Kissinger received a memo outlining American options in the nuclear negotiations with Iran. It identified the main problem facing the administration as the need to balance between imposing too many restrictions on Iran and risking the Shah taking his business elsewhere, and imposing too few restrictions and provoking congressional intervention. It then listed four options for a new nuclear agreement with Iran:

1. The standard nuclear agreement that the USA had already signed with twenty-nine countries in which IAEA safeguards were applied.
2. As option one but with extra bilateral safeguards to ensure non-diversion of US-supplied material.
3. As option two but with the additional requirement that the USA have the right to insist on storage and/or reprocessing of spent fuel outside Iran or have a say in how it was reprocessed in Iran.
4. As option three but excluding any possibility of reprocessing inside Iran and adding the right for the US to 'buy-back' spent fuel.

The memo recommended Kissinger approve the third option, since it was felt that the fourth would lead the Shah to break off negotiations whilst the first two would not satisfy Congress.[59]

By the time Kissinger approved the new policy, Gerald Ford had replaced Richard Nixon as president, the latter having resigned as a result of the Watergate affair. Roham Alvandi has argued that this change was critical to the evolution of the nuclear negotiations on the grounds that Nixon's commitment to the Shah was such that he would have resisted demands to impose extra constraints on Iranian reprocessing.[60] Whilst such a counter-factual claim cannot be either proved or disproved, it is unlikely that the change of president was as significant as Alvandi implies. In the first place, his argument is belied by the timeline of events, with the shift in US non-proliferation policy beginning before Nixon resigned in August 1974. By that point the US had already begun to organise the NSG and the State Department had informed the US embassy in Tehran that the US would insist on a veto on reprocessing of US-supplied fuel. This, in turn, reflects the fact that it was the Indian PNE, rather than Nixon's resignation, which changed everything. It was the PNE that led the administration to review and then alter its non-proliferation policy and it was the PNE which mobilised Congress to take the hard line on reprocessing that greatly constrained the administration's room for manoeuvre on the issue.

US–Iranian Nuclear Negotiations 1975–6

The memo outlining US options in the negotiations with Iran had stated that Tehran would not be happy with option three. Its accuracy was confirmed when the first meeting of the nuclear energy committee of the recently established US–Iranian Joint Economic Commission was held in January 1975. When the American team presented Etemad with the draft agreement they had brought with them he objected vigorously to the inclusion of any requirements going beyond standard IAEA safeguards, on the grounds that the US was discriminating against Iran by seeking to impose conditions not included in previous agreements.[61]

Etemad's anger at the American proposal stemmed from a number of sources. In the first place there is little doubt that his stated reasons for rejecting the proposal were genuine. The *quid pro quo* in the NPT was that non-weapons states agreed not to pursue nuclear weapons, accepted IAEA safeguards and in return were allowed to have peaceful nuclear programmes and given assistance with their development. What Washington was now proposing amounted to a unilateral attempt to rewrite the non-proliferation regime by significantly extending the restrictions on the kind of assistance that could be given, thus denying NNWS control of all aspects of peaceful nuclear power generation.[62] Under the American proposal Iran would not be permitted either to enrich its own fuel or to reprocess spent fuel, leaving it wholly dependent upon the United States or another country for its fuel supply. While Iran had no plans to pursue enrichment at this point, it did intend to have the ability to reprocess spent fuel, and Etemad was adamant that Iran had to have control of all aspects of the nuclear fuel cycle in order to avoid dependence on external suppliers.[63] It was also true, of course, that without the ability to reprocess he would not be able to keep open the possibility of weapons development.

In point of fact, Etemad was less than enthusiastic about both the Shah's turnkey approach to developing nuclear power and cooperation with the USA. He would have preferred a slower approach that focused on developing indigenous capacity and cooperation with states over which Iran would have had more leverage.[64] The Shah, however, was focused on having nuclear power as quickly as possible and regarded the maintenance of a good relationship with Washington as critical to his wider ambitions. This difference between the two was clearly evident in 1975 when Etemad organised a conference on the transfer of nuclear technology in Tehran with the aim of mobilising support for his position that there should be no restrictions on such transfers to states which observed their NPT obligations. The Shah nevertheless endorsed the more restrictive Western position at the 1975 NPT review conference.[65] These differences, and the fact that the Shah generally left Etemad to conduct talks with the Americans, added significantly to the complexity of the negotiations.

With a further meeting in March 1975 producing no movement in the Iranian position, and the Shah due to visit Washington in May, Kissinger ordered a further policy review. This concluded that the current US position was likely to remain unacceptable to the Iranians, with potentially serious consequences. If the Shah decided to look elsewhere for his nuclear supplies, American firms would lose an estimated $7 billion worth of contracts, non-proliferation objectives would be undermined, and the US–Iranian relationship would be seriously damaged. The review therefore outlined a number of alternative options which were circulated amongst the bureaucracy for discussion. The outcome was NSDM 292, in which Ford approved the following position: the US would 'continue to require American approval for reprocessing of US-supplied fuel' but indicate that it would be likely to approve reprocessing if Iran set up a multinational facility (MNF) for the purpose (the logic being that in a plant run by more than one country each would monitor the other and thus prevent the diversion of nuclear material). If the Iranians were to reject the MNF idea then the US would agree to approve reprocessing in Iran if the country supplying the technology (i.e. the US) were a partner in the plant and had an equal say in the safeguards to be applied.[66]

In practice, therefore, the new position represented little more than a variation on a theme. While the suggestion that the US require that reprocessing take place outside Iran had gone, the bar on Iran having autonomous control of reprocessing inside Iran remained. The lack of movement on the American side, despite real fears that the Iranians would walk out of the negotiations, reflected a lack of room for manoeuvre. As David Elliott of the National Security Council (NSC) staff wrote to Deputy National Security Adviser Brent Scowcroft,

> our problem is that even if we can convince ourselves that a greater good would be served by falling off our plutonium veto, Congress may not approve the Agreement if (1) they think it weak, or (2) find out that we have caved. Also, our protestations to other nuclear suppliers about the importance of imposing stricter controls may be considerably less convincing if our actions don't match our words.[67]

In addition to those considerations, administration concerns that the Shah might have weapons ambitions probably also played a role. Although this concern was never openly articulated as a reason to oppose reprocessing in Iran, there was widespread suspicion within the US government about the Shah's intentions. An assessment by the US embassy in Tehran in mid-1975 concluded that the government of Iran's motivations 'to acquire this complex and extensive technology are not entirely clear', and that 'it is possible that Iran's interest in acquiring nuclear knowhow and plutonium is, in part, motivated by the desire to preserve the option of developing nuclear weapons should the region's power balance shift toward the nuclear'.[68] Kissinger also wrote in a briefing document for Ford that the Shah 'probably would like to move toward a position where he could eventually produce weapons on short notice if he believed it necessary'.[69]

American concerns about proliferation were further exacerbated in June 1975 when West Germany stated its intention to sell enrichment and reprocessing facilities to Brazil, followed shortly by the announcement of similar French sales to Pakistan and South Korea.[70] The Ford administration responded by increasing its efforts to secure multilateral agreement on nuclear exports, with American pressure leading to a series of meetings of the NSG in London at which the administration sought agreement not to export enrichment or reprocessing technology. With the French and Germans, in particular, resisting that demand, it was all the more essential for Washington to maintain its tough line with Iran if it was to have any hope of cajoling the other nuclear suppliers into line.[71]

However, any hope the administration might have had that their attempt to finesse the reprocessing issue would meet Iranian concerns was quickly dashed. While the Iranians claimed that they welcomed the MNF idea they immediately sought to find a way round it, arguing that if they made 'good-faith' efforts to involve other states in a reprocessing plant but failed to secure partners, they should nevertheless be allowed to go ahead with a national facility. An unmoved Washington insisted that 'the actual establishment of such a multinational plant – not only an effort' would be the precondition for reprocessing.[72] Further talks in Vienna in September and October 1975 only confirmed the stalemate. Etemad complained that US proposals would 'tie [Iran's] hands for thirty years' and said that Iran would not buy US reactors 'unless the United States [was] prepared to base cooperation only on principles of the NPT, and unless it was clear that Iran was not being treated as a second class citizen'. Iran had to have the 'final decision' on reprocessing.[73] In an attempt to bypass Etemad, Kissinger asked the American ambassador to Iran, Richard Helms, to explain the US position to the Shah directly. He instructed him to articulate the advantages to Iran of taking a strong stance against proliferation and to tell the Shah that 'we are not in any way singling out Iran for special, disadvantageous treatment'.[74] Shortly afterwards, however, the Shah was quoted in an Iranian newspaper as saying the US demands were 'incompatible' with Iranian sovereignty and that the French and Germans would never make such demands. Helms wrote to the State Department that 'Iranian sensitivities in this area of nuclear cooperation run deeper than we thought.'[75]

By the start of 1976, therefore, the nuclear negotiations were still stuck at square one and the Ford administration once more decided to review its options. David Elliot again summed up the situation for Scowcroft: the nuclear negotiations were stalled because Iran was insistent on having the right to reprocess spent fuel in Iran and

> we have told Iran that we would approve . . . reprocessing only if the plant were multinationally owned and operated. We would accept, as a minimum commitment, a binational plant, if a company of one of the major nuclear supplier nations, including ourselves, was the partner with Iran.[76]

He reiterated that 'it is the view of the agencies that an Iranian agreement for cooperation which contains no special control on reprocessing would be disapproved by Congress, and the President would be criticized as being irresponsible in nuclear matters'.[77]

To make matters worse, after a year of negotiations, the administration was still unclear as to what the Iranian bottom line was. In particular, 'we really are uncertain as to the Shah's basic views and his flexibility'. Although an inter-agency working group had already identified a range of possible modifications to the US negotiating position, the administration decided that it was pointless to draw up a new proposal only to see it rejected once more. Instead it was decided to send a delegation to meet directly with the Shah, in the hope both that he would prove more flexible than Etemad and that the administration would finally be able to determine precisely what his minimum demands were. Subsequently, 'a report should be submitted to the President describing those alternate approaches which would be consistent with our objective of avoiding the spread of national reprocessing facilities while permitting us to reach an agreement on nuclear cooperation with Iran'.[78]

The American delegation, led by the head of the US Energy Research and Development Administration (ERDA), Robert Seamans, met with the Shah on 23 February 1976. While they were still unable to get him to put all of his cards on the table, Seamans nevertheless concluded that the Shah would not accept a 'US veto to prevent Iranian reprocessing' and was also unlikely to accept an MNF. He therefore recommended that, while Washington should continue to press Iran to 'exert strenuous efforts toward the establishment of a multinational or binational reprocessing facility', it should also establish a new fallback position in readiness for the likely failure to achieve either outcome. Seaman's proposal was that, should that eventuality occur, the USA would consent to reprocessing in an Iranian national facility subject only to its being satisfied that effective safeguards were in place and having the right to assign American personnel to the facility to ensure that that was the case.[79]

With Etemad due in Washington to conduct further negotiations in late April, the administration needed to determine what its new position was going to be. Most of the relevant governmental agencies felt that Seaman's proposal conceded too much too quickly. They therefore proposed that if Iran failed to establish an MNF or bi-national facility, the USA should demand the right to 'buy-back' spent fuel from Iran for storage or reprocessing in the USA. If the USA chose not to exercise that right *then* Iran would have the right to reprocess the fuel in an appropriately safeguarded national facility. Only if the Iranians rejected the buy-back idea, they argued, should Seaman's proposal be put on the table.[80] Two days before Etemad was due to arrive in Washington, Ford approved the new policy. The new US bottom line was now that, 'should it prove essential, in the view of the negotiators, to the achievement of an ad referendum agreement, they are authorized to withdraw the plutonium buy-back option, i.e. we will accept a national plant with safeguards'.[81]

Between January and April 1976, therefore, the Ford administration had retreated significantly from its demand that the US retain an effective veto over reprocessing in Iran. The continued insistence of Etemad and the Shah on Iran's sovereign right to control reprocessing appeared to have paid off. The administration's fear that the Shah would go elsewhere for his nuclear supplies, its fear of losing business, and its fear of damaging this critical strategic relationship all led it to the conclusion that the concession had to be made. The belief that the United States needed the Shah more than he needed the USA was still prevalent, as indicated by Kissinger's response to one proposal to try to persuade the Shah to accept the need to forego reprocessing: 'five years from now we'll be on our knees begging him to do a tenth of the things that he now does voluntarily at a heavy price'.[82]

Nevertheless, given that they were not yet certain of the Shah's bottom line, the administration did not offer up its concession unprompted. In their meetings with Etemad in April, American negotiators emphasised the buy-back option. The AEOI chief appeared to be more receptive to the idea than he was to the MNF and, in the light of these discussions, a new draft of the nuclear agreement was sent to Tehran on 28 May. This complicated document comprised what the administration hoped would become their standard nuclear cooperation agreement along with an accompanying note spelling out conditions specific to the proposed agreement with Iran. Article VIII (c) of the draft agreement stated that if reprocessing could not take place in a facility that both parties deemed to be acceptable, then the US government would have the right to require spent fuel to be transferred to the United States in exchange either for an equivalent amount of fuel or appropriate financial compensation. The accompanying note spelled out what would constitute an 'acceptable' reprocessing facility in this case, namely that it was a multinational or bi-national plant involving the active participation of the supplier of the nuclear material being reprocessed, that the US government had been offered the opportunity to participate in its operation, and that it was placed under the safeguards spelled out in Article XI of the agreement (which went beyond the standard IAEA safeguards). However, the note also went on to state that, should it not prove possible to establish a multinational or bi-national facility, reprocessing could still go ahead in a facility that 'the parties jointly determine to be acceptable'.[83]

It took the Iranians the best part of two months to digest the proposal and formulate their response. This took the form of a redrafting of the proposed agreement in which they firstly suggested that Article VIII be rewritten to remove any mention of buy-back, and state simply that when material required reprocessing this should 'take place in appropriate facilities'. The bulk of the redrafting then focused on the note. Here Iran rewrote the US document to state that, while it would be happy to consider inviting the US to participate in any reprocessing facility it chose to establish, Iran 'shall have the right to effective control' of the facility and America's 'active participation' would not include a veto power. The draft went on to say that, should the Iranian government conclude that reprocessing was not desirable then, 'at the request of Iran', reprocessing could take place in facilities in the USA or elsewhere, with Iran having the right to the reprocessed material or appropriate financial compensation. In short, reprocessing in Iran, in a facility controlled by the Iranian government, over whose operation the US would have no veto power, was to be the first recourse. Only if Tehran decided not to exercise that option would buy-back of spent fuel become a possibility.[84]

The Iranian response demonstrated the continued inability of US negotiators to read their Iranian counterparts. Buoyed by Etemad's perceived receptivity to the buy-back concept, they had chosen not to reveal their willingness to abandon it if necessary and instead put on the table a deal which would ensure that the US would be in a position to exercise the buy-back option. The Iranian response, which constituted a flat rejection of the key US propositions on reprocessing and a bold assertion of Iran's sovereign right to reprocess, thus came as a real shock. As Robert Oakley of the NSC staff wrote to Scowcroft, it returned 'our negotiations to the starting point'.[85]

Nevertheless, for all Etemad's defiance, the immovable object that he sought to present was doomed to be overwhelmed by the irresistible force of the pressures bearing down on the Ford administration. For its part, Congress was still considering how best to prevent further nuclear proliferation, with a number of competing bills at various stages of the legislative process. All sought to tighten controls over nuclear exports by imposing unilateral constraints and reducing the autonomy of the executive branch to make nuclear agreements.[86] In early May 1976 the Senate Foreign Relations Committee passed an amendment proposed by Senator Symington that would cut off military and economic aid to any country that imported reprocessing equipment, unless the facility was multilateral and all its nuclear facilities were under IAEA safeguards.[87]

To make matters worse, 1976 was a presidential election year and the Democratic candidate, Jimmy Carter, was making great play of both the danger of nuclear proliferation and what he alleged was the Ford administration's laissez-faire attitude toward it. In a speech at the UN on 13 May he warned of the 'fearsome prospect that the spread of nuclear reactors will mean the spread of nuclear weapons to many nations', and claimed that if the West did not act, by 1990 the developing nations would be producing enough plutonium to build 3,000 Hiroshima-size bombs.[88] During the campaign he went on to assert that the Ford administration had 'ignored the increased risks of nuclear war' posed by the spread of nuclear technology, and to state that if elected, he would seek an international ban on the export of enrichment and reprocessing technologies.[89] A Department of State analysis concluded that, while Carter's allegations were unfounded, the charges were sticking and 'the Administration is pictured as callous to security, public safety and environmental concerns and oversensitive to the feelings of our allies who are engaged in selling dangerous technology to dangerous governments'.[90]

That last point highlighted the third factor constraining the administration. Despite American pressures, both France and West Germany had refused to agree to a complete ban on the export of enrichment and reprocessing technologies, and in July 1976 Bonn announced a nuclear agreement with Iran which envisaged the eventual transfer of reprocessing technology when Iran required it. The Ford administration was privately furious with the Germans and publicly stated its opposition to the deal. If it was to have any hope of forcing Bonn to back out of the agreement, it had to hold the line on reprocessing in its own negotiations with Iran.[91]

Oakley's memo to Scowcroft suggested that the two sides were 'now so far apart that it may be better for the Secretary [Kissinger] to discuss this exclusively with the Shah' when he visited Iran in August, rather than hold another round of fruitless negotiations at a lower level.[92] In the event more negotiations took place in Tehran immediately before Kissinger's arrival, but it was in the latter's meeting with the Shah that an agreement was, seemingly, reached. On 8 August Kissinger reported that he had told the Shah that there were three possible options in relation to nuclear reprocessing. These were: a binational plant in Iran with the US as a partner, though 'I made it clear that under current and foreseeable conditions this would not be possible'; reprocessing in 'an acceptable third country'; or buy-back of spent fuel/exchange of spent fuel for new fuel. Iran would choose which option it preferred in the first instance but the US would have a veto and 'I made it clear that reprocessing in Iran on a purely national basis would not be an acceptable solution.' Apparently the Shah 'seemed agreeable' to the proposal while Etemad also indicated that 'Iran would be prepared to go along with this solution' in a separate meeting.[93]

The agreement apparently reached during Kissinger's visit presents something of a conundrum, and one to which there is ultimately no answer, since Kissinger's summary of events is all that we have to go on. In the first place we have the fact that Kissinger, previously amongst those most inclined to plead the Iranian cause, presented the Shah with a set of options which were not those previously agreed within the administration and which represented a considerably more restrictive offer than the agreed position.[94] One can only speculate that Kissinger had now come to recognise that political realities meant that he had no choice but to take a tough line in order to avoid domestic political fallout, get the deal past Congress, and keep up pressure on the other members of the NSG. On the Iranian side we are confronted with the fact that, two weeks after Etemad had robustly rejected the American draft agreement, Tehran now folded its hand. To a large extent this would appear to be due to the direct intervention of the Shah in the process. Always more preoccupied with maintaining a good relationship with Washington than Etemad, the Shah, seemingly persuaded by Kissinger and by the political realities constraining the American negotiating position, apparently came to the conclusion that he needed to concede to American demands to keep relations on an even keel.[95]

Confirmation of the accuracy of the Shah's perceptions was provided in late October 1976. In response to Carter's continued criticism, which was being echoed in the media, and in order to shore up his electoral prospects, Ford initiated a nuclear policy review. The result of the review was announced in a major speech on 28 October. For the most part, Ford reiterated existing policy, calling for increased cooperation between nuclear exporters to achieve 'maximum restraint in the transfer of reprocessing and enrichment technology'. In addition, however, Ford also announced a moratorium on the export of reprocessing and enrichment technology for 'at least three years'.[96]

Carter and the End of the Shah's Nuclear Programme

Ford's defeat in the 1976 presidential election meant that his nuclear policy review would never be implemented. It also meant that any agreement reached by Kissinger and the Shah was moot as the new Carter administration initiated its own nuclear policy review.

When Carter announced the results of that review he confirmed that the administration would halt reprocessing in the USA 'indefinitely', while conceding that the other members of the NSG had the right to reprocess if they so wished. He hoped, nevertheless, to persuade them to limit the spread of reprocessing technology and his objective was 'that those countries that don't now have reprocessing capability will not acquire that capability in the future'.[97] The administration's approach to nuclear exports was given more concrete form when it submitted a bill to Congress on 27 April 1977. The essence of the policy therein was very similar to the position reached by the Ford administration by the second half of 1976. While seeking to act as a reliable supplier of fuel for civilian reactors, the administration would 'continue to embargo the export of enrichment and reprocessing plants' and impose 'a requirement that no fuel exported from the United States be reprocessed without the prior approval of the United States'.[98]

Despite the clarity of the Carter administration's position and his own apparent acceptance that Iran would not be allowed to pursue national reprocessing, Etemad continued to present a conundrum to American negotiators. When he met Deputy Assistant Secretary of State for Near Eastern Affairs Sidney Sober in May 1977, he reiterated that Iran had abandoned the idea of reprocessing 'with the expectation that the supplier countries will fully recognize Iran's legitimate needs' for fuel supply and technology.[99] However, when the American representatives presented him with a new draft agreement and a paper on alternatives for spent fuel disposition in August, he 'launched into a long, emotional and at times bitter monologue' about how Iran 'must manage independently the end of the fuel cycle'. Efforts to 'get him to be more precise about what was bothering him' and what he wanted changed were 'simply rebuffed'. The US negotiating team confessed itself 'frankly somewhat bewildered' as to whether this was some form of negotiating tactic or simply an emotional outburst.[100]

In contrast, in a meeting with Treasury Secretary Michael Blumenthal on 27 October 1977, the Shah 'categorically assured' him that Iran had 'no intention of making atomic weapons' and had no interest in having an indigenous reprocessing plant in the absence of any economic rationale for such.[101] When negotiations continued during the Shah's visit to Washington in November and Carter's reciprocal visit to Tehran in December, the US team confirmed to their Iranian counterparts that the legislation currently going through Congress would require the administration to terminate all nuclear cooperation with any state which pursued national reprocessing.[102] They did offer some minor adjustments to the text of the draft agreement but these were largely designed to salve Iranian pride. Thus, the new text made clear that Iran would receive 'most favored nation' status in regard to nuclear cooperation, including reprocessing, but this simply meant that Iran would not be treated differently to any other state with which the USA made an agreement. When it came to the question of reprocessing itself, the options offered to Iran in mid-December were (a) storage of spent fuel in Iran; (b) storage of spent fuel in the US and the transfer of equivalent new fuel or financial compensation to Iran (buy-back); or (c) storage or reprocessing in an agreed third country and return of any reprocessed fuel to Iran. In another sop to Iran, the new draft stated that these provisions would be reviewed in 1985.

Two weeks later, at the end of Carter's visit to Iran, it was announced that the two sides had reached a new bilateral nuclear agreement.[103] The rapidity with which the agreement was reached, and its timing, suggest that once again it was the personal intervention of the Shah which was decisive and that his desire to preserve his relationship with Washington overcame his, and Etemad's, desire to protect Iran's 'sovereign rights'. Even then, there were still disagreements about the exact wording, as the Iranians continued to push for maximum leeway with regard to future reprocessing, and only in July 1978 did representatives of the two governments initial the new US–Iran nuclear agreement.[104]

The agreement would never be ratified, however. The Shah had relaunched the nuclear programme in 1974 on a wave of oil money, but by 1978 the tide was on its way out after Western governments sought to diversify their energy sources and instigated energy-saving measures, leading Saudi Arabia to force a production cut on OPEC in an effort to maintain prices. The Iranian economy, after a decade and a half of dramatic growth, was now in serious trouble. The lavish spending of petrodollars had produced soaring inflation and corruption while growth began to slow and government deficits began to rise.[105] Under these circumstances, the nuclear programme came to be seen by some as an expensive and unnecessary luxury.

One of those inclined to that view was Jamshid Amouzegar, who replaced Amir Abbas Hoveyda, a strong supporter of the nuclear programme, as prime minister in August 1977. Amouzegar instigated a review of the nuclear programme by a panel of economists and energy policy specialists which resulted in a highly critical report. They highlighted a number of key flaws in the programme, especially the lack of a guaranteed fuel supply and a national electricity infrastructure capable of utilising the production of the proposed reactors. With the cost of the nuclear programme escalating at a dizzying rate (the estimate of $30 billion to build twenty reactors in 1974 had risen to $80–120 billion by 1978) they argued that Iran would be better off supplying its increasing energy needs from its vast natural gas reserves for a fraction of the cost. They recommended that there should be a moratorium on all new nuclear activities until a full-scale assessment of the utility of nuclear power could be completed.[106] The already sceptical Amouzegar was readily persuaded and, as part of his effort to cut government spending and reduce inflation, proceeded to dismantle the nuclear programme. Etemad was forced from his post and the AEOI stripped of most of its responsibilities.[107]

Had he wished to the Shah could, of course, have prevented Amouzegar from taking this course of action. By mid-1978, however, with the political crisis that would eventually become the Iranian Revolution steadily escalating, all of the Shah's attention was devoted to his doomed attempts to prevent the demise of his regime. In October 1978 he postponed the purchase of four additional reactors from KWU and it was announced that funds would be transferred from the nuclear programme to increased social spending.[108] As the political crisis deepened the nuclear programme continued to crumble. In November strikes halted work at reactor construction sites and in January 1979 the Shah's last prime minister, Shapour Bakhtiar, announced the annulment of the contracts for the two French reactors under construction.[109] In the same month the Shah fled into exile and as revolution engulfed Iran his nuclear programme was also brought to an end.[110]

Lessons of the 1970s

The US–Iranian nuclear deal initialled in July 1978 died with the Shah's regime. While the Iranian Revolution struck the final blow, negotiations had been tortuous even before that point. Despite the alliance between the two countries, and the desire of both to reach a new agreement, it had proved extraordinarily difficult to do so. While from 1979 onwards the US–Iranian relationship would take a very different turn, many of the factors that were at play between 1974 and 1978 and which made agreement so difficult would continue to be central to the nuclear relationship in the coming decades.

The issue which lay at the heart of US–Iranian disagreements between 1974 and 1978 was the nuclear fuel cycle. Etemad and the Shah were insistent that Iran must have the right to reprocess spent fuel in order to ensure that it had a reliable, renewable source of fuel for its reactors. The US government, for its part, sought to deny Iran the right to control reprocessing on the grounds that weapons grade plutonium would be one of the products of that process. Although the focus of concern would subsequently shift from reprocessing to enrichment, this conflict over the fuel cycle remained central when the United States later confronted the Islamic Republic of Iran (IRI) over its nuclear programme, and for the same fundamental reasons – the inevitable commonalities of civilian and weapons programmes.

Despite the transformations wrought by the Iranian Revolution, the factors shaping the policy preferences and decisions of both sides would also demonstrate a significant degree of continuity. In this first episode domestic political factors proved to be of great importance in shaping the American negotiating position.

The deep hostility of Congress to further nuclear transfers after the Indian PNE and the requirement that any new nuclear agreement with Iran receive congressional ratification imposed very clear constraints on American negotiators. The fear that an agreement that did not prevent Iran from having autonomous control of reprocessing would not get past Congress was arguably the key reason that Washington refused to compromise on its demands. The difficulty of identifying a compromise that was acceptable both to the other government and to one's own domestic audience would remain a defining feature of the US–Iranian nuclear relationship.

The importance of domestic political considerations to the American negotiating position raises the question of whether, had that congressional pressure not existed, the Nixon–Ford administration would have gone ahead with a deal that allowed Iran control over reprocessing (Carter, clearly, would not have done). This question is of interest because it addresses the widespread allegation that the United States was blithely unconcerned about nuclear proliferation when Iran was an American ally and only became preoccupied with it when Iran had become America's sworn enemy. While there can be no definitive answer to the question, there is sufficient evidence to permit informed inference. On the one hand, we have seen the lengths to which the Nixon–Ford administration went to try and find a compromise acceptable to Iran – constantly adjusting American demands in regard to reprocessing – and how concerned it was about doing damage to the US–Iranian relationship. Given that evidence it is hard to believe that, had fears about congressional action not existed, the administration would not have offered Iran greater control of reprocessing than it actually did.

That is not to say, however, that it would have allowed Iran full control of reprocessing without any extra safeguards beyond the standard IAEA arrangements. The Indian PNE clearly affected the administration's views, and the conclusion of NSSM 202 that the USA needed to pursue an 'intensified program' to prevent proliferation was not driven solely by fear of Congress taking control of nuclear export policy. The administration took the lead in organising the NSG and took much the most restrictive position on the transfer of nuclear materials and technology within that group. While it is reasonable to conclude that, absent domestic political pressures, the Nixon–Ford administration would have offered Iran greater autonomy with regard to reprocessing, its concerns about proliferation were real and it would most likely have sought safeguards (probably US involvement in a reprocessing plant in some form) beyond the IAEA norm. The allegation that US policy toward Iran's nuclear programme has been hypocritical – demonstrating concern about proliferation only when it has been opposed to the regime in power – is exaggerated at best.

While concerns about proliferation and domestic politics drove the American stance in the negotiations, the Iranian stance on reprocessing was rooted in a strong belief that, as a great power, Iran ought to have mastery of advanced technologies. It was also driven by the belief that Iran had an absolute right to complete control of the fuel cycle under the NPT, provisional only on its complying with standard IAEA safeguards. A third factor underpinning the Iranian desire to control reprocessing was the recognition that, without it, they would be dependent on external powers for their fuel supply and a fear that those powers would not prove to be a trustworthy or reliable source of that fuel.[111] Finally, without control of the whole fuel cycle Iran would not be in a position to pursue weapons status should it deem it necessary to do so.

In all these aspects the Islamic Republic's attitude toward nuclear power would be consistent with that of Etemad and the Shah. The one critical difference was that the Shah wanted nuclear power in order to join the club of advanced Western nations rather than in order to challenge it, leading him to put his relationship with the United States ahead of his desire for control of the fuel cycle. Even under those circumstances, however, he and Etemad abandoned their demand for national control of reprocessing only under great pressure and with extreme reluctance. It should hardly have come as a surprise, therefore, that the IRI, shorn of any desire to appease Washington, proved to be so utterly intractable in its insistence on control of the fuel cycle.

Another area in which there would prove to be considerable continuity is in the great difficulty that American negotiators had in understanding their Iranian counterparts and in establishing precisely what their bottom line actually was. Etemad proved to be a source of constant irritation and confusion to his interlocutors, repeatedly shifting his stance and appearing to accept US conditions at one meeting only to reject them at the next one. The Shah also proved to be an elusive negotiator for much of this period. This, moreover, was under circumstances in which American diplomats had excellent access to Iran and to the regime, as opposed to later decades in which they had virtually no contact with their Iranian interlocutors. The mutual misunderstanding and distrust that subsequently characterised so many US–Iranian interactions was thus predictable.[112]

The final aspect of the first episode of the nuclear relationship which prefigured what was to follow was the tension between unilateralism and multilateralism in US policy, and the difficulties incumbent on the pursuit of either approach. The Nixon–Ford administration's opposition to congressional desires to impose unilateral constraints on nuclear exports was rooted in the understanding that such an approach would be self-defeating. Iran would simply look elsewhere for its nuclear supplies while US companies lost valuable business. That logic would apply equally well to the unilateral imposition of US sanctions on Iran following the Iranian Revolution, but antipathy to the new regime and domestic political pressures would come to override logic. The preferred alternative of the administration (and of Carter, despite his imposition of some unilateral measures) was for the establishment of effective multilateral controls on the transfer of nuclear material and technology. Such controls would certainly have been a more effective means of managing proliferation, but as the July 1976 West German agreement to supply Iran with reprocessing technology demonstrated, other nuclear suppliers took a more sanguine view of the dangers of proliferation. An inability to persuade other advanced states, not least its European allies, to put controlling proliferation ahead of their narrow economic or strategic interests would prove to be another recurring problem for Washington.

Notes

1. US Department of State, *Report on the International Control of Atomic Energy*, p. 4.
2. US Department of State, *Documents on Disarmament: Volume 1*, pp. 7–16.
3. Ibid., pp. 17–24.
4. Dwight D. Eisenhower, 'Address before the General Assembly of the United Nations on peaceful uses of atomic energy', 8 December 1953, US President, *Public Papers of the Presidents of the United States (PPPUS)*.
5. IAEA, 'Statute of the IAEA'.
6. Poneman, *Nuclear Power*, p. 27.
7. United Nations, 'Agreement for cooperation'.
8. Walker, 'Nuclear power and non-proliferation', pp. 217–18.
9. United Nations, 'Treaty on the Non-Proliferation of Nuclear Weapons'.
10. The IAEA's safeguarding role is defined in IAEA, 'Structure and content of agreements between the agency and states'.
11. Kuniholm, *Origins of the Cold War in the Near East*.
12. Gasiorowski, '1953 coup d'etat in Iran'.
13. Alvandi, 'Nixon, Kissinger and the Shah'.
14. Alam, *The Shah and I*, p. 48.
15. 'Editorial note', US Department of State, *Foreign Relations of the United States (FRUS) 1969–1976 (FRUS 1969–1976): Vol. I*, Document 29.
16. 'Memorandum of conversation', Washington, 1 April 1969, *FRUS 1969–1976: Vol. E-4*, Document 6.
17. 'Memorandum from Kissinger to President Nixon', 22 October 1970, *FRUS 1969–1976: Vol. E-4*, Document 91; 'National Security Decision Memorandum (NSDM) 92', 7 November 1970, *FRUS 1969–1976: Vol. E-4*, Document 97.
18. 'Memorandum of conversation', Tehran, 31 May 1972, *FRUS, 1969–1976: Vol. E-4*, Document 201.
19. Poneman, *Nuclear Power*, p. 84; Patrikarikos, *Nuclear Iran*, pp. 16–20.
20. *Kayhan International*, 24 March 1974, p. 1; Patrikarikos, *Nuclear Iran*, p. 21.
21. *Kayhan International*, 30 November 1974, p. 1.
22. US Embassy Tehran, Airgram A-69 to State Department, 'The Atomic Energy Agency of Iran', 11 May 1977, National Security Archive, *The Iranian Nuclear Program (NSA: Iranian Nuclear Program)*.

23. US ERDA, 'Iran: Atomic Energy Programme', p. 3.
24. *Kayhan International*, 3 August 1974, p. 4.
25. Mossavar-Rahmani, 'Iran', p. 204; Afkhami, *Life and Times of the Shah*, p. 357; Etemad, 'Interview', p. 94.
26. Sagan, 'Why do states build nuclear weapons?'; Suchman and Eyre, 'Military procurement as rational myth'; Husbands, 'Prestige states'; Hymans, 'Theories of nuclear proliferation'.
27. The Shah, quoted in Karanjia, *Mind of a Monarch*, pp. 242–3.
28. Abrahamian, *Iran Between Two Revolutions*, pp. 430–1.
29. M. R. Pahlavi, *Besouyeh Tamadun-e Bozorg* (Tehran: n.d.), quoted in Ansari, *Modern Iran*, p. 191.
30. Prem 15/1684, 'Meeting Shah – Rothschild December 2 1972', quoted in Ansari, *Modern Iran*, pp. 63–4.
31. See, for example, McGlinchey and Choksy, 'Iran's nuclear ambitions'.
32. US Embassy, Paris, cable 15305 to Department of State, 'Interview with the Shah', 24 June 1974, *NSA: Iranian Nuclear Program*; Alam, *The Shah and I*, p. 353.
33. Cahn, 'Determinants of the nuclear option', pp. 188–9.
34. Poneman, *Nuclear Power*, p. 133.
35. IAEA, 'Text of the agreement between Iran and the agency for the application of safeguards'; *Kayhan International*, 8 July 1974, p. 1.
36. Tahtinen, *Arms in the Persian Gulf*.
37. Frey, 'Of nuclear myths and nuclear taboos'.
38. Etemad, 'Interview'; Patrikarikos, *Nuclear Iran*, pp. 64–8.
39. Zubeida Malik, 'The man who turned Iran nuclear', *BBC Today Programme*, 28 March 2013, <http://www.bbc.co.uk/news/world-middle-east-21938310> (last accessed 27 September 2016).
40. *Kayhan International*, 20 September 1975, p. 4; see also the Shah's reported comments in *Der Spiegel*, 8 February 1975.
41. Golnaz Esfandiari, 'The father of Iran's nuclear programme recalls how it all began', *Radio Free Europe*, 3 July 2015, <http://www.rferl.org/a/father-of-iran-nuclear-program-recalls-how-it-began/27108228.html> (last accessed 27 September 2016). See also Homayounvash, *Iran and the Nuclear Question*, pp. 169–72.
42. 'US–Iran Cooperation', Department of State Telegram, 11 April 1974, Digital National Security Archive (*DNSA*).
43. 'Summary of developments in Secretary's absence', Department of State, memorandum, 30 May 1974; 'US–Iran Joint Statement', unclassified briefing paper, 3 November 1974, *DNSA*.
44. Paper prepared by an interdepartmental working group, 25 April 1974, *FRUS 1969–1976: Vol. XXVII*, Document 59; 'Telegram

from the Department of State to the embassy in Iran', 11 March 1974, *FRUS 1969–1976: Vol. XXVII*, Document 55.

45. Hamblin, 'Nuclearization of Iran in the seventies'.
46. Brown, 'Presidential leadership and US nonproliferation policy', p. 564.
47. 'Westinghouse gets Korea Electric order for two nuclear plants' *Wall Street Journal*, 4 April 1978, p. 13.
48. Mossavar-Rahmani, 'Iran', p. 203.
49. National Security Study Memorandum 202, 23 May 1974, *Nixon Presidential Library: Virtual Documents*.
50. Walker, 'Nuclear power and non-proliferation'.
51. US Congress, Joint Committee on Atomic Energy, 'Proliferation of nuclear weapons', pp. 30–1.
52. US Congress, Senate Committee on Government Operations, 'Hearings on the Export Reorganization Act – 1975', p. 1.
53. Special National Intelligence Estimate 4-1-74, 'Prospects for further proliferation of nuclear weapons', 23 August 1974, *NSA: Iranian Nuclear Program*.
54. National Security Decision Memorandum 255, 3 June 1974, *Nixon Presidential Library: Virtual Documents*.
55. Burr, 'A scheme of "control"'.
56. Telegram from the Department of State to the embassy in Iran, 28 June 1974, *FRUS 1969–1976: Vol. XXVII*, Document 63.
57. NSC Under Secretaries Committee to Deputy Secretary of Defense et al., 'US nuclear non-proliferation policy', 4 December 1974, enclosing Memorandum for the President from Robert S. Ingersoll, Chairman, 4 December 1974, and NSSM 202 Study, 'Executive summary', *NSA: Iranian Nuclear Program*.
58. Testimony of the former Chairman of the AEC, Dixy Lee Ray, US Congress, Senate Committee on Government Operations, 'Hearings on the Export Reorganization Act – 1975', p. 125.
59. Executive Secretary Samuel R. Gammon to Sidney Sober, Bureau of Near Eastern Affairs, and Thomas Clingan, Bureau of Oceans, International Environmental, and Scientific Affairs, 'Nuclear energy agreement for cooperation with Iran', 11 December 1974, enclosing memorandum to Secretary Kissinger from Alfred Atherton, Bureau of Near Eastern Affairs and Nelson F. Sievering, Bureau of Oceans, International Environmental, and Scientific Affairs, 'Nuclear energy agreement for cooperation', 6 December 1974, *NSA: Iranian Nuclear Program*.
60. Alvandi, *Nixon, Kissinger and the Shah*, p. 6.

61. 'Cable 1393 to Department of State from embassy Tehran', 21 February 1975, US National Archives and Records Administration, *Department of State General Records, Record Group 59, Central Foreign Policy Files 1973–1976*.
62. Embassy Tehran to Secretary of State Washington DC, 'Iranian atomic energy chief rebukes supplier nations', 20 April 1976, US Department of State, *Department of State Central Policy Files 1973–1977* (*Central Policy Files 1973–1977*), Document 1976STATE095264.
63. Etemad, 'Interview'.
64. Esfandiari, 'Father of Iran's nuclear programme'.
65. Patrikarikos, *Nuclear Iran*, p. 57.
66. National Security Decision Memorandum 292, 'U.S.–Iran nuclear cooperation', *NSA: Iranian Nuclear Program*.
67. 'Memorandum from David Elliott of the National Security Council Staff to the President's Deputy Assistant for National Security Affairs (Scowcroft)', 12 March 1975, *FRUS 1969–1976: Vol. XXVII*, Document 112.
68. Embassy Tehran to Secretary of State, 'Multinational nuclear centers: Assessment of Iranian attitudes toward nuclear reprocessing', 17 July 1975, *NSA: Iranian Nuclear Program*.
69. 'Kissinger to Ford', 15 May 1975, *Ford Presidential Library, National Security Adviser, Box 9*. Kissinger's observation is probably based on Special National Intelligence Estimate, 9 May 1975, *FRUS 1969–1976: Vol. XXVII*, Document 121.
70. Walker, 'Nuclear power and non-proliferation', p. 224.
71. In the end, the US failed to convince the other suppliers to take a hard line, with the French and Germans arguing that it was simply seeking to deny them legitimate commercial opportunities. When the agreement on nuclear exports was announced in March 1976 it merely stated that the NSG had agreed to 'apply restraints in the transfer of such sensitive technologies as uranium enrichment and reprocessing to separate plutonium'; 'Officials confirm reports on seven nation pact', *Nuclear News*, 19 April 1976, pp. 105–6.
72. Sidney Sober, 'Your meeting with the Shah at Blair House', Confidential Briefing Memorandum, 9 May 1975, *DNSA*.
73. US Mission, Vienna, to Department of State, 'US–Iran nuclear cooperation', Cable 8210, 25 September 1975, *DNSA*.
74. State Department cable 254826 to embassy Tehran, 'Nuclear agreement for cooperation', 25 October 1975, *NSA: Iranian Nuclear Program*.

75. Embassy Tehran to State Department, 'Shah's interview by *Business Week* given prominent coverage by English language Kayhan', 13 November 1975, *NSA: Iranian Nuclear Program.*

76. 'Memorandum from David Elliott of the National Security Council Staff to the President's Assistant for National Security Affairs (Scowcroft)', 20 January 1976, *FRUS 1969–1976: Vol. XXVII*, Document 160.

77. Ibid.

78. 'Memorandum from the President's Assistant for National Security Affairs (Scowcroft) to President Ford', 26 January 1976, *FRUS 1969–1976: Vol. XXVII*, Document 159; 'Memorandum by the President's Assistant for National Security Affairs (Scowcroft)', 4 February 1976, *FRUS 1969–1976: Vol. XXVII*, Document 162.

79. 'Meeting on nuclear negotiations with Iran', memorandum for the Secretary, 16 April 1976, *NSA: Iranian Nuclear Program.*

80. Ibid.

81. National Security Decision Memorandum 324, 20 April 1976, *FRUS 1969–1976: Vol. XXVII*, Document 173.

82. 'Secretary's staff meeting', incorrect date of 12 January 1975 on document, minutes c. 12 January 1976, *DNSA*.

83. State Department to Embassy Tehran, 'Iranian nuclear power agreement', 28 May 1976, *NSA: Iranian Nuclear Program.*

84. 'Iranian counterproposals for atomic energy agreement', 23 July 1976, *NSA: Iranian Nuclear Program.*

85. Oakley to Scowcroft, 26 July 1976, *Ford Presidential Library, National Security Adviser, Box 1.*

86. Walker, 'Nuclear power and non-proliferation', pp. 233–4.

87. 'Proposed cable to Tehran on Pakistani nuclear reprocessing', 12 May 1976, *DNSA*.

88. 'Address by Governor Jimmy Carter at the United Nations', 13 May 1976, 'Nuclear issues', *Carter Presidential Library, Folder, Box 25.*

89. Ellis, 'Carter would shift toward solar energy'.

90. 'Memorandum from Stuart S. Janney and Paul L. Ahern of the Office of the Deputy Under Secretary of State for Management to the Deputy Under Secretary of State for Management (Eagleburger)', 21 July 1976, *FRUS 1969–1976: Vol. XXXVIII*, Document 81.

91. Memorandum of conversation, 'The Secretary's meeting with FRG Ambassador Von Staden on the FRG/Iran Agreement for nuclear cooperation', 2 July 1976, *NSA: Iranian Nuclear Program.*

92. Oakley to Scowcroft, 26 July 1976, *Ford Presidential Library, National Security Adviser, Box 1.*

93. 'Nuclear cooperation with Iran', 8 August 1976, *Central Policy Files 1973–1977*, Document 1976SECTO20089.

94. Memorandum for the Secretary from Charles W. Robinson, 'Nuclear negotiations with Iran', 18 August 1976, *NSA: Iranian Nuclear Program*.

95. Roham Alvandi suggests the Shah had reached the conclusion that a nuclear agreement with the USA was not going to be possible and therefore decided to cut his losses and protect the core US–Iranian relationship; Alvandi, *Nixon, Kissinger and the Shah*, p. 167.

96. Gerald Ford, 'Statement on nuclear policy', 28 October 1976, *PPPUS*.

97. Jimmy Carter, 'Nuclear power policy remarks and a question-and-answer session with reporters on decisions following a review of U.S. Policy', 7 April 1977, *PPPUS*.

98. 'Fact sheet on the proposed Nuclear Non-Proliferation Policy Act of 1977', 27 April 1977, *PPPUS*.

99. 'US–Iran nuclear cooperation agreement and US–Iran energy discussions', 16 May 1977, *Central Policy Files 1973–1977*, Document 1977TEHRAN04313.

100. 'Negotiations on bilateral agreement on nuclear energy', 12 August 1977, *Central Policy Files 1973–1977*, Document 1977STATE191592.

101. 'Secretary Blumental's discussions with the Shah', 28 October 1977, NLC-16-109-3-2-9-Laserfiche, Jimmy Carter Presidential Library, quoted in Homayounvash, *Iran and the Nuclear Question*, pp. 108–9.

102. The Nuclear Non-Proliferation Act was signed into law by Carter on 10 March 1978. Amongst other things, it contained a prohibition on the reprocessing of US-supplied fuel without US approval. See Public Law 95-242, available at <https://www.gpo.gov/fdsys/pkg/STATUTE-92/pdf/STATUTE-92-Pg120.pdf> (last accessed 22 November 2016).

103. 'Negotiations with GOI concerning nuclear cooperation', 15 December 1977, *Central Policy Files 1973–1977*, Document 1977TEHRAN11031; 'Draft press release', 30 December 1977, *Central Policy Files 1973–1977*, Document 1977STATE310441.

104. Homayounvash, *Iran and the Nuclear Question*, pp. 114–17; Department of State Memorandum, 'Iran: The US–Iran nuclear energy agreement', 20 October 1978; 'Country Team Minutes', 12 July 1978, *DNSA*.

105. Axworthy, *Revolutionary Iran*, pp. 97–8.

106. Mossavar-Rahmani, 'Iran's nuclear power programme revisited', p. 199. Mossavar-Rahmani was one of the panel members.
107. *Kayhan International*, 29 June 1978, p. 1. For a more detailed account of the 'retrenchment' of the Shah's nuclear programme, see Homayounvash, *Iran and the Nuclear Question*, pp. 144–54.
108. Poneman, *Nuclear Power*, p. 96; *The Wall Street Journal*, 11 October 1978.
109. *Le Monde*, 30 January 1979.
110. Poneman, *Nuclear Power*, p. 96.
111. Hamblin, 'Nuclearization of Iran in the seventies ', pp. 20–1.
112. Bar, 'Iran'.

2 The 1980s: Developing Hostility and the Origins of the Islamic Republic's Nuclear Programme

It was always likely that the relationship between the United States and the Islamic Republic of Iran (IRI) would be one of conflict, since not only were the two regimes driven by antithetical ideologies but each was also intent on being the dominant power in the Persian Gulf. Nevertheless, between 1979 and 1988 events, some of which were avoidable, also conspired to ensure that the conflict between the two would become an exceptionally bitter one. The lack of mutual understanding that had been evident under the Shah's regime evolved into a relationship of pathological mistrust, in which the worst was always assumed of the other whilst the reasonableness of one's own actions and intentions was rarely questioned.[1] The 1980s thus saw the forging of the relationship of profound hostility and distrust which formed the essential context in which the nuclear relationship would develop over the next three decades. Both the IRI's nuclear programme and the American response to it have been fundamentally influenced by this antipathy, both at the elite level and through its pervasiveness in their wider societies. This chapter traces the development of that antipathy as well as examining the decision of the new Iranian leadership to reconstitute the country's nuclear programme in the context of its developing confrontation with the United States.

Before the Revolution

The Iranian antipathy toward the United States that bloomed in the 1980s was borne in no small part from a sense of disillusion. Before the Cold War the United States had been viewed favourably in Iran because of its anti-colonialism. Russia and Britain were Iran's imperialist bogeymen while America was viewed as a potential saviour. That hope was reinforced by American support for Iranian national self-determination during World War II and in the face of Soviet pressure in 1946.[2] Consequently, 'on the eve of the American moment in Iran, the Iranians held an idealised image of the United States. The expectation was that the Americans would do what they could to allow Iranians to take control of their own destiny.'[3]

Iranian perceptions were changed, and their hopes dashed, by the events of 1953. The American role in the overthrow of Mossadegh is viewed as an act of betrayal by Iranians regardless of their political allegiance. For supporters of the IRI it is proof that the United States is just another 'imperial' power bent on exploiting Iran for its own ends. For the regime's opponents Washington's action killed off the development of secular nationalism and democracy in Iran and guaranteed that the country would be ruled first by one autocracy and then another. The consequence of the American decision to back the coup was that 'in little more than one generation, American policy toward Iran had succeeded in replacing what was probably unreasonably strong goodwill toward the United States with unreasonably strong resentment'.[4]

Between 1953 and 1979 continued American support for the Shah served to cement Iranian resentment toward the American government. Washington's decision to rely on the Shah as the best guarantor of Iranian political stability and reliability as a Cold War ally made it unwilling to press for political change, despite widespread recognition that the Shah's continued failure to reform made him, in many respects, his own worst enemy. Thus tied to an increasingly unpopular autocrat, everything Washington did was turned against it. The US aid programme, rather than being evidence of American generosity, was resented because of its focus on military, rather than economic, aid and the way that it fuelled corruption. There was also anger at the way that aid was doled out in response to compliant behaviour such as Iran's signing of the hugely resented 1964 Status of Forces Agreement.[5] Abdolhassan Ebtehaj, the former head of the Iranian seven-year plan organisation, told an American audience in 1961:

not so many years ago in Iran, the United States was loved and respected as no other country, and without having given a penny of aid. Now, after more than $1 billion of loans and grants, America is neither loved nor respected; she is distrusted by most people and hated by many.[6]

As the Shah's regime became more repressive, so the bond between him and the United States seemed to Iranians to become ever closer. In the 1970s the Shah abandoned any pretence of political reform and sought to maintain his rule through increasing repression. As the disappearance, arrest and torture of political opponents escalated, American support for the Shah became less and less equivocal. Nixon's decision to make Iran the US proxy in the Gulf ended any American efforts to press the Shah to reform. Allowing him to buy whatever conventional weapons he wanted then led to a massive spending splurge that created a field day for US corporations and further fuelled already rampant corruption. Typically, it was also perceived as evidence of American power and cunning, rather than weakness. According to the Shah's opponents, this was all a cunning American plan: 'the United States government, by frightening the Iranian people with the specters of their neighbors, by selling us used weapons at exorbitant prices, has poured billions of rials in to pockets of US military cartels'.[7] The Shah's spending also resulted in a rapid escalation in the number of Americans working in Iran, from 8,000 in 1970 to almost 50,000 by the end of 1977, further reinforcing the increasingly indelible association of the USA with his regime.[8]

Iranian hopes were briefly raised with the accession of Jimmy Carter to the presidency. In his campaign for office Carter had emphasised the importance of human rights and condemned the fact that the United States had become the world's leading arms supplier. Once in office, however, his administration 'decided early on that it was in our national interest to support the Shah so he could continue to play a constructive role in regional affairs'.[9] Consequently, the Shah's human rights record went unexamined and arms sales continued unabated. Iranians whose hopes had been raised by Carter's earlier statements found them crushed by American hypocrisy once again.

The Hostage Crisis and the 'Mad Mullahs'

To a great extent, therefore, anti-Americanism was built into the Iranian Revolution, with Washington held to be as much or more to blame for the inequities of the Shah's regime as the Shah himself. As the first president of the IRI, Abdolhassan Bani-Sadr, put it, 'all that happened in Iran: It was not the imperial court that made the decision. It was the United States embassy.'[10] Iran's new Supreme Leader, Ayatollah Ruhollah Khomeini, made the same point more pithily, asserting that 'all our problems come from America'.[11] This perception that the Shah was an American puppet reflected tendencies already discussed. A highly developed sense of national pride, a recent history of humiliating 'imperialist' interventions, and a 'paranoid' readiness to attribute Iran's problems to the malign manipulation of Iranian politics by outside forces all predisposed Iranians to see the hand of the United States behind the policies of the Shah.[12]

The extent to which the new Iranian regime held the American government responsible for the actions of the Shah was dramatically demonstrated by the text of the new Constitution of the IRI, which denounced 'the American conspiracy known as the "*White Revolution*" which was a step intended to stabilize the foundations of despotic rule and to reinforce the political, cultural and economic dependence of Iran on world imperialism' and identified one of the primary goals of the new regime as 'the complete elimination of imperialism and the prevention of foreign influence' in Iran.[13]

Despite the bellicose anti-American rhetoric of the Revolution's leaders, the Carter administration hoped to establish a working relationship with the new regime. For there to have been any chance of this effort succeeding, however, the representatives of the US government would have needed unequivocally to accept both the outcome of the Revolution and the legitimacy of some of the charges the revolutionaries made against the United States. That, in turn, required a degree of understanding of the Revolution and of Iranian perceptions of the United States which simply did not exist in Washington. In the words of CIA Director Stansfield Turner, 'we did not know beans about who made up the Revolutionary Council'.[14]

Instead of acting in ways which would have appeased the new regime, in the course of 1979 the Carter administration and Congress took a series of actions which served to deepen the revolutionaries' distrust of Washington. After initially continuing to honour economic agreements made with the Shah, the administration halted the selling of spare parts for American equipment previously sold to Iran. It also refused to return funds sent overseas by the previous government and allowed its fleeing representatives to claim exile in the United States. These actions were rationalised, in part, as a response to the new regime's human rights violations and in May Senator Jacob Javits introduced a resolution in the Senate condemning the revolutionaries for executing prisoners without due process.[15] This action provoked outrage in Iran, where it was seen as an act of gross hypocrisy given the blind eye Washington had turned to the Shah's depredations. Some 150,000 protestors marched on the US embassy in Tehran while the Iranian government informed the Carter administration that its newly appointed ambassador to Iran, Walter Cutler, would not be welcome 'until such time as the political atmosphere between Iran and the United States is cleared'.[16]

On 22 October 1979 the Shah arrived in the United States. After much agonising, and despite great concern about the potential ramifications of his decision, Carter had decided that the Shah's urgent need for medical treatment overrode those concerns. In doing so he set in train a series of events that would kill any possibility of a rapprochement between the United States and Iran stone dead. On 4 November 1979, in response to Carter's decision, Iranian students occupied the US embassy in Tehran and took US diplomatic personnel hostage. Fifty-two Americans were subsequently held for 444 days before being released on 20 November 1981. During the course of those 444 days American diplomatic relations with Iran were broken and an image of the new Iranian regime was forged in the American mind such that relations remain broken to this day.

The admission of the Shah, more than any other action, demonstrated the American ignorance of the paranoia of the Iranian revolutionaries. As Mohsen Sazegara, a founder of the IRI's Islamic

Revolutionary Guard Corps (IRGC), put it, 'everyone believed that the United States wanted to overthrow the revolution and reinstall the shah. . . . It was a universal truth as far as we were concerned.'[17] In that febrile atmosphere Carter's decision was seen as a signal of intent and the embassy as a fifth column in the heart of Tehran. The occupation of the embassy was an attempt to nip Washington's assumed plot in the bud. It would not have lasted so long, nor have had such a profound impact on US–Iranian relations, nevertheless, had it not also served Khomeini's purposes to prolong the American agony. Though he knew nothing about the planned seizure of the embassy beforehand, Khomeini exploited it ruthlessly. Once he realised its popularity he extended his support and worked to prolong the crisis, using it to undermine more moderate political opponents and to ensure the dominance of Islamic radicals in the new regime.[18]

If Carter's decision to admit the Shah to the United States demonstrated a misunderstanding of the revolutionaries, however, the latter's decision to hold US diplomats hostage for over a year demonstrated their own insularity and ignorance. They saw their actions as a necessary response to illegitimate American efforts to restore the Shah, and as such the hostage crisis was deemed to be the fault of the Americans and, in the overall scheme of events, a relatively insignificant episode in recent Iranian history.[19] In drawing this conclusion they demonstrated a complete failure to understand the incomprehension and outrage amongst Americans that their actions provoked.[20]

Though the Iranians failed, and perhaps still fail, to realise it, the hostage crisis 'may be one of the most devastating non-war related events to have ever occurred between two nations'.[21] In taking American diplomats hostage and violating one of the most fundamental of international norms the revolutionaries committed an act that was profoundly shocking not just to Americans but to governments and peoples around the world. For 444 days Americans followed the crisis in the media every day. They saw their fellow Americans subjected to repeated public humiliation by the revolutionaries, baying crowds chanting 'death to America' while burning the American flag, and bearded clerics spewing hatred toward the United States. All of this was branded on the consciousness of the American public, and they understood none of it. To them the United States was a source of good in the world. The Americans in the US embassy in Tehran had been helping Iran and supporting its modernisation and development. The incomprehensibility of events, when combined with widespread racism and a profound ignorance of Iranian history, led inevitably to the conclusion that the only possible explanation for events lay in the wickedness of the Iranian revolutionaries and their 'fanatic Islamic fundamentalism'.[22]

If the hostage crisis led most Americans to conclude that the new regime was comprised of a bunch of fanatical, irrational thugs, then the IRI's early foreign policy brought American policymakers to the conclusion that they were also a critical threat to American interests in the Middle East. The Carter administration had hoped to restore a working relationship with the IRI because the fall of Washington's main proxy in the Gulf threatened to undermine the American strategic position in the region. To make things worse, the loss of the Shah was compounded when, within twelve months of his fall, the USSR invaded Afghanistan, bringing Soviet troops significantly closer to the Gulf.

Under those circumstances, the last thing Washington wanted was an Iranian foreign policy that directly challenged its interests in the Middle East, but that was exactly what it got. Though Khomeini rejected alignment with the USSR as well as the United States, this was of little comfort to American officials who feared that an Iran in internal turmoil was ripe for Soviet invasion.[23] Moreover, Khomeini also sought to extend the Iranian Revolution across the Middle East, with some initial success, provoking anti-regime demonstrations by Shiites in Kuwait, Bahrain and Saudi Arabia between September 1979 and February 1980.[24] A CIA analysis of the situation concluded that the survival of the Saudi regime 'could not be assured beyond the next two years'.[25] As well as seeking to mobilise Gulf Arabs against America's client regimes, moreover, the IRI also challenged American interests and allies in the Levant. Israel's June 1982 invasion of Lebanon led Syrian President Hafez al-Assad to allow Iranian forces to cross Syria into Lebanon, where they busied themselves supporting the development of Hezbollah. That involvement, in turn, implicated Iran in the bombings of the US embassy and Marine Corps barracks in Beirut in 1983 and in the varied kidnappings of Americans and other nationals carried out by Hezbollah. Iranian support for Hezbollah also brought it into proxy conflict with Israel, a conflict further fuelled by Khomeini's efforts to 'Islamicise' the Israeli–Palestinian conflict as another means to increase his influence in the Arab world.[26]

Within a few years of the Iranian Revolution, therefore, in addition to outraging American opinion in the hostage crisis, the IRI had adopted a set of policies that systematically challenged every key US interest and ally in the Middle East. Consequently, in one of the earliest invocations of the 'rogue state' concept, President Ronald Reagan identified Iran, along with Libya, North Korea, Cuba and Nicaragua, as an 'outlaw government'.[27] Far from the reestablishment of a working relationship, Iran had rapidly become Washington's regional enemy number one.[28]

The Iran–Iraq War and the 'Great Satan'

Many of the Iranian foreign policy actions that so angered Washington were, in Iranian eyes, legitimate responses to American aggression. Central to their reaching that conclusion was the Iran–Iraq War, which is for Iranians in many ways what the hostage crisis is for Americans. Indeed, for many Iranians it was 'the defining event of their lives' and 'their anti-Americanism and deep suspicion of the West generally can be traced directly to their understanding of the Iran–Iraq War' as much as it can to the 1953 coup.[29] If the revolutionaries were convinced from the start that the United States was bent on overthrowing them then the war provided them with any further confirmation they needed. In Iran it is known as 'the imposed war' because of the widespread belief that Washington prompted Saddam Hussein to invade Iran and then continued to back his war effort in a sustained attempt to destroy the Iranian Revolution.[30] The fact that this belief persists is testament to the fact that Iranian perceptions of American actions are typically as distorted as are American perceptions of Iran.

Contrary to Iranian beliefs, the Carter administration did not give Saddam Hussein a 'green light' to invade Iran.[31] Nor was it, or its successor, bent on using the war to overthrow the IRI. Nevertheless, the reaction of the United States to the invasion, and its actions in the following eight years, starting with Washington's failure to condemn Saddam's unprovoked aggression, provided ample grist to the mills of Iranian conspiracy theorists. As Iran's foreign minister reminded the Security Council nearly thirty years later:

> When Saddam Hussein invaded Iran 27 years ago, this Council waited seven days so that Iraq could occupy 30,000 sq kilometers of Iranian territory. Then it unanimously adopted resolution [sic] asking the two sides to stop hostilities, without asking the aggressor to withdraw.[32]

What Tehran thus saw as a conspiracy was in fact largely the consequence of its actions during the hostage crisis. Its alienation not just of the USA but of most of the international community resulted in a profound lack of sympathy for Iran's subsequent plight. Nevertheless, the Carter administration made an error in not pressing for an immediate ceasefire and a return to the *status quo ante* since, had a continuation of the war been prevented, there was at least a possibility that the future course of US–Iranian relations would have been different.

The consequences of the failure to demand a ceasefire became painfully clear in mid-1982, as the war began to turn against Iraq. The possibility of an Iranian victory sowed panic amongst Washington's Gulf allies, who called upon the administration of Ronald Reagan to do everything necessary to prevent it.[33] In doing so they were pushing at an open door, since an Iranian victory would have led to the fall of Saddam's regime, the probable installation of a pro-Iranian regime in Baghdad, possible Shiite uprisings across the wider Middle East, a threat to the oil supply and the collapse of America's dominant position in the Persian Gulf. In short, in the words of Assistant Secretary of State Richard W. Murphy, 'our feeling [was] that an Iranian victory in the war would become some sort of Middle East Armageddon'.[34]

Far from seeking to overthrow the Iranian regime, therefore, the Reagan administration was trying desperately to prevent its victory over Iraq.[35] From 1982 until 1987 Washington lived in constant fear that Iran might win and that 'the Middle East as we knew it would soon be overrun by anti-Western fanatics'.[36] It therefore took whatever actions it deemed necessary to prevent that outcome. To begin with this meant supplying Baghdad with satellite intelligence showing the Iranian order of battle. In addition, the administration removed Iraq from the State Department's list of state sponsors of terrorism, making it eligible for the extension of US government credit guarantees. Over the next six years the Commerce Department's Commodity Credit Corporation, and the Export-Import Bank, approved hundreds of millions of dollars' worth of credits for US exports to Iraq, enabling Saddam to divert his dwindling oil revenues to the war effort. The exports thus guaranteed were non-military in nature (though the administration became increasingly laissez-faire about licensing the export of dual-use technology) because of the restrictions of the Arms Export Control Act, but Washington encouraged its allies, who were not so constrained, to sell Iraq whatever materiel it required.[37]

From 1982 to 1986 the Reagan administration thus extended increasing support to Iraq, albeit at arm's length. In 1987–8, however, the United States was brought into direct conflict with Iran as a result of the escalation of the 'Tanker War'. Initiated by Iraq, this conflict involved the targeting of oil tankers and facilities in the Gulf. In response to escalating Iraqi attacks, Iran decided to retaliate not only against Iraq but against the tankers of the latter's Saudi and Kuwaiti backers. Increasingly worried about the threat to the oil supply from the Gulf, the Reagan administration agreed to a Kuwaiti request to 'reflag' its tankers and to send US warships to the Gulf to protect shipping. When Iran continued its attacks Washington took the opportunity to retaliate, and between September 1987 and April 1988 US forces sank at least nine Iranian ships and gunboats and destroyed a series of oil rig platforms.[38] By 1988 the United States was thus, to all intents and purposes, at war with Iran.

Even more devastating to Iran than the actions of the US navy was Washington's response to Iraqi use of chemical weapons (CW). Iraqi forces used CW repeatedly from 1983 onwards, in clear violation of international law and with horrific results, yet received nothing more than a slap on the wrist for their trouble. Western countries provided Iraq with the materials and technology to produce CW and ignored the use to which it put them.[39] While Iraqi use of CW was rhetorically condemned, this made no practical difference whatsoever to continued American support for Iraq. Even more aggrieving for the Iranians was the disingenuousness of the American response. A 1984 Department of State statement 'condemning' Iraq's use of CW spent one sentence doing that before focusing most of its effort on implying that Iran's refusal to accept a ceasefire was the real problem.[40] Similarly, after Iraq used CW against Iranian troops at Halabja in 1988, the Reagan administration initially blamed Iran. When the UNSC did finally condemn the use of CW it failed to identify Iraq as the culprit and called on both sides to stop using CW despite the fact that Iran had never done so.[41] When the attack at Halabja was shortly followed by the shooting down of an Iranian airliner by the USS *Vincennes* on 3 July 1988 the Iranian leadership was forced to the conclusion that 'they [the USA] will not allow us to win the war'.[42] Iran again took its grievance to the UN only to be rebuffed. Khomeini therefore concluded he had no choice but to drink from the 'poisoned chalice' and agreed to a ceasefire on 18 July 1988.

Ali Ansari has described American support for Iraq between 1982 and 1988 as 'an indictment of the shortsightedness of their policy, and the utter failure of intellect which could not see beyond the religious dimension of the Revolution'.[43] Yet while the long-term consequences of American support for Iraq were decidedly negative, it is not clear that there was much else that Washington could have done once it had failed to prevent the war escalating in 1980. An Iranian victory would have been a disaster for US interests in the Gulf because Tehran was bent on driving American influence from the region. Once the war escalated, therefore, the US could not contemplate the possibility of an Iraqi defeat, whatever the rights and wrongs of who started it or who was violating international law. Given that Saddam was well aware of this, American leverage over Iraq was also extremely limited.

Nevertheless, the consequences of Western support for Iraq, and particularly the failure to condemn or punish Iraq's use of CW, would be profound and long-lasting. Iran's leadership would not forget what had happened. As President Mahmoud Ahmadinejad reminded the world in 2005:

> for eight years, Saddam's regime imposed a massive war of aggression against my people. It employed the most heinous weapons of mass destruction. . . . Who armed Saddam with those weapons? What was the reaction of those who claim to fight against WMDs regarding the use of chemical weapons then?[44]

The Origins of the IRI's Nuclear Programme

Not the least of the consequences of Western support for Iraq during the Iran–Iraq War was its role in the decision of the leadership in Tehran to revive Iran's nuclear programme. On coming to power in 1979 the new regime demonstrated an unsurprising hostility toward the existing nuclear programme, given the latter's close personal association with the Shah, high costs, widespread unpopularity and extensive dependence on the West.[45] It was this last point, in particular, which seems to have been the key factor in the IRI leadership's initial antipathy, rather than any ideological or theological objection to nuclear power *per se*. The new Head of the Atomic Energy Organization of Iran (AEOI), Fereydun Sahabi, announced in April 1979 that the nuclear programme would be reviewed because it was reliant on foreign assistance which 'would bind us economically and industrially to those countries'.[46] The following month he stated that in future no foreign manpower would be used by the AEOI and in July he announced that the mission of the AEOI was to 'enhance the country's knowledge of nuclear energy with a view to self-sufficiency'.[47]

This initial burst of autarkic sentiment led to the breaking off of Iranian cooperation with its foreign partners. The United States had unilaterally ceased cooperation in the aftermath of the Revolution, and when the new regime refused to extend the work permits of foreign workers and then stopped paying foreign contractors, Kraftwerk Union (KWU) halted work at the Bushehr site. It subsequently announced that it would withdraw from its contract to build the reactors.[48] When Tehran then 'cancelled' the agreement the Shah had signed with France for a share in the

Eurodif enrichment plant at Tricastin, and demanded repayment of his $1 billion loan, the French government announced that it would not be refunded.[49]

The departure of the foreign contractors, along with a great many Iranian nuclear scientists and engineers, meant a huge reduction in the capacity of the Iranian nuclear programme. Nevertheless, while the new regime rejected the Shah's turnkey approach to developing nuclear power and the grandiose scale of his plans, it never rejected nuclear technology and soon had its own programme up and running. This was first indicated by the appointment as head of the AEOI of nuclear physicist Reza Amrollahi in 1981, replacing Sahabi, a geologist with no knowledge of nuclear science. In 1981–2 Iran imported uranium ore, in the form of 'yellowcake', and began conducting experiments on how to convert the ore into uranium hexafluoride gas (UF6), a first step toward being able to enrich uranium via the centrifuge method. It was also decided to begin research and development on a heavy water reactor programme.[50] The formal public announcement of the programme's recommencement came in March 1982, with the AEOI emphasising that there would be no repetition of the reliance on foreign sources of technology that there had been under the Shah and that the programme would go 'very slowly'.[51]

Despite the declared intent to develop an indigenous nuclear programme, the 1982 relaunch also demonstrated a degree of pragmatism on the part of the Iranian leadership. While Tehran did not wish to be dependent on foreign suppliers, it had evidently realised that there were limits to such an approach. Since the reactors at Bushehr had been designed and part-constructed by KWU they would be very difficult for anyone else to complete, and in April 1982 it was announced that a deal had been struck for KWU to finish the reactors.[52] In a similar vein, despite an ongoing dispute with France over the latter's refusal to return the Shah's loan to Eurodif, Iran came to an agreement with France for the supply of equipment and fuel.[53] In 1983 Iran also informed the IAEA of its intentions and invited it to inspect its nuclear facilities as a prelude to providing technical assistance. The inspection duly took place and in his report its head, Herman Vera Ruiz, recommended that the IAEA assist Iran in its new programme.[54]

Iran's initial efforts to secure international assistance came to nothing, however, in large part because of the efforts of the United States. On 9 September 1982 the Reagan administration announced its intention to tighten export controls and named sixty-three countries, including Iran, to which the transfer of nuclear technology would be put under more scrutiny. That position soon evolved into a complete bar on the sale or transfer of US-produced nuclear materials to Iran.[55] Simultaneously, the Reagan administration also called for a global ban on such transfers and applied diplomatic pressure to that end. The West German government subsequently blocked KWU's efforts to restart work at Bushehr and the deal with France agreed in 1982 failed to go ahead. The IAEA also pulled back from its offer to aid the Iranian programme: 'we stopped that in its tracks', according to an unnamed American official.[56]

Precisely what they had stopped in its tracks, however, the Reagan administration had no idea. After 1979 the US had no diplomats inside Iran and no other sources of intelligence, having failed to recruit any spies amongst the Iranian population for fear of upsetting the Shah. As far as understanding what was going on inside Iran was concerned, therefore, the US intelligence agencies were reduced to using the sources available to any outside observer – public statements, documents and the media.[57] A lack of intelligence, nevertheless, was no hindrance to a non-proliferation policy which was based less upon evidence of an intention to proliferate than on the nature of the relationship between the United States and the potential proliferator.

During the course of the Reagan administration a number of states continued to pursue actual or possible undeclared nuclear weapons programmes, yet only some of them prompted a restrictive American response. The Reagan administration turned a blind eye to Pakistan's evolving weapons programme, conspired in the myth that Israel did not have nuclear weapons, opposed motions passed by the Board of Governors of the IAEA to suspend South Africa's rights and dismissed the idea that Iraq had a weapons programme.[58] This approach was rationalised by the administration on the grounds that, while proliferation was a technical and a political problem, technical restraints alone (embargoes on exporting technology, IAEA safeguards, etc.) would not stop nations pursuing weapons and that 'political measures are more important in the long term than technical measures'. Moreover, they argued, it was reasonable to make 'rational distinctions' between 'close friends and allies who pose no real proliferation risk' and other countries that supposedly did.[59] The administration further justified its policy toward the countries listed above by arguing that isolation and embargoes would be ineffective – 'severing all ties in the nuclear field eliminates the possibility of affecting their policies in the nuclear field'. Instead, it was preferable to pursue a 'pragmatic' policy which sought to dissuade them from pursuing weapons by offering continued nuclear cooperation and 'technically feasible alternatives to sensitive activities'.[60]

The Reagan administration thus argued for a policy of engagement and the proffering of carrots, rather than sticks, to would-be proliferators, as long as they were also friends of the United States. Governments which were not in that fortunate position, in contrast, were apparently susceptible only to an entirely different logic involving the technical isolation and threats which were deemed to be doomed to failure if applied to Israel or Pakistan. Iran was therefore to be subject to a total embargo of nuclear technology whilst Washington's friends were allowed to pursue their covert weapons programmes largely unhindered.

On purely pragmatic grounds a case might have been made for such an approach if it could be demonstrated to be effective. However, as was already abundantly clear by the 1980s, denying a state access to nuclear technology and knowledge is impossible. In addition to being doomed to fail, moreover, the approach also had a number of further significant downsides. In the first place, by so obviously violating its commitments under the Treaty on the Non-Proliferation of Nuclear Weapons (NPT), the Reagan administration only encouraged other states to do likewise while providing them with a justification for their actions. Consequently, this approach also encouraged states to develop programmes outside of the NPT regime without any safeguards in place. Finally, the Reagan policy was a crude exercise in *realpolitik* which only served to undercut American pretensions to upholding international laws and rules such as the non-proliferation regime.[61]

None of which is to say that, had the Reagan administration pursued a policy of nuclear engagement toward Iran, everything would have been different. Indeed, given the wider context of the US–Iranian relationship, such a policy was inconceivable. Nevertheless, it remains the case that the hypocritical nature of the Reagan approach only served to further reinforce Iranian perceptions about Washington's double standards and determination to deny Iran its rights. Just as Etemad and the Shah had been, the leadership of the IRI were quite clear in their understanding that, as a signatory to the NPT, Iran had a right to a peaceful nuclear energy programme, hence their invitation to the IAEA to assist them in its development. As far as Tehran was concerned, therefore, just as Washington ignored international law when it came to Iraqi use of CW, so it was doing so again in obstructing Iran's exercise of its right to nuclear technology under the NPT.

With the assistance of Western nuclear suppliers denied it, Iran began to look to regimes less likely to be responsive to American pressure for assistance. An Argentinian company, Investigaciones Aplicadas, signed a deal to provide a replacement core and fuel for the research reactor at Tehran University in 1987. Talks with the USSR began in the same year, leading to a commitment from Moscow to build 'several' new reactors in Iran. A nuclear agreement with China which led to the latter providing equipment and designs for nuclear reactors, as well as training for Iranian technicians, followed in 1989.[62] Here again, the Reagan administration's approach to non-proliferation proved self-defeating – enabling Moscow and Beijing to dismiss American requests that they cease such cooperation as the rankest hypocrisy.

By far the most important partner for Iran, however, was one that the US government was not even aware of. Initially, Iran had hoped to secure uranium enrichment technology from Pakistan, and in 1986 senior Iranian officials met with its leader, General Zia ul-Haq. However, while Zia agreed to support nuclear cooperation, he rejected Iranian requests for the transfer of fuel cycle technology.[63] Undaunted, Iran looked to the black market to meet its needs and specifically to the network run by the Pakistani nuclear scientist Abdul Qadeer (A. Q.) Khan. Khan visited Iran in early 1987 and offered to sell the Iranians the designs for a

P1 centrifuge. After further negotiations the Iranians were offered a complete gas centrifuge plant, including disassembled centrifuges and designs for their assembly, by Khan's business partner, Gotthard Lerch. Iranian Prime Minister Mir Hossein Mousavi authorised the purchase in March 1987 and gas centrifuge research and development testing began at the Tehran Nuclear Research Centre in 1988.[64]

Weapons Programme?

By the late 1980s, therefore, Iran was engaged in extensive research and development efforts aimed at mastering the nuclear fuel cycle. It was working on conversion, enrichment and fuel fabrication as well as conducting experiments in the production of heavy water. But was this being done with the intention of eventually developing nuclear weapons?

In 2011 the IAEA reported that there was 'credible' evidence that Iran had engaged in nuclear weapons development. However, it placed the unambiguously weapons-related research and development in the period between 1999 and 2003, and there is very little in the record of Iranian nuclear activity in the 1980s which points conclusively toward a weapons programme at that point.[65] All of the activities that we know Iran was engaging in had civilian uses, primarily as parts of the nuclear fuel cycle. The only concrete piece of technical material pointing toward a weapons programme is a document, supplied by the A. Q. Khan network in 1987, along with the centrifuge designs, describing procedures for turning uranium metal into hemispheres, which are components of nuclear weapons. Iran subsequently claimed that it had not asked for the document.[66]

The fact that the Iranian programme was covert might be seen as reasonable grounds for suspicion in itself. As the IAEA noted, 'all of the materials important to uranium conversion had been produced in laboratory and bench scale experiments between 1981 and 1993 without having been reported to the Agency'.[67] Iran, however, could respond that it had approached the IAEA to ask for its assistance in pursuing the fuel cycle and that it was only when the United States prevented it from receiving such assistance (to which Iran was entitled under the NPT) that it was forced to secure the assistance it required through covert means.

As far as the content of the actual programme goes, therefore, the evidence is inconclusive. Regime intent, however, might be better understood through an analysis of what regime members had to say about the purposes of the programme. In international institutions the IRI was consistent in its stated opposition to nuclear weapons throughout the 1980s and voted in favour of disarmament measures on all available occasions. In addition, despite its being increasingly depicted as a 'rogue state', the regime retained Iran's membership of the NPT. Evidence from Iran's internal debates, however, provides a somewhat different picture. Mohsen Rafighdoost, Minister for the IRGC from 1982 to 1989, has admitted that he established a programme within the IRGC to explore the possible development of weapons of mass destruction, including nuclear weapons, during the Iran–Iraq War. In addition, IRGC commander Mohsen Rezaei, in a letter written in early 1988 outlining what Iran needed if it was to win the war, included 'atomic weapons' in his requirements. According to Rafighdoost, however, when he informed Khomeini about his plans the Supreme Leader told him that nuclear weapons were 'haram' (forbidden by Islam) and 'we don't want to produce nuclear weapons'. Khomeini repeated the injunction to him in 1987 and rejected Rezaei's request for further resources in favour of signing a ceasefire in 1988.[68]

While it thus seems that Khomeini may have been personally opposed to the development of nuclear weapons, the same was clearly not true of everyone within the regime, including some of its most senior leaders. Along with Rafighdoost and Rezaei, Ayatollah Ali Khamenei, then President of Iran and Khomeini's successor as Supreme Leader, apparently favoured a weapons programme. In a speech to the AEOI in February 1987 he reportedly told them:

> Regarding atomic energy, we need it now. . . . Our nation has always been threatened from outside. The least we can do to face this danger is to let our enemies know that we can defend ourselves. Therefore every step you take is in defense of your country and your revolution. With this in mind you should work hard and at great speed.[69]

While the source of that alleged statement was less than impeccable, that for the following speech by Speaker of the Iranian Parliament Akbar Hashemi Rafsanjani was Tehran's own main news service. Speaking to the IRGC in October 1988, Rafsanjani told them that 'we should fully equip ourselves both in the offensive and defensive use of chemical, bacteriological and radiological weapons'.[70]

It would seem, therefore, that at the very least there was by the late 1980s significant support amongst key Iranian leaders for the development of nuclear weapons. To what extent the actual nuclear activities then being pursued were initiated with that purpose in mind is, however, impossible to say. There is no compelling evidence that research and development begun in the early to mid-1980s was pursued with the purpose of weapons development specifically in mind. Nor is it possible to conclude that there had yet been a clear and unambiguous decision by the regime to pursue nuclear weapons. Indeed, if we take Rafighdoost's claim seriously, the most powerful figure in the regime was actively opposed to weapons development. With his death in June 1989, however, and the subsequent accession of Rafsanjani to the presidency and Khamenei to the Supreme Leadership, the key positions of power were both held by men who had expressed support for the development of nuclear weapons.

It thus seems reasonable to conclude that, by the time of Khomeini's death, Iran had the beginnings of a nuclear weapons programme, albeit not one of any significant scale and not one that was the product of any sustained internal debate or authoritative formal decision. The final question worth asking at this stage is why at least some members of the IRI elite were in favour of weapons development at this point.

There is little by way of consensus about why states choose to proliferate.[71] This is perhaps unsurprising when we consider the fact that nuclear decision-making is one of the most secretive areas of state policy. Inevitably, therefore, testing of theories is hampered by the lack of access to reliable information about why weapons programmes were or were not pursued. Initial theories of proliferation were dominated by realist theories of international relations which seemed to offer an intuitively plausible explanation: states seek nuclear weapons for reasons of power and security and once one state has nuclear weapons others will inevitably follow as they seek to offset the power imbalance and eliminate the security dilemma created by the nuclear-armed state. Thus, once the USA had nuclear weapons the USSR was bound to follow, which in turn led the UK and France to arm and so on.[72]

However, whilst the logic of the realist argument is compelling, the empirical evidence does not support its utility as a universal explanation of nuclear proliferation. Only about 20 per cent of those states with the technological capacity to build nuclear weapons have done so, and many of those which have chosen not to do so face security threats and dilemmas which ought, according to realist logic, to have driven them to proliferate.[73] For example, if the UK and France developed nuclear weapons for security reasons then why did West Germany and Japan not do so when their security dilemma as a US ally facing the Soviet threat was fundamentally the same? The realist model of proliferation assumes that all states are the same. Driven by the inescapable logics of anarchy and security, all states will respond in similar fashion to the same external pressures. However, the fact that in practice they do not do so indicates that we cannot treat 'the state' as a universal, interchangeable unit which behaves in a consistent fashion when faced with a certain type of external input. In short, 'a growing body of research suggests that one cannot properly understand nuclear weapons (non)proliferation without reference to the domestic context in which nuclear decisions are made'.[74]

Once we open the 'black box' of the state, however, we inevitably find that there is a dramatic expansion in the range of potential explanatory variables which can be brought to bear on any given decision. Etel Solingen's 'economic' model of proliferation links decisions about whether or not to proliferate to different modes of 'political survival' which in turn are connected to alternative economic policies. According to her research, based on a comparison of states in the Middle East and East Asia, 'outward oriented' governments, which seek to ensure their political survival through securing economic growth for their populations, are much less likely to proliferate than 'inward oriented' regimes which base their survival primarily on repression and an effective security state. In the former case the international response to proliferation – diplomatic isolation and sanctions – would undermine the economic growth strategy upon which political survival is premised. Inward oriented states, in contrast, have much less to lose by international isolation and have greater incentives to exploit nuclear weapons as symbols of national defiance and as a means of staying in power.[75]

Scott Sagan, in contrast, proposes a 'domestic' model of proliferation which emphasises the importance of powerful bureaucratic actors in the decision to develop nuclear weapons. This approach is shaped by the literature on bureaucratic politics and the social construction of technology. Groups of domestic actors who stand to benefit from the development of nuclear weapons, notably the nuclear establishment itself, but also parts of the military (often the air force) promote weapons development for parochial reasons. According to this approach security threats are rarely so clear cut that the decision to pursue nuclear weapons is a foregone conclusion. Rather, security threats are ambiguous and nuclear weapons programmes result from domestic actors exploiting those uncertainties to successfully advance the case for nuclear weapons. 'Security threats are therefore not the central cause of weapons decisions . . . they are merely windows of opportunity through which parochial interests can jump.'[76]

In the same article Sagan outlines a 'norms' model of proliferation which focuses on the symbolic function of nuclear weapons. According to this model, proliferation is shaped by norms in one of two ways. In most cases the effect of norms considerations is to prevent states from proliferating. The devastating effects of nuclear weapons are argued to effectively delegitimise them, resulting in the development of a powerful 'nuclear taboo'. This is held to be a key reason explaining why so many states that have the technological capability to build nuclear weapons have chosen not to do so.[77] For a minority of states, however, these negative norms have been trumped by a set of norms that valorise nuclear weapons as status symbols and markers of technological advancement or great power status.[78] Itty Abraham's account of India's development of nuclear weapons, for example, places New Delhi's nuclear decision-making in the context of its status as a post-colonial state. He argues that India 'fetishized' nuclear technology and came to view the development of nuclear weapons as connoting sovereignty and independence and as a symbol of India's status as a major global power.[79]

Finally, there are theories of nuclear proliferation which emphasise the role of individual policy-makers or leaders. The most well known of these is that developed by Jacques Hymans. In *The Psychology of Nuclear Proliferation* Hymans employs the concept of 'national identity conceptions' (NICs) to explain (non)-proliferation. He postulates that differing NICs amongst leaders explain whether or not they are likely to support weapons development. Those most likely to do so are what he terms 'oppositional nationalist' leaders – those whose worldview combines a high level of fear of foreign threats with an equally high level of national pride and belief in the ability of their nation to confront those threats.[80]

If we test these various models against what we know about the 1980s Iranian nuclear programme we can see, in the first instance, that Hyman's theory about oppositional nationalist leaders does not seem to fit. Khomeini certainly fits his template of an oppositional nationalist leader but, if we accept the evidence above, was nevertheless opposed to the development of nuclear weapons. The power of key bureaucratic actors also lacks purchase at this point in the evolution of the Iranian nuclear programme. The AEOI had been reduced to a shadow of its former self in the aftermath of the Revolution and clearly lacked the bureaucratic weight to determine policy choices. There is some evidence of IRGC interest in the nuclear programme, but while this would become important later, there is no indication that it was significant at this point.

The relevance of the norms model is also somewhat uncertain. We can certainly conclude that the nuclear taboo was not a concern for many key Iranian decision-makers but we do not have any evidence that those individuals saw nuclear weapons as status symbols either. There is also no strong evidence to suggest the applicability of Solingen's economic orientation model in the 1980s. The IRI can certainly be argued to have been an 'inward looking' state at this point since it was economically isolated and not pursuing greater economic integration with the global community. However, Iran's inwardness at this point was not a product of free choice so much as of the actions of the rest of the world in isolating it. It is not, therefore, a useful gauge of regime orientation.

Iran's being at war, in fact, provides the most convincing explanation for an Iranian interest in nuclear weapons in the 1980s. The stark reality facing Iranian policy-makers at that point was that they were at war with an adversary which from 1983 onwards repeatedly used CW against Iranian forces. Moreover, despite Iranian protests in international institutions, the international community had chosen to turn a blind eye to Saddam's CW use. Finally, Tehran was fully aware that, in addition to CW, Iraq also had an active nuclear weapons programme.[81] Iran thus had a clear security motive for developing nuclear weapons and this is reflected in the available evidence. All of the statements in which Iranian policy-makers referred to a need for nuclear weapons cite security and/or the threat from Iraq as the reason to do so. Rafighdoost and Rezaei of the IRGC both argued for the development of nuclear weapons in order to defeat Iraq. Khamenei, in his speech to the IRGC quoted above, referred to external threats and defence, and Rafsanjani, when he told the IRGC Iran needed nuclear weapons, offered the following rationale for doing so:

> It was made very clear during the war that these weapons are very decisive. It was also made clear that the moral teachings of the world are not very effective when war reaches a serious stage and the world does not respect its own resolutions and closes its eyes to the violations and all the aggressions which are committed in the battlefield.[82]

While the realist model of proliferation may not be universally relevant, therefore, it offers the best explanation of the origins of the Iranian nuclear weapons programme given the available evidence. That conclusion, in turn, further emphasises the significance of

American decision-making in relation to the Iran–Iraq War for the subsequent evolution of the US–Iranian nuclear relationship. If the origins of the Iranian nuclear weapons programme lie in the war with Iraq and the latter's use of CW then the significance of Washington's failure to try to prevent the war's escalation, subsequent support for Iraq and ignoring of Iraqi CW use is obvious. To a considerable extent, when it later found itself faced with the problem of how to halt the Iranian nuclear programme, the United States government was the author of its own misfortune.

The Consequences

The experiences of both the United States and Iran between 1979 and 1988 would have a profound impact on the future course of the US–Iranian relationship and on how each country approached the nuclear issue in the future. For its part, Washington's belief that Iran posed a mortal threat to American interests was confirmed by Tehran's perceived determination to overthrow Saddam Hussein, while the conviction that Iranians were irrational religious fanatics was reinforced by Iran's conduct of the war and its use of 'human wave' attacks.[83] The 'lessons' learned about Iranian 'fanaticism' and 'irrationality' would have a significant influence on the American response to the IRI's nuclear programme. As Dennis Ross, who was involved in Iran policy-making in several administrations, noted:

> Certain images get formed, and when they are formed, even when there are behaviours which seem to contradict the image, if there are other images [sic] which tend to confirm it, you give much more weight to those that tend to confirm it. . . . The behaviours that actually tended to fit with the traditional images were treated as if that was the real Iran.[84]

And if those images influenced policy-makers then they were even more significant at a popular level, where hostility and distrust of Iran became deeply entrenched amongst ordinary Americans. Traumatised by the hostage crisis and with their perceptions of

Iran fuelled by consistently negative media coverage and (later) the constant anti-Iranian lobbying of groups like the American Israel Public Affairs Committee, the American public developed deeply negative views of Iran.[85] Thus disposed always to think the worst, American popular opinion, and its reflection in Congress, would become an important constraint on US policy toward Iran.

The 'lessons' Iranian leaders took from the Iran–Iraq War were that the United States was bent on the destruction of the Islamic Republic and that its claims to uphold international laws and principles were hypocritical lies. In addition, 'the experience reinforced the belief that Iran could depend only on her own resources, and that fine words in international institutions counted for little'.[86] The Reagan administration's non-proliferation policy only served further to reinforce this understanding of how the world worked, with one set of rules for Washington's friends and another for its enemies. This perception of discrimination and isolation, and the distrust of the United States, the West and the United Nations that resulted from the experience of the war inevitably shaped Iran's response to international efforts to constrain its nuclear programme.

Notes

1. Blight et al., *Becoming Enemies*, pp. 26–8; Ansari, *Modern Iran Since 1921*, pp. 10–11; Beeman, *'Great Satan' vs the 'Mad Mullahs'*.
2. Hess, 'Iranian crisis of 1945–46'.
3. Cottam, *Iran and the United States*, p. 54.
4. Ibid., p. 3.
5. Bill, *Eagle and the Lion*, pp. 114–15, 156–61.
6. Bostock and Jones, *Planning and Power in Iran*, pp. 160–1.
7. Majlis Deputy Qorbani-Nasab, 14 January 1979, US Department of Commerce, *Foreign Broadcast Information Service, Daily Reports, Middle East Area (FBIS-DR-MEA)*, 15 February 1979.
8. Bill, *Eagle and the Lion*, pp. 209–11.
9. Vance, *Hard Choices*, p. 317.
10. Abdolhassan Bani-Sadr, *Tehran Radio*, 11 November 1979, *FBIS-DR-MEA*, 13 November 1979.

11. Ayatollah Khomeini, 'Speech to Islamic students in Qom', 28 October 1979, *FBIS-DR-MEA*, 29 October 1979.
12. Abrahamian, *Khomeinism*, pp. 113–20.
13. *Constitution of the Islamic Republic of Iran*. The 'White Revolution' was the name given to the Shah's ambitious programme of social and economic modernisation launched in the early 1960s.
14. Moses, *Freeing the Hostages*, p. 89.
15. US Congress, *Congressional Record*, Proceedings and Debates of the 96th Cong., 1st Sess., May 10–17 1979, pp. 11674–6.
16. Bill, *Eagle and the Lion*, p. 284; Edward Cody, 'Angry Iran tells US not to send new Ambassador', *The Washington Post*, 21 May 1979.
17. Crist, *Twilight War*, p. 91.
18. Ansari, *Modern Iran Since 1921*, pp. 227–8; Keddie, *Modern Iran*, pp. 248–9.
19. Ansari, *Confronting Iran*, pp. 71–2.
20. Blight et al., *Becoming Enemies*, p. 258.
21. Beeman, *'Great Satan' vs the 'Mad Mullahs'*, p. 138.
22. Ibid., pp. 120–1; Little, *American Orientalism*, ch. 1; Ansari, *Confronting Iran*, pp. 83, 90; Reagan, *American Life*, p. 218.
23. According to former CIA official Bruce Riedel, in the early 1980s US intelligence picked up what was, in his view, 'absolutely reliable information' that the Soviets were conducting a 'command post exercise' which simulated an invasion of Iran and which many feared was preparation for the real thing, Blight et al., *Becoming Enemies*, pp. 69–70.
24. Behrooz, 'Trends in the foreign policy of the Islamic Republic of Iran'.
25. *The Washington Post*, 22 July 1980.
26. Ehteshami, 'Foreign policy of Iran', p. 298.
27. 'Remarks at the Annual Convention of the American Bar Association', 8 July 1985, US President, *Public Papers of the Presidents of the United States (PPPUS)*.
28. Which is not to deny that some in Washington held out hope that a rapprochement was still a possibility. Such hopes, however, rested on an increasingly implausible belief that the revolutionaries would somehow 'come to their senses' or be supplanted by a set of, as yet unidentified, 'moderates'. See, for example, Jimmy Carter, 'Interview on *Meet the Press*', 20 January 1980, *PPPUS*.
29. Bruce Riedel, quoted in Blight et al., *Becoming Enemies*, p. x, and see the comments of former UN Under-Secretary General Giandomenico Picco at p. 78.

30. See, for example, the comments of former Iranian President Akbar Hashemi Rafsanjani in 'American did not start the war', interview with *Tabnak* news magazine, 14 September 2008, available at <http://nsarchive.gwu.edu/NSAEBB/NSAEBB394/docs/2008-09-14-Interview-Rafsanjani-Tabnak.pdf> (last accessed 10 January 2017).
31. Blight et al., *Becoming Enemies*, pp. 63–9.
32. 'Statement by H. E. Manouchehr Mottaki, Foreign Minister of the Islamic Republic of Iran before the United Nations Security Council', UN Press Release, 23 March 2007.
33. 'Your meeting with Israeli Defence Minister Ariel Sharon 4–5pm Tuesday May 25', 21 May 1982, National Security Archive, *Iraqgate*.
34. Blight et al., *Becoming Enemies*, p. 95.
35. The Iranians made their own mistake in 1982 when they had driven Iraq back over the border. Saddam was ready to accept a ceasefire at this point but the leadership in Tehran, after some debate, decided to continue the war. The result was another six years of war, further alienation of the international community, the expenditure of vast resources and the loss of up to a million lives for no gain; Ansari, *Modern Iran Since 1921*, pp. 235–6.
36. Bruce Riedel, quoted in Blight et al., *Becoming Enemies*, p. 104.
37. Jentleson, *With Friends Like These*; Friedman, *Spider's Web*; Timmerman, *Death Lobby*.
38. Chubin and Tripp, *Iran and Iraq at War*, pp. 217–18.
39. Timmerman, *Death Lobby*, pp. 106–12.
40. 'Chemical weapons and the Iran–Iraq War', *Department of State Bulletin*, 5 March 1984.
41. United Nations, UN Security Council Resolution 612.
42. Rafsanjani, quoted in Alfoneh, 'War over the war'. The shooting down of the plane was an act of incompetence on the part of the captain of the *Vincennes* rather than a deliberate act of aggression.
43. Ansari, *Modern Iran Since 1921*, p. 236.
44. Ahmadinejad, 'Address by H. E. Dr. Mahmood Ahmadinejad'.
45. Patrikarikos, *Nuclear Iran*, pp. 93–5.
46. 'Atomic Energy Organization projects to be discontinued', *Tehran Domestic Service*, 9 April 1979, *FBIS-DR-MEA*, 10 April 1979.
47. 'Scale down for Iranian nuclear programme', BBC *Summary of World Broadcasts* (*BBC SWB*), 28 May 1979; 'Iran's reconsideration of its nuclear policy', *BBC SWB*, 19 July 1979.
48. 'KWU official confirms withdrawal from nuclear plants', Hamburg, Deutsche-Presse-Agentur (DPA), 31 July 1979, *FBIS-DR-Western Europe*, 31 July 1979.

49. 'France denies Iran a refund, 1980', *The New York Times*, 19 February 1980.
50. IAEA, 'Implementation of the NPT safeguards agreement in the Islamic Republic of Iran', GOV/2004/83, pp. 4–5, 15.
51. *Nucleonics Week*, 25 March 1982, p. 3.
52. 'Iran: Nuclear power agreement with FRG firm', *BBC SWB*, 6 April 1982.
53. 'Iranian nuclear power project', *BBC SWB*, 6 July 1982.
54. Hibbs, 'US in 1983 stopped IAEA'.
55. Milton R. Benjamin, 'Administration will list 63 countries subject to nuclear export restrictions', *The Washington Post*, 9 September 1982, p. A4; Bernard Gwertzman, 'US urges ban on atom sales to Iran', *The New York Times*, 26 April 1984.
56. Hibbs, 'US in 1983 stopped IAEA'.
57. Crist, *Twilight War*, p. 15; Blight et al., *Becoming Enemies*, p. 189.
58. Smith and Cobban, 'Blind eye to nuclear proliferation'; 'US–USSR Non-proliferation bilaterals: Regional aspects of non-proliferation', Department of State background paper, 20 July 1987, *DNSA*.
59. Thompson, 'NPT regime, present and future global security', pp. 153–4. Thompson was part of the US delegation to the IAEA under the Reagan administration.
60. Ibid., pp. 158, 160.
61. Betts, 'Paranoids, pygmies, pariahs', pp. 171–3.
62. Richard Kessler, *Nucleonics Week*, 14 May 1987, pp. 6–7; *Nuclear News*, July 1987, pp. 4–5; Mark Hibbs, 'Iran negotiating with USSR for supply of "several" PWRs', *Nucleonics Week*, 25 October 1990, pp. 1–2; Mark Hibbs and Neel Patri, *Nucleonics Week*, 21 November 1991, pp. 2–3; Garver, *China and Iran*, pp. 143–4.
63. International Institute for Strategic Studies, *Nuclear Black Markets*, p. 66; 'Khamenei submits report to Khomeini', *Tehran Domestic Service*, 22 January 1986, *FBIS-DR-MEA*, 23 January 1986.
64. IAEA, 'Implementation of the NPT safeguards agreement and relevant provisions of Security Council resolutions 1737 (2006) and 1747 (2007) in the Islamic Republic of Iran', GOV/2007/58; Corera, *Shopping for Bombs*, pp. 65–7; IAEA, 'Implementation of the NPT safeguards agreement in the Islamic Republic of Iran', GOV/2004/83.
65. IAEA 'Implementation of the NPT safeguards agreement and relevant provisions of Security Council resolutions in the Islamic Republic of Iran', GOV/2011/65, p. 8.
66. IAEA, 'Implementation of the NPT safeguards agreement in the Islamic Republic of Iran', GOV/2004/83.

67. IAEA 'Implementation of the NPT safeguards agreement in the Islamic Republic of Iran', GOV/2003/75, p. 17.
68. Gareth Porter, 'When the Ayatollah said no to nukes', *Foreign-policy*, 16 October 2014, <http://foreignpolicy.com/2014/10/16/when-the-ayatollah-said-no-to-nukes/> (last accessed 13 January 2017); 'Letter from Ayatollah Khomeini regarding weapons during the Iran–Iraq war', available at <http://www.cfr.org/iran/letter-aya-tollah-khomeini-regarding-weapons-during-iran-iraq-war/p11745> (last accessed 13 January 2017).
69. David Segal, 'Atomic Ayatollahs', *The Washington Post*, 12 April 1987. It should be noted that the source of the quote was the Tudeh Party, an exiled opposition group with plenty of reasons to depict the IRI in the most negative light possible.
70. 'Hashemi-Rafsanjani speaks on future of IRGC', *Tehran Domestic Service*, 5 October 1988, *FBIS-DR-MEA*, 6 October 1988.
71. Ogilvie-White, 'Is there a theory of nuclear proliferation?'; Singh and Way, 'The correlates of nuclear proliferation'; Potter and Mukhatzh-anova, *Forecasting Nuclear Proliferation*.
72. Frankel, 'Brooding shadow'.
73. Hymans, 'Theories of nuclear proliferation', pp. 455–6.
74. Potter and Mukhatzhanova, *Forecasting Nuclear Proliferation*, p. 5; Reiss, *Without the Bomb*.
75. Solingen, *Nuclear Logics*, p. 5.
76. Sagan, 'Why do states build nuclear weapons?', pp. 63–5.
77. Tannenwald, 'Stigmatizing the bomb'.
78. Frey, *Nuclear Weapons as Symbols*; Suchman and Eyre, 'Military procurement as rational myth'.
79. Abraham, *Making of the Indian Atomic Bomb*.
80. Hymans, *Psychology of Nuclear Proliferation*, p. 2.
81. As demonstrated by Iran's attempt to destroy the Iraqi nuclear research centre at Tuwaitha eight days after the war started; National Intelligence Daily, Director of Central Intelligence, October 1, 1980, *DNSA*.
82. 'Hashemi-Rafsanjani speaks on future of IRGC', *Tehran Domestic Service*, 5 October 1988, *FBIS-DR-MEA*, 6 October 1988.
83. While such tactics were seen as evidence of Iranian religious mania, they were arguably, as Alia Ansari has pointed out, a rational mea-sure based on the resources available to Iran. Nor were they nec-essarily that different from tactics used by other, non-theocratic, regimes in other wars. The Soviet Union, for example, sent infantry through minefields to clear them, rather than risk the lives of combat

engineers, during World War II; Ansari, 'Civilizational identity and foreign policy', p. 244.

84. Quoted in Parsi, *Treacherous Alliance*, p. 152.
85. Jeffrey M. Jones, 'Iran, North Korea still Americans' least favourite countries', *Gallup*, 11 February 2011, <http://www.gallup.com/poll/146090/Iran-North-Korea-Americans-Least-Favorite-Countries.aspx> (last accessed 18 January 2017).
86. Axworthy, *Revolutionary Iran*, p. 293.

3 The 1990s: Clinton and the Failure of Containment and Engagement

The 1990s in some ways represent a kind of 'phoney war' before the real conflict over the Iranian nuclear programme broke out in the early twenty-first century. Washington continued to insist that Iran had a nuclear weapons programme yet regarded it as sufficiently embryonic not to require much attention or extensive reflection as to how it might best be dealt with. Existing policies of diplomatic isolation and economic sanctions were extended despite Washington's failure to persuade the rest of the world to join with it and the consequent ineffectiveness of those policies.

The inertia of US policy was sustained by a combination of a lack of any pressing need to change it – the policy was ineffectual but Iran was still years away from having the bomb – and political considerations that militated against change. As the experience of the first Clinton administration clearly demonstrates, there was a widespread and powerful domestic consensus in favour of taking a hard line with Iran, as well as an Israeli government for which such a hard line was the price of its readiness to negotiate with the Palestinians. In his second term Clinton, encouraged by the election of President Mohammad Khatami, would nevertheless make a tentative effort to engage Iran diplomatically, but that only served to demonstrate that the domestic constraints preventing Iranian leaders from compromising with Washington were as powerful as those in the United States.

Bush and Rafsanjani

Shortly before his death in June 1989, Ayatollah Khomeini approved changes to the Constitution of the Islamic Republic of Iran (IRI) which eliminated the post of prime minister, enhanced the powers of the president and weakened those of the Majlis. Perhaps most significantly, the changes also removed the need for the Supreme Leader to be a *marja*, the highest-ranking form of Grand Ayatollah in the Shia clerical hierarchy. In pushing through these changes Khomeini sought to stabilise the regime and ensure its survival after his death.[1] The change to the qualification requirement for Supreme Leader ensured that Khomeini's preferred candidate, Khameini, would succeed him. The newly enhanced presidency was also filled by the candidate Khomeini endorsed before his death, with Rafsanjani winning a landslide vote in July 1989. The changes thus engineered ensured that the two most powerful positions in the state were occupied by men who had both expressed support for the development of nuclear weapons.

While parts of the Iranian nuclear programme remained covert,[2] with the ending of the Iran–Iraq War the regime sought to restart the civil nuclear programme – the Atomic Energy Organization of Iran (AEOI) announcing that it would build ten power plants to produce 20 per cent of Iranian electricity by 2005.[3] To achieve such an ambitious goal Iran would need external assistance which it knew Washington would seek to deny it. While Tehran did try, once again, to secure the services of Kraftwerk Union to complete Bushehr (which the company was prevented from doing by the German government), the two countries to which Iran increasingly looked were China and Russia, countries whose leaderships were presumed to be less likely to be susceptible to American pressure.[4]

Sino-Iranian nuclear cooperation had begun in the mid-1980s, but the scope and extent of the relationship expanded significantly under Rafsanjani. In 1989 China agreed to provide Iran with an electromagnetic separator for isotope production (a calutron) and the following year the two countries signed an agreement under which China would assist in the construction of a nuclear research facility at Isfahan. In January 1992 a further agreement, under which China would construct a 27 MW plutonium reactor at Isfahan, was signed, and later that year China agreed to build two full-scale 300 MW reactors.[5]

If anything, Russia was even keener than China to assist the Iranian nuclear programme. As the Soviet Union collapsed and its successor state went into economic freefall, nuclear exports became an increasingly attractive source of desperately needed income. With the German option closed off, Russia stepped in to complete the two reactors at Bushehr. It also signed a deal to build two further reactors in exchange for the supply of natural gas and agreed to cooperate on nuclear research for peaceful purposes.[6] In August 1992 the two countries signed a long-term agreement covering cooperation in a range of areas including radioisotope production and the construction and operation of nuclear power plants.[7]

All of these agreements were made openly and had International Atomic Energy Agency (IAEA) safeguards built in. Nevertheless, the administration of George H. W. Bush expressed strong opposition to the agreements and urged China and Russia to end nuclear cooperation with Iran. The administration argued that, given the considerable overlap between the nuclear technologies required for the production of energy and those involved in the production of nuclear weapons, even purely civilian projects would 'likely be seen as contributing to a nuclear weapons capability'.[8] In addition, Washington was concerned that agreements for supposedly peaceful nuclear cooperation would create an infrastructure of collaboration, with technologies and people going back and forth between the partners, within which it would be easier to hide covert, weapons-related activities.

Nor were those suspicions without foundation. As we have seen, Iran had already established a number of undeclared nuclear programmes and in 1989 'organizational structures and administrative arrangements for an undeclared nuclear programme' were centralised in the Physics Research Centre (PHRC) at Lavisan-Shian on the outskirts of Tehran. The PHRC was in turn overseen by the Defense Industries Education Research Institute in the Ministry of Defense.[9] Thus there was indeed a covert nuclear programme, controlled by the military, running in parallel to the overt programme under the leadership of the AEOI. In 1991 China secretly supplied Iran with 1.8 tons of uranium ore which the latter used to begin larger-scale experiments on conversion into UF6.[10]

While he sought to push the nuclear programme forward, Rafsanjani simultaneously sought to ease tensions with the USA and Iran's regional neighbours. Underlying this decision was a recognition that eight years of war had devastated the Iranian economy and that access to foreign direct investment (FDI) would be vital to effective economic reconstruction. More fundamentally, Rafsanjani was seeking to shift the legitimising foundations of the regime away from the depleting resource of revolutionary ideology on to the potentially more solid basis of economic performance and prosperity.[11] To that end he took a number of steps designed to appease Washington: Iran remained neutral during the 1990–1 Gulf Crisis, and in the aftermath of the war Rafsanjani indicated that Iran would accept any outcome of the Madrid Peace Conference that was acceptable to the Palestinians. He was also instrumental in securing the release of the remaining US hostages in Lebanon while publicly condemning terrorism.[12] In 1992 Rafsanjani passed a message via Hossein Mousavian, Iran's ambassador to Germany, that Iran was ready to establish a working group to discuss terrorism, the peace process, weapons of mass destruction (WMD) and human rights.[13] The invitation was ignored by the Bush administration.

Rafsanjani's message had been encouraged by Bush's inaugural address, in which the new president had declared that 'there are today Americans who are held against their will in foreign lands, and Americans who are unaccounted for. Assistance can be shown here, and will be long remembered. Goodwill begets goodwill.'[14] Given Rafsanjani's positive response to that invitation to help, it must have come as a surprise to Tehran when the Bush administration rejected Rafsanjani's offer of dialogue. The problem, however, was the timing. While the administration did ease some sanctions imposed during the Iran–Iraq War and allowed Iran to establish an interests section in the Pakistani embassy in Washington, it was not willing to pursue a more extensive rapprochement until the hostages were released.[15] Because that process was not completed until late 1991, the Bush administration did not review Iran policy until early 1992, an election year. While senior officials within the administration were interested in exploring a possible rapprochement, the conclusion of the review was that any gesture that 'might be politically meaningful in Tehran ... would have been politically impossible at home'.[16]

The key substantive reason that the administration offered for refusing to engage with Iran at this point was the latter's continued involvement in terrorism. In August 1991 former Iranian Prime Minister Shapour Bakhtiar was assassinated by Iranian agents in Paris. The following year Iran was assumed to be behind the bombing of the Israeli embassy in Buenos Aires and the assassination of three Iranian Kurdish leaders in Berlin. According to Bruce Riedel, who had been charged with putting together the options paper on Iran, the assassinations killed the policy review process and ensured that there would be no further progress in relations with Iran during the Bush administration.[17]

In Riedel's words, the assassinations 'boxed in' Bush. With an election coming up he could hardly risk being accused of courting a terrorist state. Moreover, his room for manoeuvre in relation to Iran was, if anything, even further restricted by the failure of the US policy of engagement with Iraq and the revelation of how close Saddam Hussein had come to possessing nuclear weapons. One consequence of that was a new congressional preoccupation with the dangers of nuclear proliferation and a dismissal of the utility of engagement based on the analogy, however questionable, with Iraq. The House Foreign Affairs Committee led the charge, with Democrat member Howard Berman attacking Bush for allowing continued trade with a 'terrorist country' and declaring his amazement that Bush 'still believes we can influence the behavior of these countries by trying to build closer economic relations'.[18] The outcome of this concern was a series of pieces of legislation, including the Non-Proliferation and Arms Transfer Control Act and Omnibus Nuclear Proliferation Act of 1991 and the Iran-Iraq Arms Non-Proliferation Act of 1992. The latter was the most extensive piece of sanctions legislation imposed on Iran since 1980, banning foreign military sales and the issuing of licences for military items and material controlled for national security reasons.[19] This combination of continued Iranian support for terrorism, a heightened preoccupation with nuclear proliferation and an upcoming presidential election ensured that the Bush administration chose not to respond to Rafsanjani's invitations. As Scowcroft put it to UN negotiator Giandomenico Picco, 'Gianni, this is a presidential election year. What do you expect? Do you expect us to give something to Iran during a presidential election? It can't happen.'[20]

That refusal, in turn, further undermined whatever desire to engage there was on the Iranian side, a waning of enthusiasm that was driven not just by the lack of a positive American response but by the domestic political risks and costs involved in attempting to reach out to Washington. Rafsanjani's desire to establish a less confrontational relationship was far from universally shared and his actions exposed the differences between his developing pragmatism and the views of Iranian hardliners for whom Washington remained the 'Great Satan'.[21] The fact that it took Rafsanjani until late 1991 to secure the release of the final American hostages in Lebanon was one consequence of his opponents using their ties to Hezbollah to undercut his efforts. In that instance Rafsanjani succeeded in getting his way because the Supreme Leader eventually backed his position.[22] For the most part, however, Khamenei was one of the principal obstacles to Rafsanjani's plans. Although the latter had been instrumental in helping Khamenei secure his position, the new Supreme Leader made a strategic decision to broaden his power base and cement his position by forging new alliances with hard-line and conservative factions in the Islamic Revolutionary Guard Corps (IRGC) and elsewhere in the regime.[23] As a consequence, Khamenei positioned himself in direct opposition to any effort to secure a rapprochement with the USA. In May 1990 he warned that 'those who think we should conduct talks with the head of arrogance [i.e. the USA] are either simpleminded or terrified'.[24]

Rafsanjani thus faced a powerful coalition of opponents who maintained a vigorous resistance to his efforts. An article by one of his vice-presidents, Ata'ollah Mohajerani, advocating negotiations with the US, was so widely attacked by conservative media outlets that Rafsanjani ended up publicly disassociating himself from what had been his own trial balloon.[25] This kind of attack, as well as the opposition of Khamenei, explains why Rafsanjani sought secret, rather than public, negotiations with Washington. It also helps to explain the mixed messages that he communicated in public. After Khamenei had denounced those seeking negotiations with Washington as 'simpleminded' Rafsanjani publicly declared that 'Iran does not want ties with America.'[26] In March 1991 he suggested that a 'normal' relationship with the US was possible if it abandoned its 'hostility toward Iran' only to state two months later that 'Iran is not thinking about restoring relations with the United States.'[27]

Iranian domestic politics thus served to undercut Rafsanjani's diplomatic efforts. Resistance to the release of the US hostages prevented that obstacle from being removed until just prior to an American election year. The hostility to rapprochement with Washington also led Rafsanjani to move very cautiously and to offer mixed messages in public as well as sometimes contradicting what he was trying to communicate in private. Most crucially, Rafsanjani lacked either the power or the will to prevent the various acts of terrorism conducted by Iranian agents throughout 1991 and 1992 which were central to the Bush administration's decision not to attempt any further engagement with Iran.

Thus, despite a clear desire on both sides to explore whether some improvement in relations was possible, the first Bush administration ended with no significant alteration in the *status quo*. On the American side, while there was some interest in exploring the possibility of change, the Bush administration simply did not see improving relations with Iran as sufficiently urgent to justify taking significant political risks.[28] Despite the recognition that there were those in Iran more eager than they to engage in a dialogue, they were nevertheless convinced that it was the Iranians' fault that relations did not improve. The continuation of terrorism made engagement impossible and the feeling was that despite all the hints, ultimately 'nobody was prepared to stick his neck out and actually have a conversation with the Great Satan'.[29] While that perception was hardly unfounded, however, that was not how things were seen amongst those in Iran who had risked sticking their necks out. From their point of view they had taken the risk of making a series of gestures indicating a willingness to compromise and received nothing in return. Consequently, 'the willingness to do positive work for America almost ended, because they never reciprocated. Whatever positive Iran did, the response was always more and more isolation.'[30]

The consequence of this episode, therefore, was to further confirm each party in its own preconceptions and to reinforce and deepen the distrust and hostility between them. As far as those Iranians who had been willing to explore improved relations were concerned, they felt that they had made concrete offers and gestures, such as securing the release of American hostages, while Washington had again demonstrated bad faith by failing to live up to the pledge that 'goodwill begets goodwill'. For Iranian hardliners, the American failure to offer anything meaningful only confirmed their wisdom in refusing to sup with the Devil. From Washington's perspective, Iranian behaviour was both self-serving and hypocritical. To the extent that Tehran was deemed to be serious about seeking improved relations, it was viewed by many as doing so simply in order to gain access to Western capital and markets. The simultaneous continuation of acts of terrorism confirmed Iran's cynical opportunism in the eyes of many observers.

Clinton and Rafsanjani

If the Bush administration was insufficiently interested in the possibility of improved relations to take any political risks to that end, the first Clinton administration was not interested in pursuing improved relations at all. On the one hand, the Iranian nuclear programme was not seen as an immediate threat while, on the other, Iran was perceived as an irreconcilable enemy with whom there was no point in trying to pursue a rapprochement. Consequently, the administration chose to pursue an ill-considered and ineffectual policy of containment designed largely to 'park' the Iranian issue and allow it to focus on other priorities.

This policy was rationalised in terms of the emergent 'rogue states' concept. In the aftermath of the Cold War American policymakers sought to identify new threats to the emerging international order. Most prominent amongst these were so-called rogue states – governments which failed to conform to the liberal, democratic, capitalist order, actively sought to challenge and subvert it, and which had the means to do so by virtue of their support for terrorism and/or pursuit of WMD.[31] The Clinton administration's review of American Middle East policy concluded that 'Iran was the archetype of a hostile rogue regime – the most important state sponsor of militant Islamic terrorism.'[32] The administration further justified its refusal to engage Iran on the less than accurate grounds that Iran had shown no interest in rapprochement and that the Bush administration's willingness to engage Iran in dialogue had been rewarded with terrorism.[33] The most important consideration determining the initial Clinton policy toward Iran, however, was Israel. Clinton was committed to pursuing the possibility of an Israeli–Palestinian peace, particularly after the signing of the Oslo Accords in September 1993, and the Israelis made it clear that, if they were going to 'take risks for peace', one of the principal *quid pro quos* was that Washington had to neutralise the alleged Iranian threat to Israel.[34]

This insistence that Washington take a hard line with Iran was a new factor complicating American policy. Throughout the 1980s Tel Aviv had actively supported Iran in its war against Iraq because it had seen the latter as the primary threat to Israeli security. In 1987 then Israeli Defence Minister Yitzhak Rabin went so far as to claim that 'Iran is Israel's best friend and we do not intend to change our position in relation to Tehran, because Khomeini's regime will not last forever.'[35] However, with the end of the Cold War the Israeli strategic calculus altered. With the USSR no longer backing the radical Arab states, and with Iraq defeated in the 1991 Gulf War, Israel saw an opportunity to make peace with the Arab world from a position of strength. The only significant potential opponent left in the region was Iran.[36] Consequently, Tehran now became the target of a systematic Israeli effort to portray it as a major threat to Israel and regional stability: 'Iran is the greatest threat', claimed Israeli Foreign Minister Shimon Peres, 'because it seeks the nuclear option while holding a highly dangerous stance of extreme religious militantism'.[37]

The Clinton administration was less than convinced by Israeli protestations about the immediacy and scale of the threat posed by Iran. According to Bruce Riedel, then the National Intelligence Officer for Near East and South Asian Affairs, 'the top agenda item was much more the terrorism, subversion issue. . . . Iran was not going to have a nuclear weapon in the next five years, or even in the next ten years.'[38] Nevertheless, Clinton wanted to pursue the possibility of a breakthrough in the peace process and was prepared to appease Israel to do so. Accordingly, rather than pursue dialogue with Iran or address the 'threat' it posed as a matter of urgency, the Clinton administration chose instead to try and isolate it while focusing on the peace process.[39] The policy, formally announced by Clinton's senior National Security Council (NSC) staffer for the Middle East, Martin Indyk, came to be known as 'dual containment'. Along with Iran, Iraq was also to be isolated, and Indyk's statement made clear that the latter was the main priority. Containment of Iran would be limited and passive – maintaining sanctions, seeking to persuade others to join them and not to aid Iran's nuclear and missile programmes.[40]

While the Clinton administration did not perceive the threat posed by Iran as immediate, Israeli efforts to demonise Iran were more persuasive at a congressional level. In 1993 the Anti-Defamation League claimed that US firms were aiding Iran's nuclear weapons programme by selling Iran computers and 'other federally listed nuclear relevant technologies' worth more than $650 million dollars a year.[41] The lobby's main focus soon became the imposition of 'comprehensive' sanctions that would bar virtually all US trade with Iran.[42] These efforts bore fruit in January 1995 when Senator Alfonse D'Amato introduced the Comprehensive Iran Sanctions Act of 1995 in the Senate. As well as seeking to bar American companies from trading with Iran the legislation sought to impose extra-territorial sanctions on foreign companies that did so.

The significance of the new legislation lay not only in the potential impact on US–Iranian relations but in what it implied about the evolution of attitudes toward Iran amongst Republicans. Historically the Democratic Party had been much closer to Israel than the Republicans (American Jews overwhelmingly voted Democrat), and Republican presidents, particularly Eisenhower and George H. W. Bush, had shown themselves to be significantly less biddable than Democratic ones as far as Israel was concerned. D'Amato and King, however, were both Republicans, and their action reflected an ongoing change within the Republican Party toward an increasingly uncritical, pro-Israeli position. That, in context, also meant an increasingly hostile attitude toward Iran and a steadily decreasing possibility that the kind of interest in improved relations shown by the first Bush administration, however circumspect, would be mirrored under a future Republican president.[43]

In a dramatic demonstration of its ignorance of American politics, on 6 March 1995 the Iranian government announced the issuing of a contract worth $1 billion to Conoco for the development of two offshore Iranian oil fields. This was another of Rafsanjani's gestures designed to improve relations by appealing to American economic self-interest, but its only effect was to embarrass the Clinton administration and seemingly legitimate the arguments underpinning the newly introduced sanctions legislation. The administration argued that unilateral legislation would damage its efforts to persuade other states to stop trading with Iran and hurt American companies without having any significant economic impact on Iran.[44] Clinton also sought to head it off by issuing Executive Order (EO) 12957, barring US companies from involvement in the Iranian energy sector.[45]

In a further effort to retain control of policy, in April 1995 Clinton announced that he would ban all US trade with Iran. In the same speech he also explicitly disavowed a policy of engagement with Iran, saying that 'there is no evidence to support' the argument that engagement was the best way to change Iranian behaviour and that, in fact, 'the evidence of the last two years suggests exactly the reverse. Iran's appetite for acquiring and developing nuclear weapons and the missiles to deliver them has only grown larger' and its support for terrorism increased.[46] The pledge made in the speech was then implemented in EO 12959 of 6 May 1995.[47]

Clinton's attempt to retain control of policy proved to be fruitless. D'Amato agreed to suspend legislative action pending efforts by Clinton to secure international support for multilateral sanctions at the G7 summit in Canada in June. Such support was not forthcoming, however, and the legislation consequently went ahead. The final version of the bill was passed by overwhelming majorities in Congress and signed into law by Clinton on 5 August 1996. The Iran and Libya Sanctions Act (ILSA) required the president to impose at least two out of a menu of six sanctions on foreign companies that made an 'investment' of more than $20 million in one year in Iran's energy sector. In a separate example of congressional antipathy toward Iran, $18 million was added to the CIA's budget at the behest of House Speaker Newt Gingrich for the explicit purpose of overthrowing the Iranian regime.[48]

The Clinton administration's initial disinterest in engaging Iran was thus powerfully reinforced by hardening Israeli and congressional antipathy toward the IRI. The combination of executive and legislative actions, however, only served to reinforce Iranian distrust and hostility. Rafsanjani had made one last effort to engage Washington only to see his plan fail dramatically. Once again there was anger at the lack of reciprocation from Washington. In the words of one Iranian official, 'this was a message to the United States which was not correctly understood. We had a lot of difficulty in this country by inviting an American company to come here with such a project.'[49] Moreover, the approach taken by Washington was a self-fulfilling prophecy. By seeking to contain Iran and making clear that one objective of the peace process was to isolate and weaken Iran, the Clinton administration gave the Iranians every 'incentive to do us in on the peace process in order to defeat our policy of containment'.[50] By identifying Iran as a rogue state, and thus implying that regime change was the ultimate objective of US policy (an impression seemingly confirmed by the funds appropriated by Congress for that purpose), the administration also gave Iran every reason to want to continue with its nuclear programme. Finally, by employing the concept of 'rogue' states and putting Iran in that category, and by failing to counter congressional and Israeli lobby efforts to demonise Iran, the Clinton administration was reinforcing a discourse and a popular perception that would only constrain the executive branch's own room for manoeuvre in the long run.

What made this worse was that the Clinton administration had no intention of seeking to overthrow the Iranian regime as it saw the objective as wholly unrealistic. However, despite the administration making it clear, when signing the bill containing funding for regime change, that it would not spend it for that purpose but to encourage Iran to change its behaviour, the Iranians still 'saw it as an American declaration of covert war against them'.[51] US policy during the first Clinton administration thus achieved the worst of both worlds, providing Iran with every incentive to leave the option of developing nuclear weapons open while doing nothing effective to persuade it to reject such an ambition.

The Iranian Nuclear Programme Continues

With no incentive, whether carrot or stick, to alter course, Iran continued to pursue its nuclear programme on all fronts in the 1990s, with a focus on developing mastery of the fuel cycle. In line with its claim that its activities were entirely peaceful and legal, much of this activity was overt and communicated to the IAEA. Iran's uranium mining efforts were not concealed and nor was its intention to learn how to convert uranium ore into UF6 gas, with China being asked for assistance with the latter.[52] Overt cooperation with Russia also continued, and in 1995 the two countries signed an $800 million contract in which Russia agreed to complete the two reactors at Bushehr, with the first to be ready within four years.[53]

Alongside the overt programme, however, there was a diverse and extensive covert effort dedicated to securing nuclear expertise and technology. While it made no secret of its desire to master the fuel cycle, Iran nevertheless experimented with conversion at a range of facilities which it kept secret from the IAEA throughout the 1990s, using uranium secretly supplied by China.[54] There is also strong circumstantial evidence of other Chinese assistance of which the IAEA was not made aware. This included providing information about plutonium separation and the sale of chemicals used in uranium conversion.[55] Russia's overt collaboration with Iran also concealed other activities which were not revealed to the IAEA. The 1995 agreement to complete Bushehr was quickly revealed to have a secret protocol in which the Russian Atomic Energy Ministry, MINATOM, had agreed to construct an enrichment plant in Iran and to supply 2,000 tons of natural uranium.[56]

In addition, Iran was able to recruit large numbers of unemployed Russian scientists and engineers to assist in its research and development efforts.[57]

In addition to Russia and China, and more important than both, was Iran's continued collaboration with the A. Q. Khan network. Although they were determined not to remain dependent on external suppliers of technology, the Iranians had struggled to master the P1 centrifuge design supplied to them in the late 1980s, in part due to the poor quality of the components originally supplied. Consequently, in late 1993 they entered into further negotiations with the Khan network which led to the supply of designs and components for the more advanced P2 centrifuge. The Iranians later claimed that no action was taken to build the P2 until 2002, due to a lack of technical and scientific resources. However, in 1994 the Khan network also supplied Iran with a new set of drawings for the P1, along with components for 500 centrifuges.[58]

Beyond these key relationships, Iran had also set up an extensive network of front companies and organisations, largely operating in Europe, for the purpose of procuring nuclear technology. The exact scale and extent of this operation is unlikely ever to be known, but some indication can be gleaned from the range of operations uncovered by European police and security services: in January 1995 Italian police seized 'ultra-sonic equipment for the testing of nuclear reactors' which had originated in Slovakia and was being shipped to Iran via Italy and Greece. The following year British customs officers impounded 110 pounds of maraging steel (a key material for centrifuge construction). In 1997 it was reported that British intelligence had uncovered a secret AEOI programme to buy 'nuclear weapons technology', including a spectrometer (used to measure levels of uranium enrichment). A year later Iran was reported to have made at least three attempts to secretly acquire nuclear components and technologies in Russia and the British government announced that it had successfully disrupted various Iranian efforts to procure British technology. In 1999 the Swedish media reported that Iran had managed to smuggle American electronic equipment used in Swedish nuclear reactors from Sweden to Iran.[59] In addition to these specific incidents, the German government published a list of Iranian front companies which had imported or attempted to import controlled items, and Western intelligence agencies identified a network of small airfields and other locations that Iran had used to smuggle nuclear technology out of Europe.[60]

US Efforts to Block International Support for Iran's Programme: The Failure of Unilateralism

American efforts to halt the Iranian nuclear programme, such as they were at this point, were based on a combination of broad sanctions designed to hurt the Iranian economy and more focused measures designed to deny Iran access to the materials and technology required for weapons development. Whilst these efforts were not wholly unsuccessful, the strategy was, nevertheless, ultimately doomed to fail due to its unilateral nature. Throughout the course of the 1990s no other major state was prepared to join Washington in imposing sanctions on Iran while China and Russia, in particular, were reluctant to halt nuclear cooperation. Moreover, whilst the latter were eventually persuaded (largely) to do so, the creation of a watertight regime preventing nuclear technology from getting to Iran was impossible, given both the extent of the Iranian procurement network and the limits of US intelligence.

The fundamental problem facing US policy at this point was the lack of any common perspective or interests amongst the major powers with regard to Iran. Washington's position was that Iran was a threat, that it had an active nuclear weapons programme and that the best means to address this problem was a combination of coercion and denial. However, all of the other key actors whose support was needed in order to make such a policy effective disagreed with at least one of those propositions. In the case of Russia and China there was a rejection of the claim that Iran had a weapons programme and an insistence that they were operating legitimately within the rules of the Treaty on the Non-Proliferation of Nuclear Weapons (NPT) in assisting it to develop peaceful nuclear energy.[61] In the case of Europe, initial scepticism was replaced by a gradual acceptance that Iran did have a weapons programme but there was a rejection of the American approach to dealing with it. Indeed, just months before the Clinton administration announced the adoption of dual containment the European Union (EU) announced a policy of 'critical dialogue' with Iran, indicating its intention to modify Iranian behaviour through engagement and the application of carrots rather than sticks.[62] In all three cases, though unstated for the most part, economic self-interest was also a major factor in the reluctance to join the United States in isolating Iran.[63]

Resistance to US pressure was further reinforced by the refusal of the IAEA to validate American allegations. IAEA inspectors visited Iran on a number of occasions throughout the 1990s and on each occasion gave it a clean bill of health. In 1991 Hans Blix, the then Director-General of the IAEA, said that there was 'no cause for concern' with regard to Iran's efforts to acquire nuclear technology. The following year an IAEA team visited six Iranian nuclear sites and concluded that 'all nuclear activities in Iran are solely for peaceful purposes'. Further visits in 1993 found no evidence of diversion, and in 1995 and in 1997 Blix again confirmed that IAEA inspections had found no evidence of weapons-related activities.[64]

Whilst the IAEA only had access to Iran's declared nuclear sites, its reports nevertheless provided legitimation for the Chinese, Russians and Europeans. Whilst America's European allies agreed as early as 1993 to examine the intelligence the administration presented to them regarding Iranian efforts to develop weapons, they never seriously considered imposing sanctions and were also resistant to American efforts to persuade them to end the export of dual-use technologies to Iran.[65] At the G7 summit in Bonn in 1992, an American proposal to implement a policy of presumption of denial on all embargoed items specified in the lists of the Coordinating Committee for Multilateral Export Controls, the Missile Technology Control Regime and the Nuclear Suppliers Group was rejected.[66] At that point, despite imposing supposedly tougher new export controls, Germany was still approving 80 per cent of licences for exports of dual-use technology to Iran.[67]

Part of Washington's problem was that, until Clinton's 1995 EOs and the subsequent passage of ILSA, Washington's requests were seen as hypocritical, given the scale of America's continued trade with Iran. Even after the USA ended that anomaly, however, its allies were unwilling to change course. After imposing his EOs Clinton sent diplomats to Europe and Japan to seek support for a multilateral trade embargo on Iran, with no success, as Washington's allies continued to argue that dialogue was the only way to change Iranian behaviour.[68] At the end of the G7 summit at Halifax in June 1995, summit host Canadian Prime Minister Jean Chrétien said that the G7 countries would cut off nuclear cooperation with Iran only if evidence of a weapons programme emerged.[69]

The passage of ILSA, with its provisions to impose extra-territorial sanctions, served to antagonise American allies while having a limited impact on their policies. Formally, the EU condemned the provisions as illegal, introduced 'blocking legislation', which would render any judgment by an American court against European firms unenforceable, and threatened to take legal action in the World Trade Organization (WTO).[70] Despite this, the act did seem to have a deterrent effect initially, with major new deals between European firms and Iran tailing off.[71] However, the Clinton administration had no interest in alienating governments it wanted to persuade to cooperate in isolating Iran, and when the French oil company Total decided to ignore ILSA and sign a $2 billion contract to develop Iran's South Pars gas field, the administration announced that it would apply the 'national interest' waiver contained in the legislation in order to avoid the imposition of sanctions.[72]

That announcement followed months of US–EU negotiations, during which the latter had agreed to increase cooperation with the United States on non-proliferation and counter-terrorism. Before the ILSA waiver was announced, the EU announced a list of new steps it was taking to prevent Iran from acquiring WMD. However, while British Foreign Secretary Robin Cook, representing the EU, stated that Europe would 'do more to stop Iran from getting hold of the sort of materials that could help it build ballistic missiles, or that could be used to make chemical or biological weapons', he also (as the quote suggests) indicated continued scepticism as to the reality of an Iranian nuclear weapons programme. In addition, he made it clear that the EU continued to regard the imposition of economic sanctions as wrong-headed. The American approach of isolating Iran 'won't hit the target we want – economic measures will not have any serious effects on Iran's attempts to acquire weapons of mass destruction'.[73]

If persuading its allies to impose sanctions on Iran proved impossible for the Clinton administration, it was never even on the cards when it came to Russia and China. In these cases the objective was simply to dissuade them from continuing to provide direct support for the Iranian nuclear programme. In the Chinese case American efforts proved to be quite successful, thanks to the significant leverage that Washington was able to bring to bear. In 1984 China and the USA had signed a nuclear cooperation agreement under which China would be eligible to receive exports of American nuclear technology for its civil nuclear programme. However, in order for the agreement to come into force, the US government had first to certify that China was conforming to non-proliferation norms. China's adherence to the NPT in 1992 was a first step in that direction but the Clinton administration indicated that Beijing's ongoing assistance to the Iranian (and Pakistani) nuclear programmes remained an obstacle to certification.[74] Faced with a choice between the economic and strategic gains deriving from continued cooperation with Iran and those resulting from complying with Washington's demands, China chose the latter. In January 1996 Beijing announced that it was cancelling plans to sell two nuclear reactors to Iran but was still interested in nuclear cooperation. However, after the Clinton administration indicated that China needed to end all nuclear cooperation with Iran, Beijing announced that it would not begin any new nuclear projects in Iran shortly before a summit between Clinton and Chinese Premier Jiang Zemin in October 1997.[75]

Russia proved a somewhat tougher proposition. While it too needed US assistance, in its case to aid its ailing economy, it also had a desperate need to earn foreign exchange and an extensive nuclear industry that was one of its few means of earning it. US efforts to limit Russian nuclear cooperation with Iran were further hampered by the chaotic nature of President Boris Yeltsin's regime and the lack of control it exercised over the various parts of the sprawling Russian nuclear infrastructure, particularly the Atomic Energy Ministry, MINATOM, which at times appeared to be willing to sell Iran

anything it wanted. The US effort to halt Russian nuclear cooperation with Iran consequently came to look like a never-ending process of plugging leaks, with each successful effort shortly followed
by a new one springing up elsewhere.

In October 1992 Russian officials agreed to impose additional
safeguards on the sale to Iran of the light water reactors (LWRs)
for Bushehr and not to supply Iran with reprocessing or enrichment technology. The following year it was also dissuaded from
selling Iran a heavy water reactor (HWR) which could have been
used to produce weapons-grade plutonium.[76] Moscow nevertheless refused to end its support for Bushehr and the Iranian civil
nuclear programme, despite a combination of economic induce-
ments and threats being deployed by the Clinton administration to
that end.[77] In January 1995 the new contract to complete Bushehr
was signed, including the secret protocol to build an enrichment
plant in contradiction of Russia's 1992 commitments. Yeltsin was
apparently wholly unaware of this side agreement, and its exposure quickly led to its renunciation and denials that it had ever
existed in the first place. An embarrassed Yeltsin announced at
the May 1995 Moscow summit that Moscow would not sell a gas
centrifuge to Iran as previously agreed and would end all 'military'
aspects of nuclear cooperation with Iran, while continuing with
the civilian ones.[78] Later that year a revised version of the agreement to provide LWRs for Bushehr was signed with Iran, including a provision that spent fuel would be returned to Russia for
reprocessing.[79]

Despite Yeltsin's promises, American government agencies continued to identify instances of illicit Russian activity. In 1997 the
administration alleged that Russian experts were advising Iran on
uranium mining and processing despite the 1995 commitments,
and the following year the administration imposed sanctions on a
number of Russian companies it accused of selling weapons-related
dual-use technology to Iran.[80] Further sanctions were imposed in
1997 and the administration warned that if the Russian government did not halt its activities, the US would consider ending collaboration on a satellite launch programme worth hundreds of
millions of dollars.[81] Whereas China had folded under American

pressure, however, Moscow became increasingly defiant, particularly after Vladimir Putin became, successively, prime minister and then president of Russia. Sanctions imposed by Washington in 1999 were followed by an announcement that Russia was increasing the number of technicians working at Bushehr, and when Congress passed the Iran Nonproliferation Act in May 2000, imposing more sanctions on Russian companies trading with Iran, Putin responded by widening the scope of nuclear materials and technology that could be exported.[82]

Even if the Clinton administration had some success in persuading China and Russia to curtail their nuclear cooperation with Iran, it completely missed the crucial Pakistani connection. Robert Einhorn, successively Deputy Assistant Secretary for Political-Military Affairs and Assistant Secretary for Nonproliferation in the Clinton administration, later admitted that while the administration believed that Iran had received some centrifuge equipment from the A. Q. Khan network,

> it was our assumption through the 90s that Iran didn't see this as a promising basis for a program. It was our impression that Iran considered the equipment to be out of date and not very effective. It was our assumption that by the early to mid-90s the Pakistani-Iranian cooperation was not a significant factor. We believed through the 1990s that Iran was looking elsewhere – Russia and China for instance. We spent a lot of time in the 90s trying to turn off Russia and Chinese connections to Iran but Pakistan was not on our radar screen.[83]

The cumulative effect of the Clinton administration's efforts to punish Iran through sanctions and to halt the flow of nuclear technology and material to Iran was thus fairly limited. No other state could be persuaded to join Washington in imposing sanctions, and efforts to persuade them to end the supply of dual-use technologies to Iran were partially successful at best. The Europeans and the Chinese gradually complied, though not, in the latter case, until they had transferred much useful material, not least the designs for a uranium conversion facility which Iran would subsequently build when Beijing withdrew from doing so. For its part Russia refused wholly to end nuclear cooperation with Iran, though the transfer of some sensitive technologies was halted, while the A. Q. Khan network's supply of centrifuge designs and parts was missed completely. At best, therefore, American efforts had a marginal impact on the development of the Iranian nuclear programme. As the administration itself acknowledged, 'current tools—economic sanctions such as the Iran and Libya Sanctions Act and the president's embargo, the missile and CBW sanctions laws, the Iran-Iraq Nonproliferation Act, and the many nuclear sanctions laws—teach the limits of effective unilateral initiatives'.[84]

Clinton and Khatami

Clinton's second term in office saw a significant change in direction in Iran policy, in large part due to the election to the Iranian presidency of the 'reformist' Mohammad Khatami in August 1997. Khatami's election, and the overwhelming nature of his victory (he won 70 per cent of the vote), came as a shock to many observers but clearly reflected important underlying trends in Iran. He surged to power on the back of a combination of disillusion and optimism amongst large swathes of the Iranian electorate – disillusion with the conservative and theocratic nature of the current regime, its corruption and its poor economic performance, and optimism that this state of affairs could be altered.

That optimism was in part a result of the liberalisation of political debate in Iran fostered under Rafsanjani. As various observers have noted, whilst he failed successfully to implement the changes he had hoped to make to Iran, Rafsanjani nevertheless ended up fostering the reform movement that swept Khatami to power in 1997. By creating the conditions in which debates about the future direction of the Islamic Republic could take place, Rafsanjani facilitated the development of a critique of the current regime by thinkers such as Abdolkarim Soroush, Mohammad Shabestari and Mohsen Kadivar who, while differing in their emphases, all argued in favour of the compatibility of Islam and democracy and for a greater emphasis on the democratic dimensions of the Iranian Constitution. They also tended to argue in favour of a more open attitude toward the outside world, including a willingness to engage with the United States.[85]

That desire to engage with the world was underpinned by important material considerations, amongst other things. As was noted above, one of Rafsanjani's key goals had been the revival of the Iranian economy after the Iran–Iraq War. To that end he had sought to liberalise the economy, privatise inefficient state-owned concerns and encourage foreign investment. After some limited initial success, however, his efforts had largely come to nothing due to a combination of factors, including a fall in the global price of oil, the inefficiency and corruption of his own government, and the resistance of powerful interests, including the bonyads and the IRGC, whose domestic monopolies were threatened by economic liberalisation. As a result, rather than raising the living standards of all Iranians, the Rafsanjani years saw a growth in income disparities between the elite and the majority of the population and growing frustration at the failure of the regime to deliver on its economic promises.[86]

Khatami's overwhelming election victory was thus driven by the economic dissatisfaction of the majority of Iranians. Groups which had backed Rafsanjani in the hope that his liberalisation would succeed, like the bazaari economic class, switched their support to Khatami and were joined by the vast majority of the professional middle classes, the intelligentsia and students. All of these groups supported a more open approach to the world, and a more pragmatic approach to dealing with the United States, in some degree because of the hope it held out of trade, investment and growing prosperity.[87]

Khatami's intention to change the direction of Iranian foreign policy was soon evident. At the Organization of the Islamic Conference in December 1997 he assured the Arab states of Iran's acceptance of their regimes and publicly condemned terrorism. He also held two meetings with Crown Prince Abdullah of Saudi Arabia, the first such meetings since 1979. In addition to working to heal the Arab–Persian divide, Khatami also sought improved relations with the EU, declaring that Iran would not in any way threaten the life of Salman Rushdie, despite the fatwa issued by

Ayatollah Khomeini in 1989.[88] Finally, in rather more oblique terms, Khatami also indicated a willingness to alter Iran's policy toward Israel. By expressing a willingness to accept a two-state solution to the Israeli–Palestinian peace process he indicated a tacit readiness to accept Israel's right to exist.[89]

All of these statements and actions indicated a desire on Khatami's part to alter Iran's relations with the outside world, and he also sought to send a similar message, in private, to the Clinton administration. According to Kenneth Pollack, then on Clinton's NSC staff, administration officials were approached by a series of informal, non-governmental emissaries acting on Khatami's behalf. The message conveyed was that Khatami wanted to explore the possibility of a rapprochement. They also said that Khatami was trying to end Iranian support for terrorism and that he understood American concerns about Iran's WMD programmes and was 'ready to accommodate' them. However, the messengers also emphasised that Khatami faced fierce resistance from Iranian hardliners and that it was crucial that the US responded to Khatami's efforts with concrete acts of reciprocity that he could utilise to prove the efficacy of his policy.[90]

In January 1998 Khatami went public with his interest in a rapprochement in his 'dialogue of civilizations' interview with CNN. He denounced terrorism, expressed regret for the Iranian hostage crisis, and expressed a desire for engagement between the USA and Iran.[91] In fact, the Clinton administration had decided to respond positively to Khatami's call for dialogue even before the interview.[92] This decision was underpinned by various factors, prominent amongst which was a belief that the change that Khatami's election represented was likely to continue. A significant body of scholarship argued that the forces of change which had brought Khatami to power were fundamental, long-term and would force the IRI in the direction of democratisation and liberalisation.[93] Moreover, that view was reflected in the administration's own analysis: in June 1998 John C. Gannon, the Chair of the National Intelligence Council, asserted that 'the social factors favoring political change will continue and power will pass to another generation of leaders'.[94]

In addition to that perception, some of the considerations which had mitigated against engaging Iran in Clinton's first term had altered. The administration spent 'considerable time' establishing the likely reaction from Israel, Congress and its allies before deciding how to respond to Khatami.[95] While congressional and wider domestic hostility to Iran was still strong, Clinton was now a second-term president who did not have to consider the electoral impact of an unpopular policy. US allies, moreover, were strongly in favour of engaging Iran and less willing than ever to support a punitive approach.[96] Even the Israelis indicated that they would not oppose Clinton's exploring the possibility of a rapprochement with Iran.[97] That, in turn, may have reflected a conclusion also reached by the Clinton administration. Attempting to isolate Iran had only encouraged it to seek to undermine US efforts to achieve an Israeli–Palestinian peace. A positive response to Khatami's overtures might end that opposition and facilitate the achievement of Clinton's key objective in the region.[98] Last, but probably not least, there was Clinton's desire to be the president who achieved what Bruce Riedel described as the 'Nixon to Beijing moment' and who transformed US–Iranian relations.[99]

Over the course of the next three years the Clinton administration made continuous efforts to indicate to Tehran that it was serious about the possibility of changing the nature of the US–Iranian relationship. In response to Khatami's overtures, Secretary of State Madeleine Albright sent a message, via the Swiss embassy in Tehran, proposing a meeting of senior officials, but the Iranians did not respond.[100] Another invitation sent via the Saudi government in May 1998 also failed to elicit a response.[101] Albright then made the administration's desires public in a major address to the Asia Society in June 1998. In this speech she stated that 'we fully respect Iran's sovereignty' and 'do not seek to overthrow its government'. Acknowledging the change that Khatami seemed to represent, she further declared that 'we must know when to engage and when to isolate, and we must always be flexible enough to respond to change and to seize historic opportunities when they arise'. On that basis she held out an invitation to Iran to engage in dialogue and to work to develop a 'roadmap for normal relations'.[102]

The administration also made a number of concrete gestures of goodwill. These included adding the Mojahedin-e Khalq, an

Iraqi-backed Iranian group seeking the overthrow of the IRI, to the Department of State's list of terrorist organisations, relaxing visa rules and encouraging non-governmental exchanges with Iran, waiving sanctions on the contract signed by Total and subsequent oil and gas deals signed by foreign firms, and removing Iran from the list of countries failing to take adequate steps to deal with drug trafficking.[103] When these efforts still failed to generate an Iranian response to the invitation to talk, Clinton offered a tacit public acceptance of Iranian criticisms of the US role in Iran under the Shah, saying that

> Iran . . . has been the subject of quite a lot of abuse from various Western nations. And I think sometimes it's quite important to tell people, 'look, you have the right to be angry at something my country or my culture did'.[104]

He followed this up by lifting the blanket embargo on the sale of food, medicine and medical equipment to Iran.[105]

American efforts were complicated in spring 1999 when the Saudi regime provided it with evidence that seemed to confirm that Iran had been behind the 1996 Khobar Towers bombing in which nineteen US servicemen had died. Even then, however, Clinton sought to turn the situation to advantage. Bruce Riedel and Martin Indyk of the NSC staff were sent to Paris to meet with Sultan Qaboos of Oman and asked him to pass on a message to Khatami. In it Clinton proposed a deal in which Iran would cooperate in investigating Khobar Towers and seeing those responsible were brought to justice in exchange for a lifting of the trade embargo and negotiations toward normalisation. The Iranian regime replied with a statement denying any involvement in Khobar Towers.[106]

Despite the repeated rebuffs, Clinton was encouraged to pursue the effort to engage Iran by the sweeping victory of reformist candidates in the February 2000 Majlis elections as well as by his desire to achieve a diplomatic landmark before the end of his presidency. The following month Albright gave another address in which she acknowledged the US role in the 1953 coup, offered a more explicit apology for American backing for the Shah, and stated that US support for Iraq in the Iran–Iraq war had been 'shortsighted'. She confirmed once again that the administration wanted 'to work together with Iran to bring down what President Khatami refers to as "the wall of mistrust"' and announced further concrete concessions including the lifting of the embargo on importing Iranian pistachios and carpets. There was a clear indication that the Clinton administration was also willing to consider ending the wider sanctions regime if Iran, in return, was willing 'to live up to . . . the pledges its leaders have made in such areas as proliferation and opposition to terrorism'.[107] The following week Khamenei responded in the most dismissive fashion, declaring that 'the confessions of American crimes are of no use to the Iranian nation' and that the American offer of talks was a 'deceitful' attempt to 'set the stage for more enmities and to regain its former interests in Iran'.[108]

Three years of repeated overtures and offers of talks thus came to nothing. Despite having indicated his desire to pursue a dialogue with Washington, Khatami failed to respond to any of the Clinton administration's invitations to do so. According to some Iranian reformists, the responsibility for this lay primarily with the Clinton administration, which had failed to offer Iran anything beyond trivial concessions. 'Khatami expected something concrete and bold', in the words of Hadi Semat, a political scientist at Tehran University. 'He had to be able to sell it to his friends, his enemies and the Supreme Leader.' Khatami's Foreign Minister Kamal Kharazi also blamed the Clinton administration, telling one interviewer: 'I regret that Clinton failed to do better to finish the job.'[109]

There is a degree of legitimacy to such accusations inasmuch as the Clinton administration's concessions to Iranian sensibilities and interests were both small-scale and qualified. Removing Iran from the list of countries failing to deal with drugs trafficking, for example, had no effect on the sanctions regime since the sanctions affected were still imposed under alternative legislation. And while the administration did offer apologies for previous US actions, these were still hedged round with criticisms of the IRI. Albright's March 2000 speech, in particular, followed its recognition of US errors with a statement about Iranian domestic politics:

> Despite the trend towards democracy, control over the military, judiciary, courts and police remains in unelected hands, and the elements of its foreign policy, about which we are most concerned, have not improved. But the momentum in the direction of internal reform, freedom and openness is growing stronger.[110]

The comment was seen as an intervention in Iran's internal affairs and an implicit attack on the legitimacy of the regime, hence Khamenei's vituperative response.[111]

The carefully qualified and hesitant nature of the Clinton administration's outreach in turn reflected continued domestic political problems when dealing with Iran. While Clinton might have been a second-term president, being seen as conceding too much too quickly to Iran would have precipitated vigorous criticism and opposition that could significantly complicate any further moves toward rapprochement. Even the tentative steps that were made were vigorously criticised by the Republican right and some members of Clinton's own party.[112] In that context the key issue that stopped Clinton moving further was Khobar Towers. There was a widespread consensus within the US political system that Iran was behind the attack, and the Iranian refusal to admit that or to engage with the administration in dealing with it 'was a real brake, constraint, on how far Clinton could move'.[113]

Domestic hostility toward Iran also hurt Clinton's efforts by constantly contradicting his administration's statements and actions. In 1998 Clinton had to veto the Iran Missile Proliferation Sanctions Act passed by Congress in order to prevent it undercutting his outreach to Iran and damaging relations with Russia. Two years later, however, he was forced to sign a modified version of the act by the size of the congressional majorities in support of it.[114] In 1999 the House of Representatives passed a measure to withhold funds from IAEA programmes that supported Iran's civilian nuclear programme.[115] The following year the National Commission on Terrorism declared that Iran remained the leading global state sponsor of terrorism and recommended that the administration make no 'further concessions' to Iran until that situation changed.[116] Finally, in October 2000 Congress passed the Victims of Trafficking and Violence Protection Act, part of which was designed to assist the parents of a US citizen killed by Islamic Jihad in 1999 to collect a $247.5 million judgment made against Iran by the US District Court in Washington.[117] While none of this stopped the Clinton administration from engaging Iran, it did undermine those efforts and feed Iranian distrust. According to Albright, one Iranian diplomat told her that these actions and others like them proved that 'all this [negotiation] is a trick' and that 'the Jews' were 'too strong' to permit US flexibility in negotiations.[118]

Nevertheless, the key factor preventing any progress in negotiations at this point was Iranian, rather than American, domestic politics. Khatami's problem in following through with his desire to engage the United States was less the unwillingness of the Clinton administration to provide sufficient incentives than the blanket refusal of hardliners in his own government to even contemplate the idea and his inability to overcome that resistance. While Khatami had won a sweeping victory in the 1997 presidential election, that only gave the reformists control of one of the key institutions of government. Many of the others remained firmly under the control of conservative hardliners who were opposed to his plans and had sufficient power to successfully obstruct them. In the context of domestic politics, the Guardian and Expediency Councils and the Judiciary worked to block Khatami's efforts to liberalise civil society while the IRGC, Ministry of Intelligence and Security, and the *basij* used the cruder means of violence and intimidation to quell the reformists.[119] In foreign policy, if anything, hardliners were even more successful in containing Khatami. He was able to make some changes to personnel, as noted above, but generally he was unable to appoint reformist candidates to the same extent as in domestic ministries. His experience with the IRGC was typical of his efforts. He managed to remove Major General Mohsen Rezaei as head of the IRGC only for him to be replaced by his former Deputy, Major General Yahya Rahim Safavi, who was just as hard-line. Moreover, Khameini then appointed Rezaei as Deputy Head of the Expediency Council. Hardliners also sought to undermine Khatami by transferring power away from bodies controlled by the reformists. Thus Khatami saw the Supreme National Security Council take over several roles previously undertaken by the Foreign Ministry while Ali Akbar Velayati, whom Khatami had removed as foreign minister, was appointed as Khameini's foreign policy adviser and acted almost as a parallel foreign minister.[120]

Most importantly, as the above suggests, Khatami never managed to win the support of the Supreme Leader for his efforts to alter the trajectory of US–Iranian relations. By the time Khatami was elected, Khamenei had been Supreme Leader for eight years and had successfully consolidated his power, primarily through forging alliances with the IRGC and other conservative and hardline groups. During that process he had shown no interest whatsoever in exploring the possibility of improved relations with the USA. Indeed, many of his statements indicated that he regarded America as fundamentally untrustworthy and bent on regime change in Iran, regardless of what the Clinton administration may have said.[121] Moreover, Khamenei believed that Washington was most likely to try and bring down the IRI through soft power and the influence of US culture and values rather than by military action.[122] Following that logic engagement with the US was to be resisted, since it risked exposing Iranian society to those corrupting influences. Finally, Khamenei's speeches revealed an overriding preoccupation with the development and preservation of Iranian 'independence', with economic power, based on scientific and technological achievement, as the foundation upon which that independence would be built. The USA and the other 'colonial powers' were assumed to be bent on preventing such independence and their efforts had to be resisted, even if the cost was sanctions and economic hardship.[123] In Khamenei's worldview, 'rights cannot be achieved by entreating. If you supplicate, withdraw and show flexibility, arrogant powers will make their threat more serious.'[124]

Consequently, Khatami found his efforts to reshape Iran's relations with the outside world repeatedly stymied by Khamenei. A week after Khatami's 'dialogue of civilizations' interview the Supreme Leader declared that 'talks and relations with America would be detrimental to the Iranian nation. . . . The American regime is the enemy of [Iran's] Islamic government and our revolution.'[125] When Khatami stated before the Camp David negotiations in 2000 that Iran would accept the decision of the Palestinians, Khameini announced that Arafat's 'negotiating away' of Jerusalem would have no validity under Islamic law.[126] And as was noted above, Albright's March 2000 invitation to talk was dismissed by Khamenei with brutal contempt.

The Iranian failure to respond to the various initiatives made by the Clinton administration was thus primarily the result of domestic political realities in Iran. Khatami wished to pursue a 'dialogue of civilizations' with Washington but he did not have enough allies in positions of power to translate that desire into policy. As Deputy Assistant Secretary of State for Near Eastern Affairs Allen Keiswetter put it, as time passed,

> it became clearer and clearer ... that the Supreme Leader wasn't really interested in this and that he was giving scope for Khatami to play out his string but ultimately he wasn't ready to see us. The Great Satan hadn't been sufficiently sanctified.[127]

The Iranian Nuclear Programme Accelerates

Khatami's relative lack of control of events was also indicated by the fact that, while he was suggesting to the Clinton administration that he would be willing to reach an accommodation in relation to the Iranian nuclear programme, that programme was actually being stepped up. Shortly after Khatami's election, Reza Amrollahi was replaced as head of the AEOI by Gholamreza Ahgazadeh, apparently at the Supreme Leader's behest. Aghazadeh's brief, according to Reza Khazaneh, Amrollahi's former assistant, was to speed up the programme, and soon after his arrival plans for an HWR at Arak that had been drawn up years earlier but left unimplemented were put into action. Ahgazadeh also informed Khazaneh that the AEOI was going to start a uranium enrichment programme in order to make its own fuel.[128] Simultaneously, beyond the purview of the AEOI, the centrifuge programme was also accelerating. The first P1 models began to be assembled in late 1998 and were tested with UF6 for the first time in 1999. That experiment proved successful and by 2000 Iran was preparing to build two enrichment facilities at Natanz – a pilot plant with 1,000 centrifuges and a full-scale plant with 50,000.[129] The late 1990s also saw the commencement of the first explicitly weapons-related nuclear research in Iran. In 1999 the PHRC was absorbed into a larger entity, known as the AMAD plan, which was directed by Mohsen Fakhrizadeh-Mahabadi, an IRGC officer and physicist. Activities which the organisation now began to pursue included work on the development of a high explosive detonation system of the type necessary to initiate the reaction in a nuclear warhead and the design of a rocket nosecone for such a warhead. Iran also began building a high explosive testing chamber at Parchin.[130]

This acceleration of the Iranian nuclear programme under Khatami is seen by some observers as evidence of a fundamental unity of purpose amongst the Iranian leadership with regard to the nuclear weapons programme. The fact that the programme continued under Rafsanjani and Khatami, according to this perspective, demonstrates that there was no difference between them and regime hardliners in regard to the objectives of the nuclear programme.[131] Khatami's indication, in his private messages to Washington, that he was willing to compromise on the nuclear programme is seen either as deliberate dissembling to buy time for the programme's evolution or evidence that he was simply not a part of the inner circle when it came to nuclear decision-making.[132]

However, whilst it is not possible, given the available evidence, to conclude definitively that this argument is wrong, it is equally difficult to demonstrate its validity. While we can be certain that the nuclear programme continued to develop steadily throughout the 1990s and thus that there was a significant degree of consensus within the IRI elite, what cannot be discerned with the confidence assumed in the sources cited above is the extent and degree of that consensus. What is clear is that all were agreed on Iran's right to nuclear energy and to the control of all the technology and processes required to that end.[133] It is not at all clear, however, that the consensus extended either to agreement that Iran should develop nuclear weapons and/or to agreement about the costs Iran ought to be willing to pay in order to achieve that end. For example, while one cannot discount the possibility that Khatami was indeed dissembling when he indicated his willingness to make concessions on the nuclear programme, the evidence offered to demonstrate his support for the development of nuclear weapons is scanty and inferential, at best.[134]

The real difficulty in drawing firm conclusions about the exact positions of the various factions within the Iranian regime at this point, however, is that the regime had not yet been faced with the need to make any real choices. In the first place, the programme was still at a very preliminary stage, and while some weapons-related experimentation had begun, any critical decision on whether to develop weapons was still a significant time away. Secondly, the regime had not yet been faced with the question of what sacrifices it was prepared to make in order to retain its nuclear programme or develop weapons, because the exposure of its violations of its agreement with the IAEA had not yet occurred and the full weight of the international community had not yet been brought to bear. Finally, neither the Bush nor the Clinton administration had been able either to bring sufficient pressure on Iran, or to make an offer sufficiently generous to it, to generate real debate within the Iranian regime about how to respond. The Iranian regime was thus not faced with making any critical choices in relation to its nuclear programme because there were no significant cost/benefit decisions being imposed by its continuation and they had not yet reached the point where the contentious decision on weapons development needed to be made. Until that situation changed, the positions of the different members and factions of the Iranian elite would remain opaque.

Thus, it is not possible to conclude that at this point the IRI leadership were as one in their desire to develop nuclear weapons or to discern whether there were, in fact, groups who were less committed to that goal and/or less willing to pay a heavy price to achieve it. At the very least, the evidence regarding the views of the leadership is ambiguous, with some indicating a willingness to consider concessions to US concerns in return for appropriate reciprocation. There is also 'no indication that a definitive decision ha[d] been made to continue [the weapons programme] irrespective of cost' or that there was any kind of clear, long-term plan to develop weapons, as opposed to a general direction of travel toward being able to develop weapons, at some point in the future, if it was deemed necessary.[135]

A Lost Decade?

As far as American policy toward the Iranian nuclear programme is concerned, the 1990s represents something of a lost decade. Hostility and mistrust between the two sides was reinforced, tentative moves toward diplomatic engagement went nowhere, and Iran's mastery of nuclear technology progressed steadily.

American policy was, for the most part, ill-designed and ineffective, with Clinton's first term a particular low point. As a report published by the Council on Foreign Relations in 1997 noted, Clinton's efforts to isolate Iran were counter-productive, with their effect being to 'increasingly isolate America, rather than their target'. The imposition of blanket sanctions and the attempt to persuade others to do likewise had been almost completely unsuccessful. The report further argued that, had the administration been less insistent on demonising Iran, and instead pursued a more nuanced policy focused on the real dangers posed by proliferation, it might have received a more favourable hearing from those it was seeking to persuade. Finally, it suggested that, rather than continuing to isolate Iran, the US should be open to the possibility of a deal in which Iran would be required to offer a verifiable commitment not to pursue nuclear weapons in return for concrete US guarantees.[136]

The latter point highlighted the rather limited nature of the first Clinton administration's approach to dealing with the Iranian nuclear programme. As Richard K. Betts had observed long before, there are five basic options available to the US government in the face of potential nuclear proliferators:

1. Do nothing.
2. Offer material incentives to states to dissuade them from proliferation.
3. Offer security guarantees or military alliances to states that might seek to proliferate due to insecurity.
4. Seek to prevent the diffusion of nuclear technology and materials.
5. Use coercive means – threats, sanctions or the use of force to stop proliferation.[137]

Of those, the Clinton administration had only attempted to employ the fourth and fifth, without success.

Nevertheless, while the first Clinton administration's approach was notably unsuccessful, it is not clear that an approach which placed more emphasis on the second and third options was either politically viable or would have had significantly greater success. On the first count, it would have been hugely problematic for the Clinton administration to have offered Iran greater incentives than it did. The response of domestic critics of Iran and Israel (and the US's Gulf Arab allies) would have been furious and their opposition would have placed major obstacles in the way of attempts to extend the kind of incentives which might have persuaded the Iranians to take the Clinton administration's offer seriously. Even if the Clinton administration had offered more generous carrots, moreover, it is unclear that they would have been well received. The experience of the second Clinton administration demonstrated the extent to which Iranian domestic politics continued to undermine efforts to engage the United States. Just as with Rafsanjani's efforts, so Khatami's were systematically undermined by the opposition of hardliners who both distrusted the USA and wished to prevent Khatami from securing a diplomatic triumph that would increase his popularity and further strengthen the political position of the reformist faction.

It is hard to escape the conclusion, therefore, that the time was not yet ripe for a successful resolution of the conflict over the Iranian nuclear programme, regardless of the wisdom, or lack of it, of American policy. The issue had not yet evolved to a point at which the stakes were sufficiently high for either side to feel the need to face up to tough choices. For the George H. W. Bush and Clinton administrations the Iranian nuclear programme was not yet threatening enough to abandon the politically safe course of sanctions and coercion and to take on Israel and the domestic enemies of Iran. Nor was it yet inescapably clear that that policy was not working. On the Iranian side, the US had marshalled neither sufficient concrete incentives nor sufficient coercive force to alter the political calculus inside Iran or to compel the regime to change course.

Notes

1. Axworthy, *Revolutionary Iran*, p. 307.
2. IAEA, 'Implementation of the NPT safeguards agreement and relevant provisions of Security Council resolutions in the Islamic Republic of Iran', GOV/2011/65, Annex.
3. *IRNA* in English, 1 September 1991.
4. Patrikarikos, *Nuclear Iran*, p. 134.
5. 'China releases details of nuclear program with Iran', *Associated Press*, 4 November 1991; *Los Angeles Times*, 17 March 1992, pp. A1, A11; 'Iran signed a nuclear cooperation pact with China', *Nuclear News*, October 1992, pp. 17–18; Elaine Sciolino, 'China will build a plant for Iran', *The New York Times*, 11 September 1992, p. A6.
6. 'USSR/Iran: Iranians say Soviets will aid in nuclear', *Nucleonics Week*, 15 March 1990, p. 18.
7. *IRNA* (Tehran), 23 September 1992, US Department of Commerce, *Foreign Broadcast Information Service, Daily Reports, Middle East Area*, 24 September 1992.
8. 'Language NEA's Libby Ward prepared for DAS Shaeffer's hearing today before Cong Hamilton's subcommittee', Department of State press guidance, 13 March 1992, *DNSA*.
9. IAEA, 'Implementation of the NPT safeguards agreement and relevant provisions of Security Council resolutions in the Islamic Republic of Iran', GOV/2011/65, Annex, p. 5.
10. Corera, *Shopping for Bombs*, p. 62.
11. Ehteshami, *After Khomeini*, p. 140; Ramazani, 'Iran's foreign policy'.
12. Picco, *Man Without a Gun*, pp. 113–14; *Iran Times*, 27 December 1991, pp. 1, 12.
13. Crist, *Twilight War*, p. 389. What Rafsanjani was prepared to offer in regard to WMD had such a dialogue taken place is unknown. There was an obvious contradiction between his desire to improve relations with the USA and a continuation of the weapons programme. It is plausible that at this early stage he was hedging his bets until it became clearer whether his efforts to engage Washington would come to anything.
14. George Bush, 'Inaugural address' 20 January 1989, US President, *Public Papers of the Presidents of the United States (PPPUS)*.
15. Crist, *Twilight War*, pp. 383–5; Discussion paper, 'Options for Iran', NSC, Robert Gates files, folder notes, August 1990, George Bush Presidential Library, *Bush Presidential Records*.

16. Pollack, *Persian Puzzle*, pp. 248, 253; Elaine Sciolino, 'After a fresh look: US decides to steer clear of Iran', *The New York Times*, 7 June 1992.
17. Riedel interview.
18. Alikhani, *Sanctioning Iran*, p. 163.
19. Ibid., pp. 171–6.
20. Blight et al., *Becoming Enemies*, p. 248.
21. Pollack, *Persian Puzzle*, pp. 250–1.
22. Seliktar, *Navigating Iran*, p. 72.
23. Ibid., p. 71; Ansari, *Modern Iran Since 1921*, p. 247.
24. Radio Tehran, 4 May 1990, *BBC SWB*, 6 May 1990.
25. Menashri, 'Iran', p. 363.
26. Radio Tehran, 5 May 1990, *BBC SWB*, 6 May 1990.
27. Elaine Sciolino, 'Distrust of US hinders Iran chief', *The New York Times*, 10 April 1992, p. A3.
28. See the comments of National Security Adviser Brent Scowcroft, quoted in Parsi, *Treacherous Alliance*, p. 134.
29. Scowcroft, quoted in Slavin, *Bitter Friends, Bosom Enemies*, p. 179. See also Pollack, *Persian Puzzle*, pp. 246–7.
30. Masoud Eslami, Iranian Foreign Ministry official, quoted in Parsi, *Treacherous Alliance*, p. 155.
31. Klare, *Rogue States and Nuclear Outlaws*; Miles, *United States and the Rogue State Doctrine*.
32. Indyk, *Innocent Abroad*, p. 39.
33. Pollack, *Persian Puzzle*, pp. 259–60.
34. Christopher, *In the Stream of History*, pp. 74–81; Indyk, 'Back to the bazaar', pp. 76–7.
35. Quoted in Souresrafil, *Khomeini and Israel*, p. 114.
36. Peres, *New Middle East*, pp. 33–4.
37. 'Iran greatest threat: Will have nukes by '99', *Associated Press*, 12 February 1993.
38. Riedel interview.
39. Indyk, *Innocent Abroad*, p. 43.
40. Indyk, 'Clinton administration's approach'.
41. Steve Rodan, 'ADL: U.S. companies helping Iran's nuclear program', *The Jerusalem Post*, 10 February 1993.
42. AIPAC, *Comprehensive US Sanctions Against Iran*.
43. Ansari, *Confronting Iran*, p. 143.
44. See testimony of Under-Secretary of State for Political Affairs Peter Tarnoff in US Congress, House Committee on International Relations, 'US Policy toward Iran'.

45. US President, Executive Order 12957, Section 1, 52 *Federal Register* 14615, 17 March 1995.
46. Bill Clinton, 'Remarks at the World Jewish Congress dinner in NY City, 30 April 1995', *PPPUS*.
47. US President, Executive Order 12959, 60 *Federal Register* 24757, 9 May 1995.
48. Tim Weiner, 'US plan to change Iran leaders is an open secret before it begins', *The New York Times*, 25 January 1996.
49. Elaine Sciolino, 'Iranian leader says US move on oil deal wrecked chances to improve ties', *The New York Times*, 16 May 1995.
50. Martin Indyk, quoted in Parsi, *Treacherous Alliance*, p. 191.
51. 'White House agrees to covert-action plan for Iran', *Agence France-Presse*, 22 December 1995, p. 1; Kenneth Pollack, quoted in Crist, *Twilight War*, p. 400.
52. Garver, *China and Iran*, pp. 156–8.
53. 'Iran, Russia agree on $800 million nuclear plant deal', *The Washington Post*, 9 January 1995, p. A18.
54. IAEA, 'Implementation of the NPT safeguards agreement in the Islamic Republic of Iran' GOV/2004/83, p. 4.
55. Garver, *China and Iran*, pp. 156–8; Harold and Nader, 'China and Iran', p. 8.
56. Aleksey Yablokov, 'Atomic energy ministry confused its own interests with national interests in signing the protocol with Iran', *Izvestiya* (Moscow), 2 June 1995.
57. Michael Dobbs, 'A story of Iran's quest for power; A scientist details the role of Russia', *The Washington Post*, 13 January 2002.
58. Corera, *Shopping for Bombs*, pp. 69–70; Braun and Chyba, 'Proliferation rings', p. 18; IAEA, 'Implementation of the NPT safeguards agreement in the Islamic Republic of Iran', GOV/2004/83, p. 8; IAEA, 'Implementation of the NPT safeguards agreement and relevant provisions of Security Council resolutions 1737 (2006) and 1747 (2007) in the Islamic Republic of Iran', GOV/2007/58, pp. 4–5.
59. Bruce Johnson, 'Iran-bound N-plant parts', *The Daily Telegraph*, 1 March 1995; Con Coughlin, 'Britain seizes bomb-grade steel cargo', *The Washington Times*, 11 August 1996, p. A8; *The Observer* (London), 31 August 1997, p. 1; 'Secret services thwart Iranian efforts to get nuclear technology', *Agence France-Presse*, 23 April 1998; 'US nuke equipment smuggled to Iran', *Middle East Newsline*, 11 October 1999.
60. Cordesman, *Iran's Military Forces in Transition*, pp. 241–2; Chris Hedges, 'A vast smuggling network feeds Iran's arms program', *The New York Times*, 15 March 1995, p. A1.

61. 'Russian Foreign Minister cited on readiness to expand atomic cooperation with Iran', *BBC*, 29 November 1994.

62. Commission of the European Communities, 'Conclusions of the Presidency'.

63. Pollack, *Persian Puzzle*, p. 264.

64. *U.S. News & World Report*, 25 November 1991, p. 42; Michael Z. Wise, 'Atomic team reports on Iran probe', *The Washington Post*, 15 February 1992, pp. A29, A30; 'Kozyrev, IAEA Director discuss nuclear cooperation, no traces of "military programs" in Iran', *Interfax* (Moscow), 3 July 1995, US Department of Commerce, *Foreign Broadcast Information Service, Daily Reports, Central Eurasia* (CE), 3 July 1995; 'IAEA: No sign of attempts to make nuclear weapons in Iran', *Voice of the Islamic Republic of Iran* (Tehran), 23 July 1997, *FBIS*, Document FTS 19970723000215.

65. Norman Kempster, 'EC will study economic sanctions against Iran', *Los Angeles Times*, 10 June 1993, p. 18.

66. Alikhani, *Sanctioning Iran*, p. 165.

67. Steve Coll, 'German exports helping Iran rebuild, rearm; Bonn approves 80% of requests to sell Tehran high-tech goods', *The Washington Post*, 6 December 1992, p. A33.

68. Fred Barbash, 'Clinton's call for boycott of Iran drawing little support abroad', *The Washington Post*, 3 May 1995, p. A27.

69. Chrétien, 'Remarks by Prime Minister Jean Chrétien'.

70. Council of the European Union, 'Protecting against the effects of the extra-territorial application of legislation'.

71. Pollack, *Persian Puzzle*, pp. 288–9.

72. Katzman, 'Iran Sanctions Act', p. 2.

73. Acronym Institute, *Disarmament Diplomacy*; *Reuters*, 16 January 1998.

74. Mark Hibbs, 'China has far to go before US will certify, agencies now say', *Nucleonics Week*, 12 December 1996, pp. 1, 8–10.

75. 'China says deals to sell Iran nuclear reactors scrapped', *Associated Press*, 9 January 1996; R. Jeffrey Smith, 'China's pledge to end Iran nuclear aid yields U.S. help', *The Washington Post*, 30 October 1997.

76. Mark Hibbs, *Nuclear Fuel*, 12 October 1992, p. 5; Steven Greenhouse, 'U.S. seeks to deny A-plants to Iran', *The New York Times*, 24 January 1995, p. A4.

77. Jim Mannion, 'US puts off nuclear agreement with Russia over Iranian nuclear deal', *Agence France-Presse*, 28 March 1995.

78. 'Russia may call off training Iranian physicists', *Interfax* (Moscow), 10 May 1995, *FBIS-DR-CE*, 10 May 1995; 'The President's news

conference with President Boris Yeltsin of Russia in Moscow', 10 May 1995, *PPPUS*.

79. 'Russian contract extended to fuel', *Nuclear News*, 1 October 1995, p. 47.

80. R. Jeffrey Smith, 'Administration concerned about Russia's nuclear cooperation with Iran', *The Washington Post*, 3 July 1997, A7; 'Kokoshin provokes Clinton to impose sanctions on Russian organizations', *Kommersant-Daily* (Moscow), 30 July 1998, p. 2, in 'Firms "perplexed" but not worried by US sanctions', *FBIS* Document FTS19980806002351, 6 August 1998.

81. Carol Giacomo, 'US warns Russia on Iranian nuclear program', *Reuters*, 16 December 1998.

82. Mikhail Kozyrev, 'Russia authorizes itself to cooperate with Iran', *The Current Digest of the Soviet Press*, 11 May 2000, p. 20.

83. Corera, *Shopping for Bombs*, p. 80.

84. US Congress, Senate Committee on Foreign Relations, 'Iran and proliferation', Statement of David Welch, Acting Assistant Secretary for Near Eastern Affairs, and Robert Einhorn, Deputy Assistant Secretary for Politico-Military Affairs.

85. Matin-Asgari, 'Abdolkarim Sorush'; Ansari, 'Iranian foreign policy under Khatami', pp. 39–40; Axworthy, *Revolutionary Iran*, pp. 331–4.

86. Axworthy, *Revolutionary Iran*, p. 309; Ansari, *Modern Iran Since 1921*, pp. 244–7. The bonyads are charitable foundations that control approximately 20 per cent of the Iranian economy. They are generally controlled by conservative-leaning clerics; Saeidi, 'Iran's para-statal organizations'.

87. Moslem, *Factional Politics in Post-Khomeini Iran*, pp. 99–105, 129; Kamrava, 'Iranian national security debates', p. 89.

88. *Associated Press*, 9 December 1997; Parsi, *Treacherous Alliance*, pp. 203–4.

89. Pollack, *Persian Puzzle*, p. 315.

90. Ibid., pp. 317–18.

91. 'President Khatami's interview with CNN', 8 January 1998, *BBC SWB*, 9 January 1998.

92. *Reuters*, 16 December 1997.

93. Wright, 'Iran's new revolution'; Zahedi, *Iranian Revolution Then and Now*; Ansari, *Iran, Islam and Democracy*, p. 219.

94. Gannon, 'Remarks to the World Affairs Council'.

95. Pollack, *Persian Puzzle*, p. 319.

96. Talwar, 'Iran in the balance', p. 61.

97. Albright, *Madam Secretary*, p. 320.

98. Keiswetter interview; Riedel interview.
99. Riedel interview.
100. Indyk, *Innocent Abroad*, p. 219.
101. Slavin, *Bitter Friends, Bosom Enemies*, pp. 188–9.
102. Albright, 'Remarks at the 1998 Asia Society dinner'.
103. Crist, *Twilight War*, pp. 419–20.
104. President Clinton, 'Remarks at the Seventh Millennium evening at the White House', 12 April 1999, *PPPUS*.
105. Alikhani, *Sanctioning Iran*, pp. 208–9.
106. Pollack, *Persian Puzzle*, p. 325; Jane Perlez and James Risen, 'Clinton seeks an opening to Iran, but efforts have been rebuffed', *The New York Times*, 3 December 1999, p. A1.
107. Albright, 'Remarks before the American-Iranian Council'.
108. 'Khamenei rejects US overtures', *BBC*, 25 March 2000, available at <http://news.bbc.co.uk/1/hi/world/middle_east/690551.stm> (last accessed 28 November 2017).
109. Slavin, *Bitter Friends, Bosom Enemies*, pp. 177, 187.
110. Pollack, *Persian Puzzle*, pp. 340.
111. Ibid., pp. 340–1.
112. Parsi, *Treacherous Alliance*, p. 213.
113. Riedel interview.
114. Rice, 'Clinton signs "Iran Nonproliferation Act"'.
115. Ceci Connolly and Tom Edsall, *The Washington Post*, 20 July 1999.
116. National Commission on Terrorism, *Countering the Changing Threat*.
117. Department of State, *Victims of Trafficking and Violence Protection Act of 2000*.
118. Albright, *Madam Secretary*, p. 230.
119. Gheissari and Nasr, 'Conservative consolidation in Iran'; Axworthy, *Revolutionary Iran*, pp. 341–8.
120. Cordesman, *Iran's Military Forces in Transition*, pp. 9–11; Seliktar, *Navigating Iran*, pp. 106–7.
121. Khamenei, 'Leader's address to Education Ministry officials'; Khamenei, 'Leader's address to students at Shahid Beheshti University'.
122. Khamenei, 'Leader's speech to residents of Qom'.
123. Khamenei, 'Leader's address to university professors and elite academics'; Khamenei, 'Leader's address to Air Force servicemen'.
124. 'Iran leader won't beg for nuke power', *Business Week*, June 2007. And see generally Sadjadpour, 'Reading Khameini'.

125. Cordesman, *Iran's Military Forces in Transition*, p. 6.

126. Seliktar, *Navigating Iran*, p. 111.

127. Keiswetter interview.

128. Patrikarikos, *Nuclear Iran*, pp. 142–3, 164–7.

129. IAEA, 'Implementation of the NPT safeguards agreement and relevant provisions of Security Council resolutions 1737 (2006) and 1747 (2007) in the Islamic Republic of Iran', GOV/2007/58, p. 4; Corera, *Shopping for Bombs*, pp. 71–2.

130. IAEA, 'Implementation of the NPT safeguards agreement and relevant provisions of Security Council resolutions in the Islamic Republic of Iran', GOV/2011/65, Annex; Albright et al., 'ISIS analysis of IAEA Iran safeguards report: Part II'; Forden, 'Iranian warhead evolution'.

131. Debs and Monteiro, *Nuclear Politics*, p. 173; Stein, 'Kilowatts or Kilotons', p. 140; Rezaei, *Iran's Nuclear Program*.

132. Rezaei, *Iran's Nuclear Program*, pp. 101–4; Stein, 'Kilowatts or Kilotons', p. 140.

133. See, for example, 'Khatami on the right of all nations to nuclear energy', *Iranwatch*, 9 February 2003, available at <http://www.iranwatch.org/library/government/iran/iran-irna-khatami-right-all-nations-nuclear-energy-2-9-03> (last accessed 18 May 2017).

134. Rezaei, *Iran's Nuclear Program*, pp. 101–4.

135. Chubin, 'Understanding Iran's nuclear ambitions', p. 47; Cordesman, *Iran's Military Forces in Transition*, p. 271.

136. Brzezinski et al., *Differentiated Containment*, pp. 6, 10–11.

137. Betts, 'Paranoids, pygmies, pariahs', pp. 167–8.

4   2001–8: George W. Bush and the Failure of Confrontation

The confrontation over the nuclear question finally came to a head during the administration of George W. Bush. Revelations about Iran's illicit nuclear activities focused the full attention of the international community on the issue for the first time. Six years of on and off negotiations, threats, proposed deals and sanctions resolutions followed, but by the time Bush left office a resolution to the conflict appeared no nearer than it had when he entered it. The failure of the Bush administration to achieve its objective of ending the Iranian nuclear programme was in large part due to the absence of a coherent policy. Initially dominated by hardliners opposed to any form of compromise with Iran, the administration pursued ends that it lacked the means to achieve. Despite subsequently becoming more pragmatic in the face of policy failure, Bush remained unable and/or unwilling to make the changes necessary to construct an effective strategy.

On the Iranian side the exposure of its secret activities meant the regime had to make real choices about the nuclear programme for the first time. What was revealed as a result were deep divisions over what Iran's nuclear goals ought to be and/or what price should be paid to achieve them. From 2003–5 Khatami's government sought to find a compromise with Washington but was rebuffed by the Bush administration. After 2005 Mahmoud Ahmadinejad instigated a policy of no compromise with American demands. The interaction of hardliners on both sides thus ensured the continuation of confrontation and a lack of progress toward a resolution of the nuclear stand-off.

George W. Bush

The incoherence of the second Bush administration's foreign policy-making process was, notoriously, laid bare by the Iraq War.[1] As Deputy-Secretary of State Richard Armitage put it, 'there was never any policy process. . . . There was never one from the start.'[2] It is not surprising to find, therefore, that its Iran policy-making process was no better, and for much the same reasons: deep divisions within the administration over how to deal with Iran and a failure on the part of the president to impose a consistent policy.

Bush's first term State Department was dominated by pragmatic Republican realists who were interested in continuing Clinton's efforts to end US–Iranian conflict through engagement and dialogue. Secretary of State Colin Powell stated in his confirmation hearings that he hoped for 'greater interaction, whether in more normal commerce or increased dialogue', and the new head of the Department's Policy Planning Staff, Richard Haass, prepared a policy paper recommending engagement with Iran.[3] The balance of power in the administration did not favour the pragmatists at State, however. The dominant axis was that between the Office of the Vice-President, Richard B. Cheney, and the Office of the Secretary of Defense, Donald Rumsfeld. Cheney and Rumsfeld are often described as 'neo-conservatives', but their worldview was closer to that of an earlier generation of right-wing Republicans such as Robert W. Taft and Barry Goldwater. That worldview, formed in the context of the early Cold War, saw containment of enemies as a weak policy that should be replaced by their 'rollback' or defeat, placed great faith in the utility of military means to achieve such ends, and regarded multilateralism and international institutions as unwarranted constraints on America's freedom of action.[4] To this wing of the administration negotiating with Iran only lent credibility to a regime that the USA should be seeking to overthrow: 'OSD [Office of the Secretary of Defense] takes a strong position on regime change and sees very little value in continuing any engagement with Iran', according to one Pentagon memo.[5]

The events of 9/11 and the Iranian response to them were thus received in quite different ways by different parts of the administration. Khatami, re-elected to the presidency with 76 per cent of the vote in June 2001, issued a strongly worded statement condemning the attacks, and thousands of ordinary Iranians staged a candlelit vigil in an expression of sympathy for the victims.[6] When it subsequently became clear that the US was going to attack the Taliban regime in Afghanistan in retaliation, the Iranians offered unqualified support for that effort. While that decision reflected Tehran's own antipathy toward the Taliban and al-Qaeda, Khatami also believed, according to an Iranian diplomat, that this issue was of sufficient importance to the US that 'the impact [of Iranian assistance] would be of such magnitude that it would automatically have altered the nature of Iran–US relations'.[7]

When Iran condemned the 9/11 attacks Powell observed that 'they, too, are shocked by what happened. . . . And so it seems to me that is an opening worth exploring.'[8] In the context of UN-sponsored meetings about the future of Afghanistan, first in Geneva and then in Bonn, State Department representatives Ryan Crocker and James Dobbins began a dialogue with their Iranian counterparts. In the course of those discussions the Iranians soon intimated that they would like to extend the dialogue beyond Afghanistan to the wider US–Iranian relationship. The State Department, in response, began planning policy options.[9] State was on its own, however, in its desire to extend the US–Iranian interaction. The hardliners in the administration had even opposed discussing cooperation against the Taliban with Iran and there was 'ferocious' opposition to any attempt to extend discussions beyond that narrow focus, according to Powell's chief of staff, Larry Wilkerson.[10] When Khatami visited the US for the opening session of the UN in November 2001 the Iranians offered to bring a delegation including experts on al-Qaeda in order to open a counter-terrorism dialogue with the US. The offer was ignored. And once the Bonn conference was over, discussions with representatives of Iran ceased. The Iranians passed a note to the US delegation at a fundraising conference for Afghanistan in Tokyo in early 2002 asking to open a formal dialogue, but there was no response.[11]

The Axis of Evil

In his 2002 State of the Union address in January 2002, Bush chose to include Iran in the so-called 'axis of evil'.[12] The decision to do so seems to have been rather careless, with Iran included largely in order to make up the numbers in a concept generated to provide a rationale for the attack on Iraq. Senior Bush administration officials, including National Security Adviser Condoleezza Rice and Powell, were opposed to its inclusion on the grounds that Iran was different to Iraq and North Korea, but to no avail.[13]

Bush's decision to ignore them stemmed from a number of factors. In the first place Iran seemingly ticked all the necessary boxes for inclusion – 'rogue state', support for terrorism and apparent pursuit of weapons of mass destruction (WMD). Distinctions between Sunni and Shiite Islam, Iran's profound antipathy toward al-Qaeda and its caution, in contrast to the recklessness of Saddam Hussein and the North Korean leadership, were apparently lost on Bush. In addition, there was a great deal of advocacy for its inclusion from Israel and the Israeli lobby. The former was quick to exploit 9/11 to advance the argument that all 'Islamic' terrorism was fundamentally the same and to assert that, in the words of former Prime Minister Benjamin Netanyahu, 'terrorist states like Iraq, Iran, Afghanistan and the Palestinian entity' were ultimately responsible for the attacks.[14] Simultaneously, the American Jewish Congress issued a statement declaring that while

> we do not yet know who did this . . . We do know the identity of those who have countenanced and even encouraged the debased notion that terrorism is an appropriate response to alleged oppression. One way or another, they are complicit in yesterday's tragedy. Afghanistan, Iran, Iraq, Syria and Libya.[15]

Israel's seizure of the *Karine-A*, a merchant ship full of weaponry sent from Iran to the Palestinian Authority, seemed to add weight to these charges.[16] Finally, the argument that Khatami, whatever his intentions, lacked the power to engineer any real change in Iranian foreign policy, was gaining traction within the administration.[17] All in all, while Iran's inclusion in the axis of evil indicated no immediate intent on Bush's part, a number of factors supported its inclusion while no compelling reason existed, in his mind, to exclude it.

If many in the Bush administration believed that Khatami was powerless to alter the direction of Iranian foreign policy then the 'axis of evil' speech was a good way of helping to ensure that they would be proved right. The administration could hardly have done more to confirm Iranian distrust of the United States and its supposed determination to destroy the Islamic regime. Bush's 'comments stunned everyone' in the Iranian government and wholly undermined Khatami's efforts to engage Washington.[18] Iranian hardliners 'used Bush's words against us', according to Mohsen Kadivar, a reformist cleric, and made it virtually unpatriotic to advocate better relations with the US.[19]

However, whilst Bush had thus ruled out engaging Iran, it did not follow that he had made a clear decision in favour of backing regime change. Rice had initiated an effort to develop a clear Iran policy, in the form of a National Security Decision Directive (NSDD), in early 2002. However, the divisions within the administration proved impossible to overcome. The hardliners pushed for regime change to become official policy – in a 19 August 2002 memo Rumsfeld wrote, 'I believe that the situations in Iran and North Korea are sufficiently interesting and unsettled that fashioning a major US government effort . . . to undermine the current regimes and encourage regime change from within is worth consideration.' The response of Powell, Rice and others was that this analysis was far-fetched and that there was no evidence of significant political instability inside Iran. In the absence of any consensus, Bush allowed the NSDD to be shelved rather than choose a side. In the words of Richard Armitage, 'we were at loggerheads . . . and the president, who has put himself up as the great decider, would never decide'.[20]

Nuclear Revelations and the Grand Bargain

On 14 August 2002 the Mojahedin-e Khalq (MEK), an Iranian opposition group, held a press conference at a Washington DC hotel in which they announced the existence of hitherto unrevealed

Iranian nuclear facilities at Natanz. The International Atomic Energy Agency (IAEA) immediately demanded further information and access to the sites. Tehran responded by conceding their existence but insisting that it had been under no obligation to inform the IAEA about them under Treaty on the Non-Proliferation of Nuclear Weapons (NPT) rules as they were nowhere near operational status. They agreed to the IAEA request to inspect the sites but then deferred the visit from September 2002 to February 2003, generating suspicions that they were seeking time to sanitise the sites.[21] When the IAEA team finally arrived in Iran further concerns arose. The Iranians claimed that all the progress they had made on centrifuge design and development at Natanz was indigenous and based on open sources, which the IAEA inspectors did not find credible. In addition, the inspectors were denied access to facilities at Kalaye that they had asked to see, with the Iranians claiming, untruthfully, that they had nothing to do with the enrichment programme.

The upshot of all this was that, in a June 2003 report, IAEA Director-General Mohamed ElBaradei concluded that Iran was in breach of its Safeguards Agreement with the IAEA (though not yet of the NPT). The grounds for this conclusion were that Iran had failed to inform the IAEA about Natanz and the heavy water reactor (HWR) at Arak and had fed fuel into the Natanz plant without informing the IAEA. It had also failed to report that in 1991 it had purchased 1.8 tons of uranium from China, and had denied inspectors access to the facilities at Kalaye. He called on Iran to sign the Additional Protocol (AP) to the NPT, giving the IAEA the right to further information and more extensive access to Iranian nuclear facilities.[22] In thus indicating that Iran was in violation of its international agreements ElBaradei initiated a new period in which the Iranian nuclear programme would come under real scrutiny and international pressure for the first time.

American officials had been aware of the existence of the facilities at Natanz and Arak before the MEK's press conference but not of exactly what was there or how far it had progressed.[23] Once it became clear that Iran had engaged in deception of the IAEA, the Bush administration's response was unhesitating, the US delegation to the IAEA lobbying for Iran to be found in violation of the

NPT and reported to the UN Security Council which could then authorise punitive action.[24]

It was in this context that Iran made the first of its 'grand bargain' offers. Despite Bush's 'axis of evil' speech, Khatami's government had continued its efforts to engage the US, especially once it became clear that Bush was intent on invading Iraq. In informal talks with retired US diplomats in New York in autumn 2002, Iranian Foreign Minister Khamal Kharrazi indicated that Khatami wanted to normalise relations with the US and was prepared to discuss the full range of American concerns. Through another channel, the Iranians also offered cooperation with any American invasion of Iraq. Both messages were relayed back to Washington but internal discussions led to their rejection. An NSC document summarised the conclusions: 'the United States should not at this point respond to overtures from the current regime'.[25]

Despite this rebuff, on 4 May 2003 a fax from the Swiss Foreign Ministry to the Department of State outlined a further Iranian offer. In this short document the Iranians offered to take the measures necessary to ensure the full transparency of the nuclear programme as well as to end support for Hamas and Islamic Jihad, to support the disarmament of Hezbollah, and to cooperate with the US 'War on Terror'. In return it sought full access to peaceful nuclear technology, a US commitment to non-interference in Iran's internal affairs, an end to sanctions and recognition of Iran's regional security interests.[26] The offer's timing was yet another indication of the mutual incomprehension that continued to plague US–Iranian relations. With the Iraq War at this point seemingly a triumph, the hardliners in the Bush administration were at the apogee of their confidence and power. Saddam had just been crushed and Iran could be next. There was no need to negotiate when regime change was the preferable, and apparently achievable, objective. In the words of one unnamed senior administration official, their message to Iran was 'take a number'.[27] This offer was also, consequently, rejected.

The Iranian offer, and the Bush administration's rejection of it, subsequently generated much debate centring on the question of whether the latter had missed a golden opportunity to limit the Iranian nuclear programme to a greater extent than proved possible twelve years later.[28] The scepticism with which the offer was received was certainly understandable, not least because of its timing. Coming so soon after the invasion of Iraq, it was easy to see it as a panicked attempt to prevent Iran suffering a similar fate. In retrospect, however, the offer was almost certainly serious and prompted by more than just fear of attack. Similar offers were made on various occasions during the remainder of the Khatami administration despite any fear of US military action then having dissipated. That the offer was serious does not, however, mean that it would necessarily have led to an agreement. There was much in it that was likely to have remained unacceptable to the Bush administration, notably the Iranian insistence on its right to peaceful nuclear technology. Nor can there be great confidence that Khatami would have been able to marshal the necessary political resources to secure acceptance of a deal along these lines at home. Instead, it seems likely that, at this point, there were still sufficient hardliners in positions of power on both sides, who felt that they could secure a better outcome, to have prevented a deal having been reached. It remains the case, nevertheless, that the rejection of the offer inevitably strengthened the hand of hard-line conservatives in Iran who argued that the US was bent on regime change and that no compromise with it was possible.[29]

Iran Gets Its Act Together

It is quite clear that, in the first year or so after the MEK's revelations, the Iranian policy response was ad hoc and disorganised. Prevarication and procrastination were combined with ostensible shows of cooperation, as the regime tried to develop a coherent policy while repeatedly being put on the back foot by new revelations. In July 2003 IAEA inspectors discovered traces of highly enriched uranium (HEU) when they were finally allowed to inspect the Kalaye site, despite Iranian attempts to sanitise it. Forced to admit that they had imported centrifuge equipment in order to explain the existence of HEU, Tehran was revealed to have engaged in another act of dissembling.[30]

The disorganised Iranian response was a product both of being caught by surprise and of internal disagreements about how best to respond to the situation. Some Iranian hardliners argued for a confrontational approach, calling for the rejection of demands that Iran explain itself, suspension of cooperation with the IAEA and even withdrawal from the NPT.[31] Others, meanwhile, called for a negotiated solution. There were also bureaucratic disagreements, with the Atomic Energy Organization of Iran (AEOI) apparently confident that matters could easily be resolved while the Foreign Ministry felt that Iran faced a dangerous situation.[32] It took until late summer 2003 for the regime to establish a more coherent decision-making process. Policy control was taken away from the AEOI and put in the hands of a high-level committee whose membership included all members of the Supreme National Security Council (SNSC) and a number of other senior figures including Rafsanjani, former Prime Minister Mir Hossein Mousavi, former Islamic Revolutionary Guard Corps (IRGC) commander Mohsen Rezaei and Khamenei's foreign policy adviser Ali Akbar Velayati. Secretary of the SNSC Hassan Rouhani was appointed as Iran's lead nuclear negotiator.[33]

In August 2003 the latest IAEA report detailed the agency's continued and growing concerns about Iran's various covert nuclear activities.[34] The main focus of the report was on the continued lack of clarity about the origins and extent of Iran's enrichment programme and the origins of the HEU particles found at Kalaye. On 12 September the IAEA Board of Governors (BOG) accordingly adopted a resolution demanding that Iran provide a comprehensive account of all its nuclear activities, allow the IAEA to conduct environmental sampling at any site it requested access to, and suspend all enrichment-related activity until such time as the IAEA could confirm that its programme was entirely peaceful. It also requested that Iran sign the AP. Iran was required to meet these conditions by 31 October.[35] The Bush administration had wanted Iran reported to the Security Council, but a substantial majority of the BOG felt that that was premature.

Nevertheless, the Iranians were shocked by a decision which seems to have made clear, even to those who had hitherto felt that this was a storm in a teacup, that they faced a serious problem.[36] Their most immediate objective now became to avoid referral to the Security Council, given the potentially dire consequences that might follow from such a development.[37] The dilemma that the regime faced, however, was that it could be damned if it did and damned if it didn't. Failure to comply with the resolution would likely lead to referral to the Security Council yet full compliance, and the revelation of the extent to which Iran had hidden its nuclear activities, might well have the same result. The objective of Iranian policy thus became to 'find a way to present a complete picture of our past nuclear activities, without being sent to the UN Security Council'.[38]

Iran was offered a path to that end by the diplomatic represen-tatives of France, Germany and the UK. Keen to avoid the escala-tion of conflict that might result from a referral to the Security Council, the 'EU3' offered Iran assistance with nuclear technology if it would abandon its enrichment programme and sign the AP.[39] The Iranians rejected the demand that they surrender the right to enrich, but with the deadline of 31 October looming they agreed to further talks. When the negotiations in Tehran began, however, they seemed likely to end in failure, with the Europeans (aware of the Bush administration's views) insistent that Iran must cease all enrichment activity and the Iranians demanding a more limited sus-pension. However, when Rouhani consulted with Khatami and the Supreme Leader he was told that he should not let the talks fail.[40] As a result, the 'Tehran Declaration' was signed on 21 October. Under the agreement Iran pledged 'voluntarily to suspend all ura-nium enrichment and processing activities as defined by the IAEA', to cooperate fully with the IAEA in order to address all 'outstand-ing issues', and to sign the AP. For their part the EU3 recognised 'the right of Iran to enjoy peaceful use of nuclear energy in accor-dance with the nuclear Non-Proliferation Treaty', and indicated that if Iran fulfilled its commitments, there would be no reason to refer it to the Security Council.[41] Iran provided the IAEA with what it claimed was a full declaration of its previously undisclosed nuclear activities before the 31 October deadline and signed the AP on 18 December 2003.

Explaining Iranian Policy

The strategy which the Iranian regime was developing by late 2003 was one of avoiding referral to the Security Council by addressing the IAEA's technical questions and easing fears about Iran's objectives while continuing to insist on Iran's right to the fuel cycle.[42] This approach is subject to competing interpretations. To some observers it is evidence that Iran was pursuing the 'North Korean option', that is, that it sought to string negotiations out as long as possible in order to reach a point at which the weapons programme was irreversible.[43] However, while Iran did continue to push the nuclear programme forward while negotiating, that fact is not necessarily incompatible with an explanation in which the more moderate factions within the regime were interested in a compromise, providing suitable terms could be agreed. *Prima facie* evidence for this interpretation includes the fact that Iran made repeated offers of comprehensive negotiations over the next two years, despite the fact that it was not under irresistible pressure to compromise. Sanctions, such as they were, were having little or no impact at this point and the threat of US military action had vanished as the disastrous occupation of Iraq unfolded. In this view, reformists and pragmatic conservatives in Iran were not bent on developing nuclear weapons at any cost and were prepared to negotiate an agreement that would guarantee that, providing they secured appropriate reciprocal concessions.

The most important of those concessions was that Iran have the right to control of the fuel cycle. Indeed, on this point there was agreement across the political spectrum. According to Hassan Rouhani, Khameini told him that 'I would never abandon the rights of this country as long as I am alive. I would resign if for any reason Iran is deprived of its rights to enrichment.'[44] Khatami, for his part, stated that 'the nation will not forgive us if we drop nuclear energy from our economic development programme just for hostile attitude [sic] of certain countries'.[45] Even Shirin Ebadi, a notable critic of the regime, acknowledged that 'no Iranian government, regardless of its ideology or democratic credentials, would dare stop Iran's nuclear energy programme'.[46] In a 2007 poll 84 per cent of Iranians said it was 'very important' for Iran to have a full fuel cycle.[47]

The ubiquity of the Iranian commitment on this point was underpinned by a number of factors, the first of which was the established Iranian belief that they had an absolute right to the fuel cycle under the NPT and that efforts to deny it to them were driven by a desire to keep Iran weak, at best, or to overthrow the regime, at worst. Whilst it is easy to see this argument as little more than a plausible excuse to hide a weapons programme, the vast majority of Iranians undoubtedly saw control of nuclear energy as a 'national right'.[48] That belief itself reflects the link that had developed between the nuclear programme and Iran's profound nationalism. As was noted in the Introduction, Iran's sense of its own history as a great power, in combination with more recent experience of humiliating foreign interventions, has resulted in it being 'inordinately sensitive of its national prerogatives and perceived sovereign rights'.[49] This was shown to be true under the Shah and it continued to be true under his successors. In the specific instance of the nuclear programme, the refusal to surrender enrichment was reinforced by the extent to which it had become emblematic of Iran's scientific progress and global status.[50] In the poll cited above, 74 per cent of those who supported Iran having the fuel cycle identified the ensuring of Iran's scientific competence as a key reason for this, with 61 per cent saying it would enhance Iran's great power status. With a domestic consensus identifying the nuclear issue as a question of fundamental rights and national status, there was no room to compromise on the fuel cycle because 'the Iranian regime's views of Iranian identity could hardly be brought in line with surrender to Western coercive measures'.[51] Any agreement had to recognise Iran's sovereign right to the fuel cycle if it was to be acceptable to the vast majority of Iranians.

Another variable common to Iranians of all factions was distrust of the United States. While some members of the regime did believe that it would be possible to come to a hard-headed deal with Washington, given the history of recent US–Iranian relations none had much faith that the latter would keep its word or its agreements. In the words of Iran's ambassador to the United Nations, Javad Zarif, were Iran to agree to a deal in which the international community pledged to supply Iran with reactors and fuel, 'we don't have any confidence that two years down the road, three years down the road, the pressure by the United States may or may not work on our suppliers' and lead to the cutting off of access to those things. It therefore followed that 'we have to create sources of self-sufficiency, which will include a fuel cycle program'.[52]

Nevertheless, whilst there was a consensus within Iran on the right to a peaceful nuclear programme, including the fuel cycle, it became evident after 2002 that there was no such consensus on the development of nuclear weapons. Although no one amongst the Iranian elite was prepared at this point publicly to admit to wanting weapons, and we lack sufficient access to primary evidence to demonstrate irrefutably what the views of the various actors were, there is sufficient evidence to support the argument that there was a division over the question of weapons development between hard-line conservatives and pragmatic conservatives and reformists.

We have already established that Iran had elements of a nuclear weapons programme and that this had had the support of Iranian hardliners to this point. There is nothing to indicate that the revelations of 2002 did anything to change their views as to the desirability of continuing with the programme, as was indicated by their condemnation of the Tehran Declaration.[53] For this group, as with their American counterparts, there was no possibility of compromise with the enemy as the conflict between the two was fundamental and not susceptible to compromise. As one unnamed Iranian official put it, 'the US is using the nuclear issue as a pretext for regime change. The issue is a diversion. The US wants to weaken Iran. Even if the nuclear issue was solved, they would want another thing and another thing.'[54] Given that analysis the only logical course of action was to push ahead with the nuclear programme as quickly as possible in order to seek an effective deterrent capacity.[55] As Ahmadinejad put it, 'if you pull back they will push ahead, but if you stand against them . . . they will back off'.[56]

This fundamental assumption of unrelenting American hostility was reinforced by further considerations. In the first place, many

Iranian hardliners clearly believed that they could achieve nuclear weapons status at an acceptable cost, particularly once the United States became bogged down in Iraq. They calculated that they could defy the international community, survive any punitive measures which might be imposed, and confront the world with a *fait accompli*.[57] In addition, many of the groups most supportive of the hard-line position had a material and political stake in the continuation of the weapons programme. The IRGC, to take the most prominent example, derived significant political power from its control of key parts of the programme in addition to massive economic benefits. Moreover, sanctions and economic isolation would only serve, at least initially, to enhance the income they made from their control of large swathes of the black market in smuggled imports.[58] Finally, continued confrontation with the USA helped to legitimise the hardliners' discourse about the threat posed to the regime and the consequent necessity of the confrontational policies they advocated. Given the political potency of the nuclear programme in Iranian domestic politics, it was a good issue on which to base confrontation with the USA. The weapons programme was a means not just of deterring the United States, therefore, but also of helping to ensure 'self-preservation at home'.[59]

If confrontation over the nuclear programme did not represent a dilemma for Iranian hardliners, however, it presented a fundamental problem for moderate conservatives and reformists. While these factions were no less committed to reasserting Iran's status as a great power – 'a proud, prosperous and independent Iran on the world scene is the common aspiration of all devoted and dedicated Iranians', according to Khatami[60] – their approach to achieving that end was fundamentally different and profoundly threatened by the revelations of 2002.

As was indicated in the previous chapter, both Rafsanjani and Khatami had sought to alter Iran's relations with its neighbours and the wider world, pursuing the goals of easing tensions and improving Iran's integration into the global political and economic systems. These efforts were premised on a combination of underlying factors and assumptions: in the first place there was an acceptance of the reality of American power and the futility of pursuing confrontation with it. As Mohammad Reza Khatami, the leader of the reformist Islamic Iran Participation Front and deputy speaker of the Majlis, expressed it:

> we believe that in the international system, the U.S. is in any case a great power and can do anything it wishes. . . . This is not a just system, but the change that has taken place among the reformists is that they now consider this a reality and are trying to prepare themselves in a way that our interests are best guaranteed.[61]

Pursuit of Iran's rightful place in the world was not to be abandoned, but nor was it to be achieved by attempting to overturn the existing international order. Instead, the policy favoured by these groups was more akin to China's 'peaceful rise' policy, in which the assertion of great power status was accompanied by reassurances that the emerging power posed no threat. 'Iran is not', Rafsanjani emphasised more than once, 'looking for adventurism',[62] while President Khatami emphasised that

> we are in favour of reducing tension throughout the world, especially in the region. We are in favour of extensive cooperation with our neighbours, with Muslims and with all the independent countries, especially those countries whose position is complementary to our economic and political situation.[63]

As Khatami's quote indicates, a further central preoccupation of both pragmatic conservatives and reformists was the development of the Iranian economy and the increased prosperity of the Iranian people. That goal was, in the first place, seen as an absolute necessity for the growth of Iranian global power. Excessive state control, a lack of free-market rigour, and a dearth of trade and investment were deemed to be the source of Iran's poor economic performance. Improvements required not only liberalisation at home but also better integration into the global economy. As Khatami's Deputy Foreign Minister Mohsen Aminzadeh put it, in a clear criticism of his political opponents, North Korea was not a very good economic model to emulate.[64] In addition, economic growth was also seen as vital to continued regime legitimacy. Whereas the hardliners sought to maintain public support through an emphasis on revolutionary ideology and nationalism, the reformists and

pragmatists saw rising prosperity, along with political liberalisation, as the key to maintaining popular support.[65] It was also, to
a significant extent, the key to their own political prosperity inasmuch as the continued support of the various demographic groups
that they represented was dependent upon their delivering the economic and political liberalisation that they hoped for.[66]

The emerging international crisis over the nuclear programme
thus posed a grave dilemma for the pragmatists/reformists. Until
2003 they had not had to choose between a weapons programme
and their goal of normalising diplomatic and economic relations
with the world. After 2003, however, they could no longer avoid
that choice. Continued pursuit of a weapons programme would
now mean confrontation and diplomatic and economic isolation.
It would destroy their strategy to advance Iran's position in the
world and undermine their political position, whilst bolstering
that of their opponents and ultimately threatening the stability of
the regime itself.

Faced with that choice, the decision they took was to reject
pursuit of nuclear weapons in favour of their larger political and
economic objectives. From this point onwards the pragmatic conservatives and reformists, while remaining committed to Iranian
control of the fuel cycle, were willing to abandon the weapons
programme because of its incompatibility with the objective of successful reintegration into the international community. To achieve
that end, and in return for policy changes that would facilitate
it, they were prepared to take steps to guarantee that the Iranian
nuclear programme was peaceful.[67] That was the essence of the
grand bargain offer and of subsequent offers made by Iran in 2004
and 2005. As Rouhani said of the decision to negotiate, 'we have
no other choice. Causing other countries to have concerns means
closing the paths to interaction.'[68]

These efforts to find an acceptable compromise were nevertheless complicated by the fact that, while the pragmatists/reformists
were largely in control of policy-making from 2003–5, they were
subject to the constant scrutiny and criticism of hardliners who
were ever ready to accuse them of selling out Iran's 'national
right'. Moreover, while the strategy pursued from 2003–5 had
the tacit, and occasionally explicit, endorsement of the Supreme

Leader, Khamenei's support was conditional and less than whole-hearted. He frequently expressed doubts about the wisdom of suspending enrichment and made speeches that resonated much more closely with the worldview of the hardliners than with those whose approach he was ostensibly backing.[69] Whilst this was typical of Khamenei's tendency to avoid committing himself wholly to any position, and to balance between factions, it nevertheless meant that Iranian negotiators were perpetually aware of the need to be able to defend their position at home, greatly limiting their room for manoeuvre and particularly their ability to offer significant concessions up front.

Explaining the International Response

In November 2003 ElBaradei issued a new report which laid bare Iran's extensive dissembling over the past two decades. He noted that Iran had admitted to pursuing a centrifuge enrichment programme for the past eighteen years, and that it now had 'a practically complete front end of a nuclear fuel cycle'. Over that period Iran had engaged in a 'policy of concealment' and had 'failed in a number of instances over an extended period of time to meet its obligations under its Safeguards Agreement with respect to the reporting of nuclear material and its processing and use'. He nevertheless concluded that there was, as yet, no incontrovertible proof that Iran had a weapons programme.[70]

ElBaradei's report exposed the divisions within the international community about how to deal with Iran's nuclear programme. Under-Secretary of State for Arms Control and International Security John Bolton described the conclusion that there was no definitive proof of an Iranian weapons programme as 'impossible to believe', while British Foreign Secretary Jack Straw sought to emphasise the positive, noting that the revelations indicated 'a pretty high level of cooperation' on the part of Tehran.[71] In his memoirs Bolton said what he really thought, namely that ElBaradei was making 'excuses all the time' and was effectively an advocate for Iran, while the Europeans were just trying to drag negotiations out in the hope that Bush lost the 2004 presidential election.[72]

Nor was it just hardliners like Bolton who thought that the Europeans were being too generous to Iran. When the EU High Representative for Foreign Affairs Javier Solana told reporters that he thought Iran had thus far been honest with the European Union, Colin Powell said that Solana's evaluation was 'premature'.[73]

These divisions were reflected in the IAEA BOG response to ElBaradei's report. The Bush administration once again pushed to have Iran reported to the Security Council, but found itself with very little support. The EU, Russia and China, along with countries from the Non-Aligned Movement, were all opposed. The most vocal opposition came from Russia, whose Atomic Energy Minister Alexander Rumyantsev declared that efforts to impose sanctions were 'unacceptable, as nothing has been discovered' that would warrant it.[74] The BOG Resolution of 26 November accordingly made no threat to report Iran to the Security Council and instead welcomed its 'offer of active cooperation' and 'positive response' to the BOG 12 September resolution.[75] The November 2003 BOG resolution thus demonstrated the degree of American isolation at this point, with all of the other key international players seeking to avoid referral to the UN and looking for alternative ways out of the impasse.

As would become clear as the crisis developed, no one wanted Iran to have nuclear weapons, but many states nevertheless had reasons for resisting the reporting of Iran to the Security Council. For their part, many EU members were not as convinced as the United States that Iran definitely had a weapons programme, if only because their own intelligence services lacked the resources to verify Washington's claims. European scepticism in this regard was fuelled by the perception that the obsessive American hostility toward Iran skewed the latter's judgement of the evidence. Secondly, the EU sought a diplomatic solution because diplomacy was the only means it had to hand. Lacking the means to pursue a coercive approach, the EU was bound to insist on a course of action which employed the resources it could draw on. Furthermore, there was a real fear that the Bush administration might pursue regime change in Iran and that that possibility had to be headed off. The EU3's diplomacy was thus designed 'not so much to contain Iran, but to contain America', according to one EU official.[76] They also felt that coercion was likely to fail and that immediate reporting to the UN would probably make Iran choose confrontation rather than cooperation. Last, but perhaps not least in some cases, EU states had significant trade with Iran that they did not want to jeopardise.[77]

Many of those reasons also applied in the cases of Russia and China. They were equally worried about the Bush administration's inclination toward regime change in Tehran and just as sceptical about the claim that Iran had a weapons programme. Russia and China also had major economic interests in Iran. The Russian contract for the reactors at Bushehr had made Iran the most important overseas market for Russian nuclear technology, and the Russian Minister of Atomic Energy at the time, Yevgeny Adamov, once described American efforts to halt the Iranian nuclear programme as designed 'to deprive Russian factories of orders'.[78] Iran was also a source of major arms sales for both countries, while China had growing economic interests in Iranian gas and oil. Finally, unlike the EU, both Russia and China had significant geopolitical reasons not to go along with the Bush administration. Russia had had good relations with Iran since the end of the Cold War and the latter had generally proved itself to be a cooperative partner in Central Asia, as well as a potentially useful ally in the Middle East. For both states the Iranian nuclear issue was also a test of their strategic independence and ability to demonstrate that the US could not simply have its own way in international relations regardless of the interests of the other major powers.[79]

All of the non-American major powers were thus determined to treat referral of the Iranian nuclear issue to the UN as a last resort, a determination that was shared by ElBaradei. He no doubt wanted to demonstrate that the IAEA, armed with the AP, could be effective in preventing proliferation, but he also felt that the US had already started one unnecessary war in the Middle East and had no desire to assist it in starting another one. Even if it did not come to that, he felt that the confrontational approach being pursued by the US risked pushing Iran into rejecting the NPT and going down the North Korean route, whereas a deal that compromised on the issue of enrichment could prevent such an outcome.[80]

The Bush administration thus found itself at odds with all of the other key players as to how best to address the problem posed by the Iranian nuclear programme. Moreover, its continued demand that the Iranian dossier be referred to the UN did little to disguise the fact that the administration had still not developed a coherent policy of its own. It remained the case, over two years after Bush's inauguration, that the NSDD on Iran policy had not been finalised because of the divisions within the administration.[81] Backing referral to the Security Council was a lowest common denominator policy response that implied no specific subsequent course of action. It was thus a way for the administration to defer serious engagement with the problem in a situation in which it was incapable of formulating a coherent policy, and so preoccupied with the unfolding mess in Iraq, that it had little or no time to do so.

That lack of a policy also meant the administration was in no position to block the diplomatic efforts of the EU3, but the administration's attitude toward the EU's diplomacy was nevertheless one of 'malign neglect' and an implicit hope that the talks would fail.[82] The administration made such an outcome all the more likely by keeping the threat of regime change alive at a rhetorical level, despite there being no credible or practical plan to pursue that option. Even more importantly, their refusal to join the negotiations more or less guaranteed the failure of the European diplomatic efforts, since the Europeans could not deliver the comprehensive deal with the United States that the Iranian moderates sought. The Bush policy in 2003–4, in sum, was to passively sabotage the diplomatic efforts of the EU3 despite having no viable alternative policy of its own.

The Paris Agreement

The problems the EU3 faced quickly became evident. In December 2003 the Libyan government admitted to the existence of its own nuclear weapons programme and agreed to abandon it in return for security guarantees and the lifting of sanctions. As part of the deal the Libyans also provided details about the origins of their programme, revealing the role of the A.Q. Khan network. That, in turn, quickly led the IAEA to identify the network as a key player in the Iranian programme, exposing Iran's November 2003 declaration of its previous activities as incomplete. Meanwhile, the Iranians were also stretching the terms of the Tehran Declaration to the limit, asserting that ongoing research on a new centrifuge did not constitute a violation of its agreement to suspend all enrichment activities.[83] The US responded by insisting once again that Iran be referred to the Security Council but received little support at the March 2004 BOG meeting, which asked only that ElBaradei report on progress again in June. That same month the Iranians agreed to widen the scope of suspension of enrichment to include the assembly and testing of centrifuges and also sent a message to Washington, delivered to Bush by ElBaradei, asking for a comprehensive dialogue on all issues. Bush did not respond.[84]

A pattern had thus been set that would continue for the next twelve months. The EU3 and Russia would make various offers and sign deals that they hoped would persuade the Iranians to abandon pursuit of the fuel cycle. The Iranians would sign some of those agreements in order to avoid referral to the Security Council whilst seeking a comprehensive agreement with the USA and pushing their fuel cycle research forward as far as they dared. The Bush administration, for its part, refused to engage and simply insisted that Iran be referred to the UN. The nuclear negotiations in 2004–5 were consequently something of a charade. Without an American presence the negotiating process could not succeed because only Washington could offer the comprehensive agreement the Iranians wanted. Nevertheless, the Iranians and the EU3 had their own reasons to keep negotiations going: both wished to avoid referral to the Security Council, Tehran sought to buy time to master the fuel cycle, and the Europeans wanted to demonstrate that they could deliver a deal.

In June 2004 the next IAEA BOG resolution identified Iranian cooperation in some areas but also that Iran's suspension of enrichment remained incomplete. The September resolution expressed continued dissatisfaction with Iranian compliance and requested ElBaradei to provide a comprehensive report on progress in November.[85] That request, and the possibility of referral to the UN, led the EU3 and Iran to engage in a further round of direct negotiations. That the Europeans recognised the weakness of the hand they had to play was evident from their dialogue with Washington beforehand, in which they argued that any incentives package offered to Iran needed to come from the whole of the G8 nations, not just the EU, and that it needed to include security guarantees.[86] Nevertheless, the Bush administration remained unmoved.

Consequently, the negotiations that led to the 'Paris Agreement' of November 2004, and the agreement itself, were just another episode in the diplomatic charade. The offer presented by the EU3 was that Iran could have peaceful nuclear power and that they would arrange the supply of reactors and fuel for them in return for Iran foregoing the complete fuel cycle. In the short term Iran had to suspend all enrichment activities until the IAEA was satisfied that Iran's nuclear programme was entirely peaceful. Failure to cooperate would leave the EU with no option but to support Iran's referral to the UN.[87] The Iranians responded by making quite clear that giving up enrichment altogether was not on the table but agreeing to further talks and a temporary suspension of enrichment, seeking to defer referral to the Security Council and create time to pursue a more satisfactory long-term agreement.[88] The Paris Agreement thus represented a diplomatic kicking of the can down the road in which the fundamental issue of future Iranian enrichment was fudged in order to avoid a breakdown of negotiations.[89]

The 2005 Negotiations

January to August 2005 saw a further period of negotiations under the terms of the Paris Agreement. While the Bush administration continued to refuse to join the negotiations, it did now announce that it would no longer oppose some of the incentives that the EU3 had offered Iran, including Iranian membership of the World Trade Organization (WTO) and the export from the US to Iran of spare parts for civilian airliners.[90] The administration also agreed to coordinate policy with the EU3, and the implacable Bolton was replaced as the administration's policy lead by Under-Secretary of State for Political Affairs Nicholas Burns.

This concession to the EU reflected Bush's gradual recognition of the limits of American power. The administration's policy to this point had been utterly ineffectual due to American diplomatic isolation and declining leverage over Iran and the other major powers in the context of the ongoing US travails in Iraq. Those travails also reduced the influence of the administration hardliners and increased Bush's receptiveness to the arguments of those, notably Condoleezza Rice, now Secretary of State, who were arguing for a change of policy. There was also a recognition on the part of Rice and others that continued non-cooperation with European diplomatic efforts risked ensuring a reciprocal European refusal to support American efforts to get Iran referred to the Security Council.[91] By supporting the negotiations the administration would shore up relations with the Europeans and demonstrate a willingness to compromise on its demands. In return it hoped that, if and when the Iranians rejected the joint EU–US offer, the Europeans would finally back Iran's referral to the Security Council.[92]

The change in the Bush administration's position was nevertheless limited, with the incentives it was prepared to offer too small to hold out any realistic prospect of a breakthrough in negotiations. The shift toward pragmatism had been forced on US policy-makers by circumstances, and the instincts of many in the administration remained to support regime change. In addition, Israel and its supporters in the US kept up the pressure on the administration not to retreat from its hard-line position. The American Israel Public Affairs Committee (AIPAC) worked unceasingly to drum the threat posed by Iran into the minds of the American public while Israel kept alive the implicit threat of military action should other means fail to halt the Iranian nuclear programme.[93] Calls for the administration to take military action to eliminate the 'threat' from Iran were also frequently heard from Bush's conservative Republican supporters.[94]

Consequently, the administration continued to send out mixed messages. Policy-makers, including Bush and Rice, continued to make statements that expressed their support for the overthrow of the Iranian regime and implied that military action remained an option.[95] In addition, when the administration finally produced a formal Iran policy in late 2005, the 'Iran Action Plan' openly supported regime change, albeit by peaceful, rather than military means. Funds were to be channelled to groups inside Iran supporting political liberalisation, while pro-democracy propaganda, via the State Department's International Information Program, *Voice of America* and *Radio Free Europe*, was to be stepped up.[96] The Bush administration clearly remained caught between a desire for regime change (and pressure from outside to hold to that objective) and a recognition of its impracticality and the need to focus on changing Iranian behaviour. Its desire for the former continued to prevent it from formulating an effective policy to do the latter, with no direct engagement with, serious incentives for, or effective pressure on Iran.

The 2005 negotiations went nowhere as a result. Iranian policy remained consistent with previous behaviour. On the one hand, the regime continued to push the nuclear programme forward and to procrastinate in its cooperation with the IAEA. Simultaneously, however, the Iranians also made no fewer than four negotiating proposals between January and July 2005. The precise content varied from one to the other but the overall thrust was familiar. The Iranians would commit not to pursue WMD and to put in place measures to allow that to be verified, including ratifying the AP and accepting limits on the scale of enrichment. They also offered cooperation in the War on Terror. In return they wanted a lifting of sanctions, guaranteed access to nuclear technology and an EU declaration recognising Iran as a major source of energy supplies to Europe.[97]

The pragmatists and reformists in Iran thus continued to seek a comprehensive deal with the international community, their ongoing non-compliance with the IAEA driven by their recognition that the continued development of the nuclear programme was their only real bargaining chip. They were not going to make significant concessions until they were promised something concrete in return, a position only reinforced by the domestic political context in Iran. Nor were they prepared to give up the right to enrich, which ensured continued American rejection of the Iranian proposals. As Assistant Secretary of State Stephen Rademaker reiterated in May 2005, the Bush administration's position remained that any solution 'must include permanent cessation of Iran's enrichment and reprocessing efforts, as well as dismantlement of equipment facilities related to such activity'.[98]

Further talks between Iran and the EU3 in May led the Iranians to agree to extend their suspension of enrichment until the end of July in order to give the Europeans time to put a new incentives package together. Having emphasised that any proposal not acknowledging Iran's right to enrich would be rejected, the Iranian negotiating team's understanding was that the EU3's desire to make a further offer indicated that they were considering that proposition.[99] They were to be disappointed, however. When the new proposal was sent it offered Iran light water reactor (LWRs) and fuel for them along with recognition of Iran as a source of energy supplies to the EU. However, it also demanded that Iran offer a 'binding commitment not to pursue fuel cycle activities other than the construction and operation of light water power and research reactors', a commitment that would be reviewed in ten years.[100] The Iranians immediately responded that the proposal 'fails to address Iran's rights for peaceful development of nuclear technology'. The offer was rejected and Tehran announced that it was resuming conversion of uranium.[101]

That announcement marked the end of the negotiations between the EU3 and the Khatami government. In its note announcing the resumption of enrichment the Iranian mission to the IAEA recited a litany of complaints about the international community's efforts to deny Iran its rights under the NPT, asserting that its cooperation with the IAEA since October 2003 had brought no reward, and that the EU3 were still to fulfil their part of the Paris Agreement. While it is easy to see this as self-justifying rhetoric, it should be taken seriously as an accurate articulation of the Iranian perspective. As one non-Iranian observer noted, the EU3's latest offer was 'vague on incentives and heavy on demands', with none of the former remotely guaranteed.[102] From an Iranian point of view it had made a series of serious offers to negotiate, making clear what they were prepared to concede and what they wanted in return, all of which had been ignored in favour of proposals that came nowhere near to meeting their minimum conditions. Almost two years of on and off suspension of enrichment had achieved nothing.

The decision to restart conversion was driven by Khamenei.[103] Whether Rouhani, Rafsanjani and others would have preferred to continue suspension in the hope of prolonging negotiations is unknown, but what is clear is that by 2005 the domestic pressure to resume enriching had become enormous.[104] As will be explained below, from 2003–5 Khatami's government had been negotiating in a context in which their power, relative to the Iranian hardliners, had been steadily dwindling. Iranian negotiators had repeatedly emphasised this point in their exchanges with the EU3 – Foreign Minister Kharrazi had warned that continued failure to reciprocate Iran's concessionary gestures 'would soon become a major internal problem in Iran', and Ali Gholampour, Second Secretary at the Iranian embassy in London, told his British counterparts that the hard line being taken on the nuclear programme was 'playing into the hands of the fundamentalists in Tehran'.[105] Analyses by Chinese, French and German diplomats reached the same conclusion.[106] There was steadily growing pressure to resume enrichment and after two years of negotiations with nothing to show for it, the pragmatists/reformists were in no position to resist that pressure.

It was not just the Iranian pragmatists and reformists who were frustrated by this outcome. Several years later, one of the EU3 negotiators, Jack Straw, claimed that a deal could have been done in 2005 had it not been for the Bush administration's refusal to bend on the question of enrichment. The EU3, he claimed, would have considered a deal along the lines that the Iranians proposed, with limited enrichment and extensive safeguards, but were hamstrung by the Bush administration's refusal to even contemplate the idea. Mousavian has also claimed that the EU negotiators indicated to him that they wanted to compromise on enrichment but were unable to do so because of the American demands.[107]

Straw's claim that a deal could have been done is certainly plausible. As we have seen, the Iranian negotiating team and the reformist–pragmatist coalition who stood behind them were prepared to accept limited enrichment and other restrictions on the nuclear programme if their own demands were met. What is less certain, however, is that had the Bush administration compromised on enrichment, that would have ensured a viable agreement. What

Straw's argument fails to take into account is the growing strength of the Iranian hardliners. Increasingly confident that they could both have their cake and eat it in the face of America's problems in Iraq, they would have strongly resisted a deal which imposed significant constraints on Iran's right to enrich. In addition, while Khamenei had supported the Iranian negotiators thus far, he clearly had little enthusiasm for compromise and his support for such a deal, had it been offered, cannot be taken for granted. In short, whether a deal along the lines proposed by the Iranian negotiators would have survived the domestic political backlash against it is uncertain.

Mahmoud Ahmadinejad

The most obvious demonstration of the growing strength of Iranian hardliners was the victory of Mahmoud Ahmadinejad in the 2005 Iranian presidential election. Ahmadinejad's election was the culmination of a conservative backlash which had been developing since Khatami's second election victory in 2001. Clearly frightened by the scale of Khatami's success, the hardliners increased their efforts to undermine him. The conservative-led judiciary began shutting down reformist newspapers and ordering the arrest of their editors and other key reformist figures outside the government. Khamenei barred the Majlis from discussing these actions and, along with the Guardian Council, blocked Khatami from implementing the key planks of his reformist programme. Khatami, rather than confront his opponents, sought to find a compromise with them that did not exist, ensuring his failure.[108]

The decline of the reformist coalition was mirrored by the emergence of a new militant hard-line conservative grouping whose objective was to reassert the revolutionary Islamist ethos of Khomeini. The so-called Islamic Developers Coalition, or 'Abadgaran', found its supporters in the IRGC and the Basij militia as well as amongst parts of the conservative clergy and some of the bonyads. That support was partly a matter of ideology and partly one of economic self-interest, since both the IRGC and the bonyads were clearly threatened by the economic reforms that the reformists wished to pursue.[109] The Abadgaran's first significant opportunity as an electoral coalition came with the February 2003 municipal elections, when Ahmadinejad was elected as mayor of Tehran. The following year Abadgaran candidates swept to victory in the Majlis elections and in 2005 Ahmadinejad won the presidency.

This series of electoral victories was characterised by two significant features. The first of these was the increasing brazenness with which hardliners used their institutional power to manipulate the election results. In 2003 the IRGC and the Basij conducted a concerted effort to intimidate reformist supporters whilst mobilising the hard-line vote, and in 2004 the Guardian Council disqualified 2,500 reformist candidates, including sitting members, from running in the elections to the Majlis. The other feature of these elections was the failure of reformist voters to engage with the electoral process. The turnout in the 2003 municipal elections was just 12 per cent and the 51 per cent turnout in the 2004 Majlis elections was the lowest ever.[110] In 2005 Ahmadinejad did galvanise support with a populist message that resonated with poorer conservative voters, but he also won because reformist voters stayed at home. On one estimate Ahmadinejad's core vote was about five million, compared with the twenty million Khatami won in both his election victories.[111]

By 2005, therefore, there was in Iran a situation in which a large proportion of the electorate, and probably a majority, was supportive of the reformist agenda but felt it had no one to vote for. While obviously opposed to the Abadgaran, these voters had also lost faith in Khatami and the reformists, who they had initially hoped could bring meaningful change. Their failure to vote was an indication of a growing belief that such change was not possible within the parameters of the existing regime.[112] Anger at the regime was further reinforced by its failure to deliver on a social and economic level as well. The Islamic Republic of Iran (IRI) had massively increased the number of Iranian university graduates but had failed miserably in its efforts to forge an economy that could employ their skills. In 2005 nearly a quarter of Iranians aged fifteen to twenty-four were unemployed.[113] Disillusion and unemployment in turn fed social problems, with Iran by 2006 estimated to have 1.2 million heroin addicts, roughly the same number as the USA despite a population a quarter of the latter's.[114] A 2005 poll found that 44 per cent of young Iranians would emigrate if they could.[115] By 2005, in short, the IRI faced a developing crisis of legitimacy, with much of its younger population unable to envisage a tolerable future under the current regime. In the long run this would prove to be an important factor shaping the domestic politics of the Iranian nuclear programme.

In the short term, however, the hardliners would dictate the course of events. Ahmadinejad's new cabinet was full of former members of the IRGC and the MOIS. In terms of nuclear policy the changing of the guard was symbolised by the removal of Rouhani as chief nuclear negotiator and his replacement by Ali Larijani. The new government adopted a philosophy of 'aggressiveness' in its foreign policy. Rather than seeking to accommodate itself to the existing international order in the manner of its predecessor, it sought to challenge and alter that order and to compel the United States to acknowledge Iran's power and sovereign rights. In concrete terms this meant seeking cooperation with the 'oppressed powers' of the world, courting socialist and anti-American governments, particularly in Latin America, and increasing support for allies like Hamas and Hezbollah.[116] In terms of nuclear policy it meant a vigorous defence of Iran's 'sovereign rights' and a full frontal assault on the hypocrisy of the 'arrogant powers', as was made clear in Ahmadinejad's address to the UN General Assembly in September 2005, where he railed against those who

> blatantly violate their obligations under the NPT, have refrained from signing the CTBT and have armed the Zionist occupation regime with WMDs, [and] are not only refusing to remedy their past deeds, but in clear breech of the NPT, are trying to prevent other countries from acquiring the technology to produce peaceful nuclear energy.[117]

Ahmadinejad's brazenness was informed by his belief that confrontation with Washington carried little risk. The USA continued to flounder in Iraq and Afghanistan and a full-scale US military attack was thus almost certainly out of the question. Limited strikes, for their part, would not halt the nuclear programme whilst multiplying America's problems in the Middle East. The new government was thus confident that Washington would have no choice but to accept their demands eventually.[118] As nuclear negotiator Sirus Naseri put it, 'Iran is not Iraq and the US is not the self-appointed policeman of the world anymore.'[119]

If the new government was confident about the strength of its position relative to the USA, however, it was also aware of its lack of legitimacy with a large part of the Iranian population and the tenuousness of its electoral mandate. Ahmadinejad's answer to this problem was a programme which combined economic populism with the revolutionary nationalist ideology of the early days of the Revolution. Central to the latter discourse was the confrontation with the USA, with the latter representing the forces of imperialist oppression and Iran playing the role of standard-bearer of the global oppressed. The nuclear issue was accordingly framed as a situation in which the US hypocritically sought to maintain its technological advantage over other nations and to deny them their rights to nuclear power. By promoting this discourse at every opportunity the government sought to rally popular support and to minimise the scope for their opponents to attack them.[120]

Referral to the Security Council

By autumn 2005 even those members of the international community who were reluctant to support Iran's referral to the Security Council were beginning to change their minds. Caught between the rock of American refusal to accept Iranian enrichment and the hard place of Iran's refusal to give it up, the latter's continued failure to cooperate fully with the IAEA, and the desire that Iran not become a weapons state pushed them to side with Washington.

At the September 2005 IAEA board meeting the EU3 introduced a resolution stating that Iran was in non-compliance with previous demands and calling for its referral to the Security Council. This action may have been influenced by the alleged evidence of Iranian weaponisation studies that Washington circulated to its allies earlier in the year, as well as frustration at the continued failure of their negotiating efforts.[121] They were eventually forced to remove the threat of referral in order to avoid a Russian or

Chinese veto, but the final resolution nevertheless found Iran to be in non-compliance with its safeguards agreement and stated that its activities and the concerns raised by them fell 'within the competence of the Security Council', implying that referral would be the next step if Iran failed to comply with IAEA demands.[122]

The Iranian response was defiant, declaring that it would not comply and that 'if the resolution is not corrected . . . Iran will have no choice but to revoke voluntary and temporary concessions it has given to the IAEA', including observance of the AP.[123] A week earlier, however, Ahmadinejad, in his address to the UN, had declared that Iran was ready to enter into a joint enrichment programme as a guarantee of its peaceful intent.[124] With the Europeans no longer willing to engage, Moscow made an effort to stave off referral to the Security Council, proposing a joint enrichment project on Russian soil. Tehran would have to forego all enrichment activity in Iran and would not have access to the technical aspects of the programme.[125] The EU and the Bush administration expressed their support for the Russian proposal and chose not to push for a referral of Iran to the UN at the November 2005 IAEA BOG meeting to give Moscow time to pursue negotiations.[126]

On 3 January 2006 Iran said that the Russian offer was inadequate and that it would resume research into nuclear fuel production (though not enrichment). Larijani said Iran was nevertheless willing to continue talking to Russia but a spokesman for the Majlis stated that it was very unlikely any offer would be accepted unless it allowed enrichment in Iran.[127] In response, the EU3 called for an emergency meeting of the IAEA BOG with the intention of pushing through a resolution referring Iran to the Security Council. Larijani, in accordance with the new Iranian approach, responded with threats rather than conciliation, warning that 'if the case goes to the Security Council, we're obliged . . . to lift all voluntary measures', and that Iran would consider resuming full-scale enrichment.[128] On 4 February 2006 the IAEA BOG nevertheless reported Iran to the Security Council. Twenty-six states voted to support the measure with only three – Cuba, Syria and Venezuela – opposed. The support of Russia, China and others who had previously opposed referral was, however, conditional on Iran being 'reported' rather than 'referred', meaning that the imposition of sanctions would not automatically follow.[129] Iran's response was nevertheless as threatened, suspending implementation of the AP and announcing that it would recommence enrichment at Natanz.[130]

In late February 2006 the first meeting of what would become known as the P5+1 was held in London. Foreign ministers of the five permanent members of the Security Council and Germany met to discuss how to deal with Iran. This development indicated a further shift in US policy toward acceptance that policy change, rather than regime change, was now the only realistic option, and that policy change could only be secured by more effective diplomacy with the other major powers. According to William Burns, there was 'a tremendous amount of internal introspection about whether to do it' (join the negotiations) but the administration concluded that 'we were the real issue here, and the only way the Iranians would have an incentive to suspend and negotiate would be if we were part of the equation'.[131]

This development demonstrated the continued atrophying of the influence of administration hardliners, but the change was still a limited and grudging one.[132] There was to be no concession on enrichment, as the Russians found out when they floated a proposal in March that would have allowed Iran to continue enrichment research and development, and the administration was still resistant to the idea of direct negotiations with Iran.[133] While there was clearly a recognition that Washington had to offer more concrete incentives, the primary objective of the new effort would seem to have been to demonstrate sufficient flexibility that, when Iran next turned down an offer, Russia and China would back sanctions. The expectation within the administration was that if only the administration could orchestrate effective sanctions, Iran would 'buckle under pressure'.[134]

In internal administration discussions, Rice proposed a two-track strategy to get the Russians and Chinese on board. Despite Iran's blatant refusal to meet the demands of previous IAEA resolutions and its announcement, on 11 April, that it had successfully enriched uranium at Natanz, the administration would not push for the immediate imposition of sanctions.[135] Instead, it would propose that Iran should be offered a set of concrete incentives (including the possibility of Washington joining the negotiations) with sanctions following only if Tehran failed to respond positively.[136] Bush backed the approach, and discussions with the rest of the P5+1 led to an announcement in early May that a new proposal would soon be forthcoming which, while it would continue to insist that Iran could not enrich, would include a more extensive set of incentives than had previously been offered.[137] Even before the formal offer was made, however, Ahmadinejad rejected it. In a speech in Arak he declared that 'your incentives are definitely not more valuable than nuclear technology', and suggested that the Iranian nation was being treated like a 'child to whom you can give some walnuts and chocolates and get gold from him'.[138] Later in the month, however, ElBaradei carried a message from Larijani to Rice in which the former expressed Iran's willingness to talk to the United States about the full range of issues that stood between the two countries.[139]

These somewhat mixed messages would seem to have been a reflection of the balance of political forces inside Iran at this point, with the hardliners prevailing but not holding sufficient power to fully impose their policy preferences. Ahmadinejad was able to pursue a more confrontational approach because Khamenei chose not to oppose it, partly because Ahmadinejad's worldview sat more comfortably with the latter than Khatami's had ever done, but also because, as ever, the Supreme Leader sought to accommodate himself to the new factional balance of power in which the hardliners had the upper hand. Nevertheless, Khamenei's support for Ahmadinejad was not unconditional, and in the aftermath of the latter's election the Supreme Leader had made a series of moves designed to limit the new president's power. Larijani had been Khamenei's, rather than Ahmadinejad's choice as nuclear negotiator, and the Supreme Leader also created a new institution, the Supreme Council on Foreign Relations, chaired by Khatami's former Foreign Minister Kamal Kharrazi. [140] Finally, he gave the Expediency Council, headed by Rafsanjani, 'supervisory' powers over all branches of government. Rafsanjani in turn appointed Rouhani and Khatami to posts in the Council's Strategic Research Center. Pragmatists and reformists thus continued to hold important posts throughout the Iranian government from which to articulate their views.[141] The fact that Iran's new negotiating position did not simply reject any and all compromise, but instead demonstrated a more incremental hardening of Iranian demands thus reflected the continued influence of policy-makers like Rouhani and Rafsanjani and Khamenei's less than complete trust in Ahmadinejad.

With Ahmadinejad deeming the May offer inadequate, the P5+1 returned on 1 June with a new version which represented the maximal position of the Bush administration. In addition to elements in the earlier package, Rice offered a tacit security guarantee by declaring that the Bush administration was 'committed to a diplomatic solution'. More explicitly, the proposal offered 'legally binding' guarantees of a supply of nuclear fuel, direct bilateral talks and, for the first time, acknowledged that Iran need not forego enrichment permanently if the right conditions could be met.[142] That concession was, however, hedged around with conditions: Iran would have to suspend enrichment indefinitely until the IAEA confirmed it had no undeclared facilities and had answered all the as yet unanswered questions about its nuclear programme. Moreover, the final decision on whether Iran had met those conditions would rest with the Security Council (where the US had a veto) rather than with the IAEA. As one EU diplomat put it, the US 'concession' implied that 'someday in some circumstances – maybe in 30 years when the mullahs disappear – there could be the end of a moratorium' on enrichment.[143]

Even with those caveats, the new offer was seen as a betrayal by American hardliners. 'Apparently Tehran has gone from being a charter member of the "Axis of Evil" to the newest market for the Bush administration's nuclear salesmen', was the sarcastic response of Representative Edward J. Markey.[144] This was a reminder of the potential political fallout for any administration which was deemed to have conceded too much to Iran. And the room for manoeuvre had, if anything, shrunk in recent months. Ahmadinejad's election and his rhetoric, particularly toward Israel, was grist to the mill of Israeli conservatives, AIPAC and American hardliners. His alleged statement that Israel should be 'wiped from the map' enabled them to claim that 'Mr Ahmadinejad and the Iranian regime are genocidal' and that regime change was the only way to prevent another Holocaust.[145] Netanyahu fanned the flames with a speech in which he said, 'it's 1938 and Iran is Germany. And Iran is racing to arm itself with atomic bombs', while Israeli officials warned of possible pre-emptive strikes and their American allies encouraged them to act.[146] All of this rhetoric, plus the Bush administration's own demonisation of Iran, had a significant impact on the American public. According to the director of the Pew Research Center, the 'threat from Iran has really penetrated, with two of three saying Iran's nuclear program represents a major threat', and Iran now identified by the public as America's number one enemy.[147]

Just as was the case for the Iranian government, therefore, there were very real constraints on the amount of ground the Bush administration could give, and the pressure on it to continue to take a hard line fed into its ongoing mixed messages to Iran. Rice's insistence that the administration sought a 'diplomatic solution' was contradicted by comments from Cheney and Bush that 'all options' remained on the table, and the administration also announced that it would step up its democracy promotion efforts in Iran.[148] Whether this was an effort by the administration to provide cover for itself domestically, or to deter unilateral Israeli action against Iran, the effect was to contradict the apparent shift in US policy evident in the two P5+1 proposals to Iran.

On 21 June Ahmadinejad announced that Iran would provide a formal response to the offer by 22 August. Some in the US and elsewhere saw this as just another Iranian effort to defer sanctions whilst they further advanced their nuclear programme. However, no significant progress would be made in two months and the delay is more plausibly explained by Iran's internal political struggles.[149] Rouhani more or less admitted this in an interview in July 2006 in which he referred to 'divisions and disagreements [that] are far wider and deeper than what ordinary members of the public can see'.[150] Thus, while Larijani described the offer as containing 'positive elements that could form the basis for renewed negotiations', and Foreign Minister Manouchehr Mottaki said that Iran was 'ready to negotiate with the Europeans all questions and ambiguities. . . . Even their demand for suspension of nuclear activities', the Speaker of the Majlis, Gholam-Ali Hadad-Adel, declared that 'Iran doesn't accept suspending its uranium enrichment.'[151] Larijani also repeatedly turned down invitations to talk during the summer of 2006, indicating that there was, as yet, no clear position to communicate.[152]

Rather than wait for Iran's formal reply, the Bush administration, in accordance with its assumption that what was needed to get Iran to comply was more pressure, pushed forward with a resolution in the UN Security Council. UNSCR 1696, passed on 31 July, demanded that Iran suspend enrichment by 31 August. Failure to do so would lead to the adoption of 'appropriate measures' under Article 41 of Chapter VII of the UN Charter.[153] The support of Russia and China for the resolution indicated that they too were running out of ideas for resolving the crisis and losing patience with Tehran. Iran's response, on 22 August, was to say that while they saw 'useful elements' in the P5+1's June proposal and were prepared to hold 'serious talks', they would not suspend enrichment.[154] Whilst it is impossible to know whether UNSCR 1696 affected this outcome, there is evidence to suggest that the resolution undermined the position of those in Iran arguing for compromise. Larijani, who was seemingly trying to find a way of compromising on the suspension question, complained to ElBaradei that the P5+1 'do not understand the domestic situation in Iran'.[155]

Resolutions 1737 and 1747

A further round of negotiations between the EU3 and Iran collapsed without progress in late September 2006 and the Bush administration then focused its efforts on securing support for sanctions at the UN. Talks began in September but it took until 23 December for UNSCR 1737 to be passed. That delay reflected the continued divisions between the US and the other major powers, with Washington proposing sweeping sanctions and Russia and China seeking to narrow their scope. Moscow, in particular, wanted to protect its contracts for the reconstruction of the reactors at Bushehr, and given the fact of the Russian veto, Washington had little option but to compromise.[156] The resolution required that all countries freeze the assets of ten Iranian organisations and twelve individuals involved in Iran's nuclear and missile programmes while prohibiting countries from transferring specific nuclear and missile-related technology to Iran. The list of items sanctioned excluded anything that could affect Russian work at Bushehr.[157]

The Iranian response was predictable. Ahmadinejad declared that 'the resolution was born dead', the Majlis passed a law requiring the government to limit its cooperation with the IAEA, and Iran banned thirty-eight IAEA inspectors from Western countries.[158] Rather than fold, in other words, the hardliners chose to double down and accept the confrontation to come.[159] At the same time they sought to mobilise public support for their chosen course, and to insulate themselves from domestic criticism by further exploiting 'nuclear nationalism'. Following the announcement of successful enrichment in April 2006, Ahmadinejad had the date made a public holiday, and on 'National Nuclear Day' in 2007 he announced that Iran could now enrich on an 'industrial' scale.[160] March 2007 saw the issuing of a new 50,000 rial note decorated with images of nuclear isotopes.

Nevertheless, if Ahmadinejad had hoped to silence his critics he was to be disappointed, with some pointed statements by Rouhani and Rafsanjani during 2006.[161] The passage of UNSCR 1737 (followed by UNSCR 1747 in March 2007), moreover, significantly emboldened his opponents.[162] On 19 January 2007 Ayatollah Hossein Ali Montazeri gave a speech in which he described Ahmadinejad's policies as 'provocative' and costly, saying that 'one has to deal with the enemy with wisdom. We should get our right in a way that it does not create problems for us or excuses for others.'[163] The Majlis, for its part, held a public debate on whether the government's policy was inviting further sanctions in which reformists called for public discussion of the costs and benefits of the current policy.[164]

Ahmadinejad's position was rendered more vulnerable by the comprehensive failure of his populist economic policies – eighteen months after his election inflation remained high, the economy was unstable and unemployment remained around 10 per cent, with significantly higher figures amongst the young. These problems eventually forced him to instigate cuts to petrol and other subsidy programmes, further increasing his unpopularity.[165] Moreover, even though the new sanctions had had no effect at this point, critics of the hardliners were happy to use their potential impact as a weapon. In June 2006, fifty Iranian economists wrote an open letter to Ahmadinejad warning that his confrontational foreign policy, along with his economic policies, was causing 'the investment atmosphere in the country to decline on a daily basis'.[166] The increasing unpopularity of Ahmadinejad's government was also reflected in Iran's election results. In 2006 the Abadgaran lost control of almost every municipal government, including Tehran, winning only 20 per cent of the seats. Salt was further rubbed into the hardliners' wounds in the elections to the Assembly of Experts, in which Rafsanjani won twice as many votes as his nearest rival and Rouhani was also elected.[167]

There was thus some logic in the Bush administration's desire to increase the pressure on Iran, inasmuch as effective economic sanctions would empower the Iranian pragmatists and reformists in their struggle with the hardliners.[168] The administration's problem at this point, however, was the very limited nature of the multilateral sanctions it had been able to secure. It thus continued to do the opposite of what President Theodore Roosevelt once recommended, with its rhetoric and threats fuelling the Iranian hardliners' confrontational discourse while its punitive measures did little to deter them or to empower their critics.[169]

By 2007, nevertheless, the Bush administration had finally begun to develop a more coherent and effective approach to sanctions. With the multilateral route still painfully slow, the administration adopted a strategy designed to leverage unilateral US sanctions so that they had more impact. The architect of this strategy was Stuart Levey, Under Secretary of the Treasury for Terrorism and Financial Intelligence. His approach was rooted in the fact that Iranian banks were involved in a variety of disreputable and/or criminal activities, from the financing of terrorism to money laundering. He sought to exploit that fact to impose pressure on the global banking system to stop doing business with Iranian banks. Firstly, the US barred its own banks from doing business with the major Iranian banks – Bank Sederat in

September 2006, Bank Sepah in January 2007 and Bank Melli in October 2007. Having thus set an example, Washington put pressure on others – both governments and banks – to follow suit. Explicitly, the argument used was that they should stop doing business with Iran because banks rely on their good reputation and banks doing business with Iran ran 'the risk of some day being exposed to the same stigma associated with banks linked to Nazi Germany'.[170] Implicit, but not openly stated, was the threat that if banks continued to deal with Iranian financial institutions, they would eventually be barred from doing business in the USA.[171] The message got through. In September 2006 three Japanese banks announced they would halt doing business with Bank Sederat, shortly followed by UBS and Credit Suisse. HSBC and ABN Amro did likewise in October 2006.[172] In June 2007 the EU black-listed Bank Melli and by late 2008 some eighty banks had publicly stated that they were cutting their business with Iran. While the effects would take time, there was no question that the new sanctions strategy significantly reduced Iran's access to international credit and investment.[173]

Despite these developments, sanctions had no overt impact on Iranian behaviour during the remainder of the Bush presidency, the last eighteen months of which were ones of stasis as far as the nuclear issue was concerned. In August 2007 Iran and the IAEA signed a 'modalities agreement' in which the former agreed to address all the outstanding issues identified by the IAEA.[174] Rather than indicating any flexibility on Iran's part, however, this was simply part of its existing strategy of asserting that Iran was ready to cooperate fully with the IAEA and observe the NPT as long as its own rights – and above all that to the fuel cycle – were respected in return. If anything, it seemed that the Iranian hardliners were strengthening their position, as was indicated by the resignation of Larijani in October 2007 and his replacement by Saeed Jalili, a close Ahmadinejad ally.[175]

A clearly frustrated Bush became increasingly bellicose as Iran demonstrated no sign of 'buckling'. In a speech to the American Legion in August 2007 he declared that 'Iran's active pursuit of technology that could lead to a nuclear weapon threatens to put a region already known for instability and violence under the shadow of a nuclear holocaust.'[176] Two months later he said in a press conference that

> we got a leader in Iran who has announced that he wants to destroy Israel. So . . . if you're interested in avoiding World War 3, it seems like you ought to be interested in preventing [the Iranians] from having the knowledge necessary to make a nuclear weapon.[177]

Clearly despairing of any negotiated solution, Bush sought to rally domestic and international opinion behind tougher action. He may also have been motivated by ongoing concerns about unilateral Israeli military action in the absence of an effective alternative. That such concerns were real was demonstrated when Israel sought to establish whether Washington would support an attack on Iran. Bush refused to do so.[178]

Bush's efforts to ratchet up the pressure were undermined by his own intelligence community who, in a National Intelligence Estimate (NIE) released on 3 December 2007, contradicted their previous conclusions that Iran had an active nuclear weapons programme. The new NIE stated that, while they were confident that Iran sought, 'at a minimum', to keep the option of a weapons programme open, the intelligence community also judged, 'with high confidence', that Iran had halted its weaponisation activities in 2003 and concluded, with 'moderate confidence', that the programme had not been resumed.[179] Whether or not the NIE was released in order to nullify the case for taking military action against Iran, as has been suggested,[180] it certainly complicated efforts to rally international support for tougher measures. A French policy-maker noted that Russia and China were soon 'using the NIE to support their arguments to slow down or not proceed to the third sanctions resolution'.[181]

2008, Plus Ça Change

In January 2008, during a visit to Iran, ElBaradei tried to persuade the Iranians to announce a temporary suspension of enrichment in order to allow for a resumption of negotiations. Now was an opportune moment, he suggested. The NIE had undermined the case for military action, Iran's cooperation on the modalities agreement had been widely welcomed and Iran's control of the fuel cycle was now complete.[182] With such a strong hand it could expect to secure a favourable deal. However, whilst it seemed that his interlocutors agreed with his assessment of their strong position, the conclusion they drew from it was that there was no need to make any concessions. Mottaki told ElBaradei that Iran had suspended enrichment in the past and got nothing so 'now it is up to the other side to also make some compromises'. ElBaradei also met with Khamenei, who assured him that Iran would continue to cooperate with the IAEA to solve all the remaining issues. But when the issue of suspending enrichment was raised the Supreme Leader dismissed it as out of the question.[183]

With Iranian defiance on enrichment continuing, March 2008 saw the passage of UNSCR 1803. The new resolution extended multilateral sanctions to additional financial institutions, including Bank Melli and Bank Sederat, imposed travel restrictions on more Iranians associated with the missile and nuclear programmes, and barred exports of nuclear and missile-related dual-use goods to Iran.[184] As a *quid pro quo* for Russian and Chinese support, the Bush administration agreed to back a revised version of the P5+1's June 2006 incentives package which was submitted to Iran on 14 June. The incentives were extended to include assistance in building LWRs and guarantees of fuel supply, cooperation on regional security and steps toward normalisation of trade relations. On the issue of suspension of enrichment, the P5+1 now offered a 'freeze-for-freeze': Iran would suspend enrichment activity in return for a hiatus in the imposition of new sanctions.[185] By this point Ahmadinejad's response was entirely predictable. UNSCR 1803 was followed shortly by Iran's national 'Nuclear Day' on which Ahmadinejad boasted that Iran now had 3,000 centrifuges in operation and was installing 6,000 new, faster IR-2 centrifuges. He also declared that US efforts to stop Iran's programme 'will fail in the same way that they have failed in the past 30 years'.[186] The revised incentives package was rejected.

Despite Ahmadinejad's defiance, however, there was evidence of considerable domestic dissent. One of the most significant developments was a fracturing of the Abadgaran. This was evident in the

March 2008 Majlis elections when a significant number of those who had previously been associated with the faction joined a new grouping led by Larijani.[187] Following the elections and the rejection of the P5+1's offer, criticism from reformists and pragmatists grew once again, leading Ahmadinejad's supporters to respond in kind. The debate became sufficiently vigorous that in mid-July Khamenei felt compelled to step in to try to put an end to it.[188]

The Iranian rejection of the latest incentives package led the US to step up its unilateral sanctions regime and the EU to join it. In July the Bush administration imposed financial sanctions on Iranian officials and businesses involved with the nuclear programme, freezing their assets in the USA and barring Americans from doing business with them.[189] Later that month the EU announced new measures directed at Iran's banking and energy sectors. These included increased scrutiny of financial transactions involving Iranian banks, bans on the export of technology and equipment for exploration and production of oil and gas, and the black-listing of forty individuals and fifty companies.[190] By now it was clear that sanctions were beginning to have an effect, albeit one that was not compelling Iran to change course. Most Western energy companies had withdrawn from doing business in Iran, which was having to turn increasingly to Russia, China and Asia for investment in its oil and gas industries.[191]

The Failure of Confrontation

Nevertheless, by the end of George W. Bush's two terms in office Iran's nuclear programme had advanced considerably, and the various efforts of the United States and the rest of the international community to bring it under control appeared to have reached a dead end. Iran had between four and five thousand centrifuges operating at Natanz and had produced approximately 1,000 kg of low enriched uranium. The HWR at Arak had begun operating in August 2006 with a capability to produce 16 tonnes of heavy water (and therefore up to 9 kg of weapons-grade plutonium) each year.[192] UNSCR 1835, passed on 27 September 2008, added to the list of black-listed individuals and companies and expanded the range of dual-use equipment banned for sale but otherwise failed to expand sanctions.[193] That reflected an increasing reluctance on the part of many states to continue with what seemed to be a fruitless attempt to coerce Iran into compliance. Moscow and China were both indicating that they saw no point in backing more sanctions and the UK Foreign Office informed Washington that it could identify only five EU states which were willing to impose new measures.[194]

Any evaluation of the policy of the George W. Bush administration toward the Iranian nuclear programme must therefore conclude that it was a resounding failure, with the only question being the extent to which the administration brought that failure upon itself, rather than being a victim of circumstances. In its defence, there were certainly factors that were beyond the ability of the administration to control, most importantly the balance of factional power inside Iran and the calculus of the other major powers, both of which hampered Washington's ability to influence Iranian decision-making. Nevertheless, even given that caveat, the administration played the hand it was dealt badly.

For some kind of resolution to have been reached there needed to be movement on the question of enrichment. Either Iran had to surrender that right until Washington was satisfied that its programme was entirely peaceful, or the Bush administration had to accept Iran's right to enrich. Between 2001 and 2008 neither side was prepared to alter its position on that critical issue. On the Iranian side that refusal was driven by a powerful national consensus on Iran's right to the fuel cycle as well as a profound animosity toward, and distrust of, the US government. The Bush administration's refusal to compromise was fuelled by an equivalent fear and distrust as well as by a failure to acknowledge the limitations of the means it had available to influence Tehran.

Successful bargaining requires the skilful employment of carrots and sticks, but the Bush administration failed to wield either effectively. On the one hand, it never offered Iran sufficient incentive to compromise. Above all, it never accepted the need to offer Iran at least some degree of enrichment on its own soil. Nor did it ever take seriously the Iranian desire to achieve a comprehensive deal in which the threat of regime change would be permanently removed. On the other hand, the administration was never in a position to exert sufficient coercive pressure to compel Tehran to concede its demands. The unfolding disaster in Iraq quickly took the threat of military action off the table and sanctions were not sufficiently effective, even with Stuart Levey's initiatives, because the administration was not able to secure the necessary multilateral support for them. The consequence was a gross mismatch between the administration's ambitions and its ability to achieve them.

Moreover, the administration's policy was self-defeating. By taking such an inflexible line on Iranian enrichment, Bush alienated the states whose support he needed to secure to impose effective coercive pressure on Iran. The Bush approach also reinforced a dynamic within Iranian domestic politics which was entirely unhelpful to American objectives. The administration's rhetoric about regime change and refusal to offer substantive concessions discredited the policy positions and diplomatic initiatives of the Iranian pragmatists and legitimated the argument of the hardliners that uncompromising resistance was the only viable course of action. Meanwhile, the inability of the Bush administration to actually impose significant costs on the Iranian regime reinforced the hardliners' claim that there was nothing to fear from confronting Washington. To succeed in its objectives the Bush administration needed either to offer substantive concessions and/or to impose real costs, but it failed to do either.

Notes

1. Woodward, *Bush at War*; Woodward, *Plan of Attack*.
2. Suskind, *One Percent Doctrine*, p. 225.
3. Powell, 'Confirmation hearing'; Haass, *War of Necessity, War of Choice*, p. 176.
4. Hurst, 'Myths of neoconservatism'.
5. Crist, *Twilight War*, p. 445.
6. Nazila Fathi, 'A nation challenged: Tehran; Iran softens tone against the United States', *The New York Times*, 21 September 2001.
7. Slavin, *Bitter Friends, Bosom Enemies*, p. 197.
8. Samii, 'Afghan war without Iran almost impossible'.
9. Crist, *Twilight War*, pp. 431–2.

10. Parsi, *Treacherous Alliance*, p. 228; Pollack, *Persian Puzzle*, p. 350; Slavin, *Bitter Friends, Bosom Enemies*, p. 196.
11. Slavin, *Bitter Friends, Bosom Enemies*, p. 194; Crist, *Twilight War*, p. 433.
12. George W. Bush, 'The president's state of the union address', Washington DC, 29 January 2002, US President, *Public Papers of the Presidents of the United States* (*PPPUS*).
13. Woodward, *Plan of Attack*, pp. 86–8.
14. *The Jerusalem Post*, 12 September 2001.
15. *PR Newswire*, 12 September 2001.
16. Though who in Iran sent the weaponry and why is an open question; Axworthy, *Revolutionary Iran*, p. 358.
17. David E. Sanger, 'Bush aides say tough tone put foes on notice', *The New York Times*, 31 January 2002, p. 16; Rice, 'Remarks by Condoleezza Rice on terrorism and foreign policy'.
18. Hossein Mousavian, quoted in Crist, *Twilight War*, p. 437.
19. Slavin, *Bitter Friends, Bosom Enemies*, p. 12.
20. Crist, *Twilight War*, pp. 443–7.
21. 'Iran confirms building new nuclear facilities', *Iran Press Service*, 14 December 2002, available at <http://www.iran-press-service.com/articles_2002/Dec_2002/iran_confirms_new_nucke_plants_141202.htm> (last accessed 12 July 2016).
22. IAEA, 'Implementation of the NPT safeguards agreement in the Islamic Republic of Iran', GOV/2003/40.
23. Gary Samore, quoted in Corera, *Shopping for Bombs*, p. 81.
24. 'Washington lobbies for UN censure of Iran's nuclear plans', *Associated Press*, 9 May 2003.
25. 'Notes on draft NS presidential directive, "Iran Policy"', 8 October 2002, quoted in Crist, *Twilight War*, p. 459.
26. Parsi, *Treacherous Alliance*, Appendix A, pp. 341–2; 'Iran's grand bargain', available at <https://static01.nyt.com/packages/pdf/opinion/20070429_iran-memo-3.pdf> (last accessed 10 March 2016).
27. Sonni Efron, 'War with Iraq – diplomacy: Looking past Baghdad to the next challenge', *Los Angeles Times*, 6 April 2003, p. 10.
28. See, for example, American Iranian Council, 'The grand bargain', available at <http://iraniansforum.com/Document/The_Grand_Bargain_April-May_2007.pdf> (last accessed 13 July 2017); PBS, 'The "grand bargain" fax: A missed opportunity?', available at <http://www.pbs.org/wgbh/pages/frontline/showdown/themes/grandbargain.html> (last accessed 13 July 2017).
29. Parsi, *Treacherous Alliance*, pp. 255–6.

30. IAEA, 'Implementation of the NPT safeguards agreement in the Islamic Republic of Iran', GOV/2003/63.
31. Hossein Shariatmadari, 'What have they dreamt for us?', *Kayhan*, 12 July 2003, quoted in Farhi, 'To sign or not to sign?', p. 39.
32. Rouhani, 'Beyond the challenges facing Iran'.
33. Mousavian, *Iranian Nuclear Crisis*, pp. 95–6.
34. IAEA, 'Implementation of the NPT safeguards agreement in the Islamic Republic of Iran', GOV/2003/63.
35. IAEA, 'Implementation of the NPT safeguards agreement in the Islamic Republic of Iran', GOV/2003/69.
36. Mousavian, *Iranian Nuclear Crisis*, pp. 75–6.
37. Ibid., p. 97.
38. Rouhani, 'Beyond the challenges facing Iran'.
39. Paula Taylor and Louis Charbonneau, 'E.U. big three offer Iran carrot for nuclear deal', *Reuters*, 19 September 2003.
40. Mousavian, *Iranian Nuclear Crisis*, p. 102.
41. 'Tehran Declaration', *BBC News*, 21 October 2003, available at <http://news.bbc.co.uk/1/hi/world/middle_east/3211036.stm> (last accessed 10 February 2014).
42. Mousavian, *Iranian Nuclear Crisis*, pp. 98–9.
43. Rezaei, *Iran's Nuclear Program*; Patrikarikos, *Nuclear Iran*, p. 182; Pollack, *Persian Puzzle*, pp. 366–7.
44. Mousavian, *Iranian Nuclear Crisis*, p. 460.
45. Quoted in Lotfian, 'Nuclear policy and international relations', p. 163.
46. Shirin Ebadi and Muhammad Sahimi, 'Link the nuclear programme to human rights in Iran', *International Herald Tribune*, 19 January 2006. Ebadi is an Iranian lawyer, human rights activist and consistent critic of the Iranian regime.
47. WorldPublicOpinion.org, 'Iranian public ready to deal on nuclear weapons'.
48. Herzog, 'Iranian public opinion'; WorldPublicOpinion.org, 'Iranian public opinion on governance, nuclear weapons'; Elson and Nader, *What Do Iranians Think?*
49. US Congress, House Committee on Foreign Affairs, 'Iran: Briefing and hearing', Statement of Ray Takeyh, p. 77.
50. Hossein, 'Iran's assertiveness'; 'Leader says US, Europe aim to hinder Iran's scientific development', *Vision of the IRI Network 1*, 3 March 2005, *BBC Monitoring*, 4 March 2005.
51. Warnaar, *Iranian Foreign Policy*, p. 135.
52. Colum Lynch, 'Envoy: Iran to continue its nuclear power effort', *The Washington Post*, 13 March 2003.

53. Jim Muir, 'Nuclear deal splits Iran hardliners', *BBC*, 22 October 2003, available at <http://news.bbc.co.uk/1/hi/world/middle_east/3204125.stm> (last accessed 14 July 2017); 'Top cleric says Iran's "red lines" still exist over NPT protocol' (in Persian), *IRNA*, 31 October 2003, available at <http://www.irna.ir/#2003_10_3114_59_479> (last accessed 20 October 2015); Shariatmadari, 'What have they dreamt for us?'

54. Simon Tisdall, 'Atomic clock ticks down to fallout with Iran', *The Guardian*, 18 March 2005.

55. Ansari, *Confronting Iran*, p. 204; Kazemzadeh, 'Foreign policy decision making in Iran', p. 205.

56. 'Iran complains of nuclear bullying', *Associated Press*, 23 February 2007, available at <http://26sep.net/news_details.php?lng=english&sid=23607> (last accessed 6 October 2017).

57. See, for example, Hossein Shariatmadari, 'There is crisis, but on which side?' (in Persian), *Kayhan*, 19 February 2007, available at <http://www.kayhannews.ir/851130/2.htm> (last accessed 10 May 2016).

58. 'Iran's conservatives are now underpinned by military ideologues', *The Economist*, 17 June 2004; Nader, 'Influencing Iran's decisions', p. 222.

59. Milani, 'US policy', p. 48.

60. Khatami, 'Covenant with the nation', inaugural speech to the Iranian Majles, 3 August 1997, in Khatami, *Islam, Liberty and Development*, pp. 76–82.

61. *ISNA*, 12 October 2003, available at <http://www.isna.ir/news/NewsCont.asp?Lang=P&id=294267>, quoted in Farhi, 'To sign or not to sign?', p. 42.

62. *Kargozaran*, no. 218, 5 February 2007.

63. 'Khatami election address', *Islamic Republic of Iran Broadcasting (IRIB-TV)*, 10 May 1997, US Department of Commerce, *Foreign Broadcast Information Service (FBIS)*, FBIS-NES-97-091, 13 May 1997.

64. Mohsen Aminzadeh, 'Siasat Hastehee Iran Va Peyamadhay Aan' ('Iran's nuclear policy and its consequences'), *Gooya*, 7 March 2006, quoted in Kamrava, 'Iranian national security debates', p. 95 and Kazemzadeh, 'Foreign policy decision making in Iran', p. 208.

65. Haghighatjoo, 'Factional positions on the nuclear issue'; Kazemzadeh, 'Foreign policy decision making in Iran'.

66. Moslem, *Factional Politics in Post-Khomeini Iran*, pp. 99–105, 129. In terms of the models of proliferation discussed in Chapter 2,

therefore, the argument here suggests that Solingen's model offers the most plausible explanation of Iranian policy after 2002. Hardliners with little interest in Iran's integration with the global economy continued to back a weapons programme, while those factions who saw economic openness as the key to regime survival supported a compromise and pursuit only of a peaceful nuclear programme.

67. Aminzadeh, 'Iran's nuclear policy and its consequences'.

68. 'Iran's nuclear chief denies rumours of resignation', *Sharq*, 14 July 2005, *BBC Monitoring*, 15 July 2005.

69. See, for example, 'Iran's Supreme Leader rejects US "lies", urges continued nuclear work', *Vision of the IRI Network 1*, 21 March 2005, *BBC Monitoring*, 22 March 2005.

70. IAEA, 'Implementation of the NPT safeguards agreement in the Islamic Republic of Iran', GOV/2003/75.

71. Carol Giacomo, 'U.S. seeking consensus approach with allies on Iran', *Reuters*, 12 November 2003; 'Straw breaks ranks with U.S. over Iran', *Reuters*, 12 November 2003.

72. Bolton, *Surrender Is Not an Option*, pp. 135–51.

73. 'Powell says Solana went too far calling Iran "honest" on nuclear program', *Agence France-Presse*, 17 November 2003.

74. 'US hopes of bringing Iran before Security Council dimming: Diplomats', *Agence France-Presse*, 17 November 2003.

75. IAEA, 'Implementation of the NPT safeguards agreement in the Islamic Republic of Iran' GOV/2003/81.

76. Parsi, *Losing an Enemy*, p. 57.

77. Spear, 'Organizing for international counterproliferation', pp. 218–20; Kaussler, *Iran's Nuclear Diplomacy*, pp. 12–13; Patrikarikos, *Nuclear Iran*, pp. 184–6; Pollack, *Persian Puzzle*, p. 365.

78. 'Russian minister rejects US "economic pressure" over Iran,' *ITAR-TASS*, 1 June 2000, *FBIS*, CEP20000601000135, 1 June 2000.

79. Arbatov, 'Inexorable momentum of escalation', pp. 70–1; Omelicheva, 'Russia's foreign policy toward Iran'; Harold and Nader, 'China and Iran'; Ghafouri, 'China's policy in the Persian Gulf'.

80. ElBaradei, *Age of Deception*; Louis Charbonneau, 'ElBaradei wary of taking Iran to Security Council', *Reuters*, 8 July 2004; ElBaradei, 'Nuclear non-proliferation'.

81. Michael Dobbs, 'Pressure builds for president to declare strategy on Iran', *The Washington Post*, 15 June 2003, p. A20.

82. Slavin, *Bitter Friends, Bosom Enemies*, p. 212; Pillar interview.

83. IAEA, 'Implementation of the NPT safeguards agreement in the Islamic Republic of Iran', GOV/2004/11; 'Iran not enriching uranium: Foreign minister', *Spacewar.com*, 17 February 2004, quoted in 'Iran nuclear

threat chronology', *Nuclear Threat Initiative*, May 2011, available at <http://www.nti.org/media/pdfs/iran_nuclear.pdf?_=1316542527> (last accessed 7 December 2017).

84. 'US again accuses Iran of hiding nuclear program', *Middle East Online*, 26 February 2004, quoted in Patrikarikos, *Nuclear Iran*, p. 204; 'Iran says it stopped building centrifuges', *Associated Press*, 29 March 2004; ElBaradei, *Age of Deception*, p. 132.

85. IAEA, 'Implementation of the NPT safeguards agreement in the Islamic Republic of Iran', GOV/2004/49; 'Implementation of the NPT safeguards agreement in the Islamic Republic of Iran', GOV/2004/79.

86. Cable from US Mission to EU to Department of State, 'Wishful thinking? EU hopes G8 can keep Iran out of UNSC', 8 October 2004, available at <https://cablegatesearch.wikileaks.org/cable.php?id=04BRUSSELS4335> (last accessed 20 May 2015).

87. 'European heavyweights pressure Iran over nuclear program; talks to continue', *Agence France-Presse*, 21 October 2004.

88. 'Iran ready to negotiate enrichment halt length', *Reuters*, 18 October 2004; Parisa Hafezi, 'Iran may resume uranium enrichment in March', *Reuters*, 10 January 2005; Rouhani, 'Beyond the challenges facing Iran'. The Paris Agreement also demonstrated the delicacy of the domestic politics of the negotiating process on the Iranian side. Apparently, Khamenei nearly killed the deal when he thought that the suspension of enrichment would be indefinite, and was only persuaded to back it when he was reassured it would be finite; Mousavian, *Iranian Nuclear Crisis*, p. 150.

89. IAEA, 'Communication dated 26 November 2004', INFCIRC 637.

90. Robin Wright, 'Rice says U.S. won't join Europe in Iran nuclear talks', *The Washington Post*, 4 February 2005, p. A10.

91. Cable from US Mission to EU to Department of State, 'EU/Iran WMD rep readout on talks, path ahead for EU-3-Iran dialogue', 23 December 2004, available at <http://www.cablegatesearch.net/cable.php?id=04BRUSSELS5396> (last accessed 20 May 2015); Cable from US Mission to EU to Department of State, 'Wishful thinking?'

92. Robin Wright, 'Bush weighs offers to Iran: US might join effort to halt nuclear program', *The Washington Post*, 28 February 2005, p. A1.

93. At AIPAC's annual conference in May 2005 the main theme was the threat posed to Israel by Iran. The conference included a 'Disney-inspired nuclear tour' which outlined the Iranian 'weapons program'; *Financial Times*, 23 May 2005; Seymour Hersh, 'The coming wars', *The New Yorker*, 17 January 2005; *The Sunday Times*, 13 March 2005.

94. 'Target Iran', *The Weekly Standard*, 24 April 2006; Joshua Muravchik, 'WE MUST bomb Iran', *Los Angeles Times*, 19 November 2006.

95. 'Bush won't rule out action against Iran over nukes', *Reuters*, 17 January 2005; Rice, 'Remarks at the American University of Cairo'; Robin Wright and Michael A. Fletcher, 'Bush denounces Iran's election', *The Washington Post*, 17 June 2005, p. A18.

96. Peter Baker and Glen Kessler, 'US campaign aimed at Iran's leaders', *The Washington Post*, 13 March 2006, p. A1; Crist, *Twilight War*, pp. 496–7.

97. Arms Control Association, 'History of official proposals on the Iran nuclear issue'.

98. Warren Hoge and David E. Sanger, 'Iran to resume nuclear plans, official states at U.N. conference', *The New York Times*, 4 May 2005.

99. Mousavian, *Iranian Nuclear Crisis*, p. 171; ElBaradei, *Age of Deception*, p. 141.

100. IAEA, 'Communication dated 8 August 2005'.

101. IAEA, 'Communication dated 1 August 2005'.

102. Ingram, 'Preliminary analysis of EU-3/EU proposal to Iran'.

103. Mousavian, *Iranian Nuclear Crisis*, p. 165.

104. See, for example, 'Ahmad Jennati: The policy trend of the nuclear file in the past two years was unsound' (in Persian), *ILNA*, 17 February 2006, available at <http://www.ilna.ir/shownews. asp?code=281793&code1=1>, quoted in Kazemzadeh, 'Foreign policy decision making in Iran', p. 207.

105. US Embassy Rome to Department of State, 'Italy on board with Iran/IAEA BoG views', 30 April 2004, available at <http://www. cablegatesearch.net/cable.php?id=04ROME1692> (last accessed 29 April 2015); US Embassy London to Department of State, 'Iranian diplomat sounds out the Brits', 18 June 2004, available at <http://www.cablegatesearch.net/cable.php?id=04ROME2363> (last accessed 29 April 2015).

106. US Embassy Beijing, 'Strong domestic pressure driving Iran's nuclear program, China looking after economic interests', 20 January 2006, available at <http://www.cablegatesearch.net/cable. php?id=06BEIJING1306> (last accessed 30 April 2015); 'EU–Iran French readout of Paris Agreement Working Group meetings January 17–18', 26 January 2005, available at <http://www.cablegatesearch.net/cable.php?id=05PARIS472&version=1314919461> (last accessed 30 April 2015).

107. David Morrison and Peter Oborne, 'US scuppered deal with Iran in 2005, says then British Foreign Minister', *OpenDemocracy.net*, 23 September 2013, available at <https://www.opendemocracy.net/david-morrison-peter-oborne/us-scuppered-deal-with-iran-in-2005-says-then-british-foreign-minister> (last accessed 19 July 2017); Mousavian, *Iranian Nuclear Crisis*, pp. 162–5.
108. Siddiqi, 'Khatami and the search for reform in Iran'; Axworthy, *Revolutionary Iran*, pp. 351–3.
109. Farhad Khosrokhavar, 'The new conservatives take a turn', *Middle East Report Online*, 2004, available at <http://www.merip.org/mer/mer233/new-conservatives-take-turn> (last accessed 25 May 2015).
110. Takeyh, 'Iran's municipal elections'; Axworthy, *Revolutionary Iran*, p. 375.
111. Ansari, *Confronting Iran*, pp. 226–7.
112. Ibid., p. 212.
113. Mahdi, 'Student movement in the Islamic Republic of Iran'; World Bank, *World Development Indicators*, available at <http://data.worldbank.org/data-catalog/world-development-indicators> (last accessed 21 July 2017).
114. United Nations Office on Drugs and Crime, *World Drug Report 2006*, p. 74.
115. Slavin, *Bitter Friends, Bosom Enemies*, p. 122.
116. Mottaki, 'Iran's foreign policy under President Ahmadinejad'; Warnaar, *Iranian Foreign Policy*, pp. 82–8.
117. Ahmadinejad, 'Address by H. E. Dr. Mahmood Ahmadinejad'.
118. Mousavian, *Iranian Nuclear Crisis*, pp. 196–9.
119. Thomas Fuller, 'Iran rejects UN nuclear concerns as "absurd"', *International Herald Tribune*, 12 August 2005, p. 3.
120. Ansari, *Confronting Iran*, pp. 212–13; Warnaar, *Iranian Foreign Policy*, pp. 145–6.
121. The evidence was a set of documents on a laptop supposedly smuggled out of Iran. The Bush administration also provided the claims to the IAEA but refused to reveal the source of the allegations or to provide copies of many of the documents, making it enormously difficult for the IAEA to seek verification of the claims; William J. Broad and David E. Sanger, 'Relying on computer, US seeks to prove Iran's nuclear aims', *The New York Times*, 13 November 2005; ElBaradei, *Age of Deception*, pp. 279–80.
122. IAEA, 'Implementation of the NPT safeguards agreement in the Islamic Republic of Iran', GOV/2005/77; 'EU backs down on Iran under Russia, China pressure', *Reuters*, 22 September 2005.

123. 'Iran's official response to the Board of Governors Resolution', *ISNA*, 26 September 2005, *BBC Monitoring*, 27 September 2005.

124. Ahmadinejad, 'Address by H. E. Dr. Mahmood Ahmadinejad'. The idea was similar to the multinational facility proposal the Nixon/Ford administration had floated in the 1970s.

125. US Embassy Moscow to Department of State, 'Security Council secretary Ivanov on Larijani talks', 25 January 2006, available at <http://cables.mrkva.eu/cable.php?id=50670> (last accessed 21 July 2017).

126. David Sanger, 'US and Europe to give Iranians new atom offer', *The New York Times*, 10 November 2005; 'U.S., Europe won't push for move on Iran', *Associated Press*, 20 November 2005.

127. Nazila Fathi, 'Iran says Russia's nuclear plan is "not sufficient"', *The New York Times*, 27 January 2006.

128. Raula Khalaf and Gareth Smyth, 'Iran warns against UN referral', *Financial Times*, 22 January 2006.

129. IAEA, 'Implementation of the NPT safeguards agreement in the Islamic Republic of Iran', GOV/2006/14.

130. Alissa J. Rubin, 'Rejecting cooperation, Iran asks IAEA to remove seals, cameras', *Los Angeles Times*, 7 February 2006; 'Iran starts injection of UF6 gas into limited number of centrifuges in Natanz', *Tehran Fars News Agency*, 13 February 2006, *FBIS*, IAP20060213011052, 14 February 2006.

131. Slavin, *Bitter Friends, Bosom Enemies*, p. 221.

132. David E. Sanger, 'Bush's realization on Iran: No good choice left except talks', *The New York Times*, 1 June 2006.

133. Elaine Sciolino, 'Russia plan for Iran upsets US and Europe', *The New York Times*, 7 March 2006; Department of State, 'Daily press briefing', 16 March 2006, available at <https://2001-2009.state.gov/r/pa/prs/dpb/2006/63271.htm> (last accessed 10 October 2017).

134. Condoleezza Rice, quoted in ElBaradei, *Age of Deception*, p. 195.

135. 'Ahmadinejad, Agazadeh announce Iranian success in uranium enrichment', *Tehran Vision of the Islamic Republic of Iran Network*, 11 April 2006, *FBIS*, IAP20060411011076, 12 April 2006.

136. Crist, *Twilight War*, p. 505.

137. Edith M. Lederer, 'UN to present Iran nuke program options', *Associated Press*, 9 May 2006.

138. Nazila Fathi, 'Iran rejects potential European incentives', *The New York Times*, 10 May 2006; 'Iran shuns EU "reactor incentive"', *BBC*, 17 May 2006, available at <http://news.bbc.co.uk/1/hi/world/middle_east/4989376.stm> (last accessed 24 July 2017).

139. Mahmoud Ahmadinejad, 'Letter to George W. Bush', 8 May 2006, available at <https://www.theguardian.com/commentisfree/2006/may/11/iran.world> (last accessed 24 July 2017); ElBaradei, *Age of Deception*, p. 194.

140. Seliktar, *Navigating Iran*, p. 149.

141. The February 2004 IAEA BOG resolution, for example, prompted significant criticisms of Ahmadinejad's policy from both Khatami and Rouhani which were widely aired in the Iranian media; 'Address by Hassan Rouhani at Imam Khomeini Holy Shrine, *ISNA*, 11 February 2006, quoted in Mousavian, *Iranian Nuclear Crisis*, p. 232; 'Interview with former Iranian president Mohammad Khatami by Al Jazeera TV', 26 February 2006, available at <http://www.payvand.com/news/06/feb/1212.html> (last accessed 24 July 2017).

142. P5+1, 'Elements of a proposal to Iran'; 'Condoleezza Rice press conference on Iran', *Scoop*, 1 June 2006, available at <http://www.scoop.co.nz/stories/WO0606/S00007.htm> (last accessed 20 August 2016).

143. Helene Cooper and Elaine Sciolino, 'US says plan offers Iran uranium option', *The New York Times*, 8 June 2006.

144. Ibid.

145. For a discussion of Ahmadinejad's statement, see Hooglund, 'Decoding Ahmadinejad's rhetoric on Israel'; Testimony of Former Director of the CIA James Woolsey and Newt Gingrich in US Congress, Senate Committee on Homeland Security and Governmental Affairs, 'Iran's nuclear recklessness and the US response', pp. 10, 17, 21.

146. Peter Hirschberg, 'Netanyahu: It's 1938 and Iran is Germany: Ahmadinejad is preparing another Holocaust', *Haaretz*, 16 November 2006; 'Israel official: Strike on Iran possible', *Associated Press*, 10 November 2006; 'Target Iran', *The Weekly Standard*; Muravchik, 'WE MUST bomb Iran'.

147. Sean Alfano, 'Americans' fear of Iran accelerates', *Associated Press*, 7 February 2006.

148. AIPAC Policy Conference 2006, 'Closing plenary leadership perspective: The U.S.-Israel relationship, Vice President Richard B. Cheney', 6 March 2006, available at <http://www.aipac.org/~/media/Publications/Policy%20and%20Politics/Speeches%20and%20Interviews/Speeches%20by%20Policymakers/2006/03/Cheney_PC_2006.pdf> (last accessed 24 May 2014); George W. Bush, 'Remarks on the nomination of Robert J. Portman to be

Director of the Office of Management and Budget and Susan C. Schwab to be United States Trade Representative and an exchange with reporters', 18 April 2006, *PPPUS*; US Congress, House International Relations Committee, 'United States policy toward Iran', Testimony of Nicholas Burns.

149. ElBaradei, *Age of Deception*, p. 197.
150. 'Ex-nuclear chief criticizes "ideological" impact on foreign policy', *E'temad*, 23 July 2006, *BBC Monitoring*, 25 July 2006.
151. *The Guardian*, 7 June 2006; 'Mottaki: Iran willing to discuss suspending its nuclear activities, Iranian Ministry of Foreign Affairs', 16 August 2006, available at <http://www.iranwatch.org/government/Iran/iran-mfa-mottaki-willing-discuss-suspension-081506.htm> (last accessed 6 June 2016); *Agence France-Presse*, 13 August 2006.
152. Patrikarikos, *Nuclear Iran*, pp. 229–30.
153. United Nations, UN Security Council Resolution 1696.
154. United Nations, 'Letter dated 11 October 2006 from the Permanent Representative of the Islamic Republic of Iran'.
155. ElBaradei, *Age of Deception*, p. 209.
156. 'World powers meet, disagree on Iran', *Global Security Newswire*, 11 October 2006; Colum Lynch, 'US, European allies at odds on terms of Iran resolution', *The Washington Post*, 26 October 2006.
157. United Nations, UN Security Council Resolution 1737.
158. Nazila Fathi, 'Iran is defiant, vowing to UN it will continue nuclear efforts', *The New York Times*, 25 December 2006, p. A10; Nazila Fathi, 'Iran to "revise" any relations with monitors in nuclear area', *The New York Times*, 26 December 2006, p. A3.
159. Shariatmadari, 'There is a crisis, but on which side?'
160. Nazila Fathi, 'Iran says it can enrich uranium on a large scale', *The New York Times*, 10 April 2007.
161. 'Ex-Iranian nuclear negotiator makes call for more balance, more reason and less emotion', *IRNA*, 20 April 2006, available at <http://www.highbeam.com/doc/IGI-145828821html> (last accessed 20 July 2015); Hassan Rohani, 'Iran's nuclear program: The way out', *Time Magazine*, 9 May 2006, available at <http://http://content.time.com/time/world/article/0,8599,1192435,00.html> (last accessed 16 March 2018); 'Ex-nuclear chief criticizes "ideological" impact on foreign policy'; Rasool Nafisi, 'The Khomeini letter: Is Rafsanjani warning the hardliners?', *Iran Press Service*, 14 October 2006, available at <http://www.iran-press-service.com/ips/

articles-2006/october-2006/khomeini_letter_131006.shtml> (last accessed 24 July 2017).

162. United Nations, UN Security Council Resolution 1747. This doubled the list of Iranian entities subject to an asset freeze and placed a ban on Iranian arms exports.

163. Nazila Fathi, 'Iran bars inspectors: Cleric criticizes president', *The New York Times*, 23 January 2007.

164. Fitzpatrick, 'Is Iran's nuclear capability inevitable?', p. 35.

165. Warnaar, *Iranian Foreign Policy*, pp. 56–7.

166. 'Economists send Ahmadinejad letter urging economic policy change', *E'temad*, 21 June 2006, *BBC Monitoring*, 22 June 2006.

167. 'Ahmadinejad appears unbowed by rivals' near sweep of local elections in Iran', *Associated Press*, 21 December 2006; 'Ahmadinejad suffers election blow', *Al Jazeera*, 21 December 2006, available at <http://www.aljazeera.com/news/middleeast/2006/12/200852513479897251.html> (last accessed 24 July 2017).

168. There is no evidence that this was the administration's plan, however.

169. Roosevelt famously advocated that in foreign policy one should 'speak softly and carry a big stick'.

170. Stuart Levey, quoted in 'Handling Iran and N. Korea cash is "like dealing with Nazis"', *Gulf News*, 25 August 2006, available at <http://gulfnews.com/business/sectors/banking/handling-iran-and-n-korea-cash-is-like-dealing-with-nazis-1.251232> (last accessed 26 July 2017).

171. Robin Wright, 'Stuart Levey's war', *The New York Times Magazine*, 31 October 2008, available at <http://www.nytimes.com/2008/11/02/magazine/02IRAN-t.html> (last accessed 26 July 2017).

172. Stephen Fidler and Daniel Dombey, 'US pushes Europe on Iran sanctions', *Financial Times*, 25 January 2007, available at <http://www.ft.com/cms/s/0/c29ee468-ac18-11db-a0ed-0000779e2340.html?ft_site=falcon&desktop=true#axzz4nvaCzyff> (last accessed 20 May 2017).

173. Gal and Minzili, 'Economic impact of international sanctions on Iran'.

174. IAEA, 'Communication dated 27 August 2007 from the Permanent Mission of the Islamic Republic of Iran'.

175. Nazila Fathi and Michael Slackman, 'Iran's nuclear envoy resigns: Talks in doubt', *The New York Times*, 21 October 2007.

176. George W. Bush, 'Remarks at the American Legion national convention in Reno, Nevada', 28 August 2007, *PPPUS*.

177. 'The president's news conference', 17 October 2007, *PPPUS*.
178. Jonathan Steele, 'Israel asked US for green light to bomb nuclear sites in Iran', *The Guardian*, 25 September 2008; David E. Sanger, 'U.S. rejected aid for Israeli raid on Iranian nuclear site', *The New York Times*, 10 January 2009.
179. US Director of National Intelligence, 'Iran: Nuclear intentions and capabilities'.
180. David Frum, 'No nukes, no war', *National Post*, 12 December 2007; Patrikarikos, *Nuclear Iran*, pp. 240–1.
181. US Embassy, Paris, 'French presidency strategic adviser discusses Iran's nuclear program', 13 December 2007, available at <http://www.cablegatesearch.net/cable.php?id=07PARIS4750> (last accessed 5 May 2015).
182. IAEA, 'Agreement and relevant provisions of Security Council resolutions 1737 (2006) and 1747 (2007) in the Islamic Republic of Iran', GOV/2008/4.
183. ElBaradei, *Age of Deception*, pp. 270–4.
184. United Nations, UN Security Council Resolution 1803.
185. 'Iran to be offered incentives', *Los Angeles Times*, 3 May 2008; Crail, 'Iran presented with revamped incentives'.
186. Nazila Fathi and William J. Broad, 'Iran says it's installing new centrifuges', *The New York Times*, 9 April 2008.
187. Nafisi, 'Iran's Majlis elections'.
188. 'The Leader: NSC is the sole authority handling the nuclear case', *FARS News Agency*, 17 July 2008, quoted in Mousavian, *Iranian Nuclear Crisis*, p. 306, n. 59.
189. 'U.S. moves against Iranian officials, companies', *Associated Press*, 8 July 2008.
190. 'EU tightens sanctions over Iran nuclear program', *BBC News*, 26 July 2008, available at <http://www.bbc.co.uk/news/world-europe-10758328> (last accessed 26 July 2017).
191. Katzman, 'Iran sanctions' (2011), pp. 46–7, Table 5.
192. IAEA, 'Implementation of the NPT safeguards agreement and relevant provisions of Security Council resolutions 1737 (2006), 1747 (2007), 1803 (2008) and 1835 (2008) in the Islamic Republic of Iran', GOV/2009/8; Nazila Fathi, 'Iran: More centrifuges reported', *The New York Times*, 27 November 2008; Director of National Intelligence, 'Iran: Nuclear intentions and capabilities'.
193. United Nations, UN Security Council Resolution 1835.

194. Steven Lee Myers, 'Russia won't meet with U.S. on Iranian nuclear program', *The New York Times*, 23 September 2008; US Embassy, London, 'Iran: UK current posture – FCO formal and informal views', 14 October 2008, available at <http://www.telegraph. co.uk/news/wikileaks-files/london-wikileaks/8304765/IRAN-UK-CURRENT-POSTURE-FCO-FORMAL-AND-INFORMAL-VIEWS.html> (last accessed 6 May 2015); US Embassy, London, 'Iran: UK's informal comments on EU dynamics and Iran sanctions prospects', 9 September 2008, available at <http://www.telegraph. co.uk/news/wikileaks-files/london-wikileaks/8304741/IRAN-UKS-INFORMAL-COMMENTS-ON-EU-DYNAMICS-AND-IRAN-SANCTIONS-PROSPECTS.html> (last accessed 6 May 2015).

5 2009–15: Obama and the Road to the JCPOA

In July 2015 the conflict between the United States and Iran over the latter's nuclear programme seemed to reach a resolution, in the form of the Joint Comprehensive Plan of Action (JCPOA). For the first time leaders on both sides, in the form of Presidents Barack Obama and Hassan Rouhani, demonstrated a simultaneous willingness to make the concessions necessary to satisfy sufficient of the other's demands for an agreement to be reached. On the American side, having managed to impose an effective sanctions regime without forcing Iran to halt enrichment, Obama decided that he had run out of options. As time progressed without a resolution, and the Iranian programme continued to advance, the choice seemed increasingly to be between accepting Iranian enrichment or risking war. By choosing the former, and thus meeting Iran's one non-negotiable demand, Obama made an agreement possible. Nevertheless, the fact that Iran took up the offer and made the necessary reciprocal concessions required other developments to have occurred. Rouhani had been ready to make the deal agreed in 2015 since 2003, but had been prevented from doing so by the American refusal to concede on enrichment and the power of Iran's hardliners. While Obama's shift removed the first obstacle, a combination of economic failure (in which sanctions played a role) and the regime's ongoing legitimacy crisis gradually shifted the balance of power in Iran toward the more moderate factions, creating the political conditions in which Rouhani could make the deal.

Obama and Engagement

In a speech in Israel in 2008, Obama outlined his views on how to deal with the Iranian nuclear programme:

> A nuclear Iran would be a game changing situation not just in the Middle East, but around the world. Whatever remains of our nuclear non-proliferation framework, I think would begin to disintegrate. You would have countries in the Middle East who would see the potential need to also obtain nuclear weapons.[1]

In order to prevent such an outcome it would be necessary 'to offer a series of big sticks and big carrots to the Iranian regime'.[2] Even if Iran were to reject the incentives offered, the latter would still

> [put] us in a stronger position to mobilize the international community to ratchet up the pressure on Iran. Our unwillingness to talk or the perception that we are trying to bully our way through negotiations, that's eliminated as an excuse for them not dealing with these issues in an appropriate way.[3]

Obama's speech suggested that he had learned from the failures of George W. Bush. The incentives offered to Iran had to be more substantive, as did the punishment for not accepting them. The only way to achieve the latter was to secure the support of the other major powers for tougher measures, and that could only be done by demonstrating that Washington was prepared to exhaust all reasonable alternatives first.

Initially, nevertheless, Obama offered Iran little in the way of 'big carrots'. His proposed adoption of a strategy of 'engagement' had caused much debate during the 2008 election campaign, yet all that Obama actually held out to Iran was a willingness to enter negotiations without the precondition that Iran first halt enrichment.[4] That apart, there was no substantive change in Washington's negotiating position. According to Trita Parsi, most policy-makers in the new administration believed that they would ultimately have to accept Iranian enrichment in order to get a deal, but that was not a concession they were prepared to make up front.[5] It was a poor bargaining strategy to concede your opponent's principal demand without first establishing whether it was possible to bring more effective pressure to bear on them. Moreover, the backlash from Israel, the Israeli lobby and the American right if the concession was made would be vicious, and Obama wanted to get re-elected in 2012.

The initial incentive that Obama offered Tehran, therefore, was that the USA would come to the table. That offer was most clearly articulated in his video message broadcast on *Nowruz*, the Iranian New Year. In it Obama stated that

> my administration is now committed to diplomacy that addresses the full range of issues before us, and to pursuing constructive ties among the United States, Iran, and the international community. This process will not be advanced by threats. We seek instead engagement that is honest and grounded in mutual respect.[6]

The offer to talk was couched in careful language – Obama's references to the 'Islamic Republic of Iran', 'mutual respect' and rejection of 'threats' were all designed to indicate an acceptance of the Iranian regime's legitimacy and a rejection of regime change – but it was still just an offer to talk. The offer was made on the same day that it was announced that the administration would take a 'seat at the table' in future P5+1 talks with Iran. The P5+1 also issued a formal invitation to Iran to resume negotiations.[7]

While Obama's language seemed to indicate some change in US policy, however, there was much in his actions which seemed to contradict that. In the first place, his key appointees in the foreign policy sphere were not noted for their willingness to accommodate Iran. Secretary of State Hillary Clinton was noticeably more hawkish than Obama, and had criticised the concept of engagement during the 2008 election campaign.[8] In early 2009 she made clear that she saw little point in talking to Tehran and warned that Iran would face 'crippling sanctions' if it failed to respond positively to US diplomacy.[9] The man appointed to be the lead on Iran policy at the State Department was, if anything, even more hawkish. Before his appointment Dennis Ross had repeatedly expressed the view that diplomacy was doomed to fail and that sanctions, or even military action, would be necessary to halt the Iranian nuclear programme.[10] In addition to making these appointments, Obama signed an order extending existing US sanctions on Iran in March, while US diplomats were already working to secure support for tougher sanctions from America's allies.[11]

From an Iranian point of view, therefore, what seemed to some in the USA to be a significant concession – the willingness to talk without preconditions – amounted to very little compared with the continuities in US policy. The Supreme Leader's response to Obama's *Nowruz* message reflected this. With regard to the supposed change in US policy Khamenei asked,

> where is the change? What has changed? . . . Has your enmity toward the Iranian nation changed? What signs are there to support this? Have you released the possessions of the Iranian nation? Have you removed the cruel sanctions? Have you stopped the insults, accusations, and negative propaganda against this great nation and its officials? Have you stopped your unconditional support for the Zionist regime? What has changed?[12]

Nor was it simply Khamenei and the hardliners in Iran who were unpersuaded by Obama's rhetoric. A September 2009 poll found that 57 per cent of Iranians had no confidence in Obama (albeit an improvement on the 72 per cent who had had no faith in George W. Bush).[13] Whilst there was, according to a 'senior Iranian official', a debate within the regime about whether Obama's overtures represented a real change in US policy or not, many in Tehran evidently felt that Obama was simply seeking to give the appearance of having 'reached out' to Tehran as a prelude to pursuing the imposition of tougher sanctions.[14] Obama tried again in May, sending a letter to Khamenei via the Swiss embassy in Tehran, offering talks and 'cooperation in regional and bilateral relations', but he received no response.[15]

Israeli Pressure

As was indicated above, one of the reasons that Obama was reluctant to make substantive concessions before he got something from Iran was the likely reaction from Israel. Pressure from Tel

Aviv, and deterring it from attacking Iran, had been a concern for Bush, but it would be a much greater one for Obama, for two key reasons: Iran would get that much closer to having the capacity to build a nuclear weapon during the Obama presidency, and the Israeli government did not trust Obama. Whilst they had had their concerns about Bush from time to time, the forty-third president had generally shown himself to be reliably hard-line on Iran and a friend of the Israeli right on most other issues as well. Obama, in contrast, for all his insistence that Iran must be prevented from having nuclear weapons and his oft-repeated commitment to Israel's security, was clearly of a different mind to the Israeli government about how both of these things were best achieved, favouring diplomacy, compromise and mutual gain over military superiority and raw power.[16]

Consequently, Obama found himself under pressure from Israel right from the start. Obama's commitment to 'engagement', while not impressing the regime in Tehran, was worrying to Tel Aviv, and the Israeli government soon began trying to curb Obama's room for manoeuvre. For the most part this took the form of issuing dire (and inaccurate) warnings about how close Iran was to having a nuclear weapon and how little time there therefore was for diplomacy. Those warnings were usually accompanied by a demand that Obama impose an unfeasibly short deadline on negotiations before taking tougher action.[17] These messages had a threefold target – the administration itself, the American public, and the regime in Tehran, whose suspicions about Obama would hopefully be exploited to undermine the possibility of successful negotiations. That the administration was concerned about the impact of Israel's efforts (and, for that matter, about the possibility of Israel taking military action against Iran) was indicated by the fact that senior administration policy-makers felt the need to call on Tel Aviv to tone down its rhetoric as well as by public statements from US officials warning that an Israeli attack on Iran would be disastrous. In response, Israeli Defense Minister Ehud Barak declared that Israel was 'not taking any option off the table'.[18]

Despite its efforts to refute Israeli arguments, the administration clearly felt constrained by the pressure being brought to bear. After a meeting with Netanyahu in May 2009 Obama gave Iran a time limit of the end of the year to take concrete steps toward halting its nuclear programme. While this was longer than Israel had been demanding, the imposition of any time limit represented a concession to the latter's pressure (as well as to that from domestic sources). Netanyahu also claimed, in a further effort to disrupt the engagement strategy, that Obama had privately reassured him that 'all options' remained on the table.[19]

The 2009 Election

As though matters were not sufficiently problematic already, the nuclear issue was further complicated by the June 2009 Iranian presidential election. During the election campaign all of Ahmadinejad's opponents sought to exploit the failure of his economic policy and frequently linked that failure to his confrontational foreign policy. All three key opposition candidates also attacked his approach to the nuclear question. Former Islamic Revolutionary Guard Corps (IRGC) commander Mohsen Rezaei asserted that 'continuing such a policy will destroy all our achievements' and that 'if the current adventurous path continues, we will be heading toward a precipice'.[20] Rezaei endorsed the idea of an international consortium controlling enrichment inside Iran. The two candidates from the reformist side of the Iranian political spectrum, Mir Hossein Mousavi and Mehdi Karroubi, both called for the renewal of negotiations. In an interview with Western journalists Mousavi, the leading challenger for the presidency, reiterated that Iran's right to a peaceful nuclear programme was 'non-negotiable' but said that nuclear weapons were a different matter: 'personally, I view this second part, which is both technical and political, as negotiable'.[21]

Polls suggested that the position of Ahmadinejad's critics was shared by the majority of Iranian voters, despite the efforts of the latter and his allies to exploit 'nuclear nationalism'. A poll conducted shortly before the election found that a majority of Iranians wanted a rapprochement with the US and better integration into the international community. To that end, 74 per cent of respondents favoured a deal in which Iran provided guarantees of a peaceful nuclear programme in return for trade and investment. Nevertheless, the same poll also found that 83 per cent of respondents 'strongly favoured' Iran having nuclear energy and another in September found only 31 per cent in favour of abandoning enrichment in return for an ending of sanctions.[22]

Despite the poor performance of the Iranian economy, Ahmadinejad was widely expected to win re-election easily (the May 2009 poll cited above had him leading by a considerable margin). In the last few days before the vote, however, there was a major surge of support for Mousavi and on polling day itself turnout was high, indicating that reformist voters who had stayed away in 2005 had decided that Mousavi offered some hope of change. In the face of this development Ahmadinejad's supporters within the regime chose to steal the election.[23] In an attempt to quell protests against this electoral fraud, Khameini immediately endorsed the result, rather than wait for confirmation by the Guardian Council as was standard practice. In his televised sermon at Friday prayers on 19 June he denounced allegations of fraud and, in what would become a standard trope, condemned those demonstrating against the result as being inspired by 'foreign elements'.[24] Rather than ending the protests, however, the speech had the opposite effect, with tens of thousands taking to the streets the following day. Mousavi and Karroubi both launched official protests and encouraged the continuation of peaceful opposition. The extent of the crisis for the regime was demonstrated by the fact that establishment figures like Larijani and Rafsanjani both expressed their doubts about the result while the latter failed to attend Ahmadinejad's inauguration.[25]

Whilst the protests would, eventually, be successfully repressed (the last major one occurring on 11 February 2010[26]), what developed in the eight-month period following the election was a crisis unlike any that the regime had faced before. The balancing act between the theocratic and democratic elements in the Islamic Republic of Iran (IRI) Constitution had long been a problematic one to maintain, and disillusion had set in amongst many reformist Iranians well before 2009. Nevertheless, in falsifying the election results, the hardliners ignored the democratic pretensions of the Constitution in a manner so blatant and contemptuous as to discredit themselves and the regime to a much greater degree than ever before. The emergence of the 'Green Movement' in the aftermath of the election demonstrated that a large segment of the population no longer accepted the legitimacy of the Islamic Republic. Never before had there been protestors on the street chanting 'death to Khamenei', and never before had internal critics been so utterly condemnatory in their charges, with Ayatollah Montazeri declaring that 'this government is neither a republic nor Islamic'.[27] By endorsing the theft of the election, Khamenei had taken Iran a step closer to naked authoritarian rule by an unrepresentative hard-line faction which lacked the support of a clear majority of voters. This was an inherently unstable situation and one that was only likely to deteriorate unless something was done to restore the democratic credentials of the regime.[28]

The Iranian presidential election also had ramifications for Obama, further reducing his room for manoeuvre by further fuelling the demonisation of the Islamic Republic of Iran (IRI) inside the United States. Obama's inclination was to avoid any inflammatory rhetoric, since he understood very well that it would only serve to legitimate the claims of Khamenei and others that the Green Movement was a front for the United States.[29] He also understood that there was little he could do to determine the course of events in Iran and did not want to burn his bridges with a government that he would still need to deal with in addressing the nuclear question.[30] Predictably, however, his nuanced response drew the ire of American hardliners, who demanded that he condemn the Iranian regime wholeheartedly.[31] More importantly, it significantly reduced the willingness in Congress to allow time for Obama's engagement policy to work. In the words of one senior White House official, after the Iranian presidential election 'skepticism in Congress against our strategy turned to outright hostility'.[32]

The Geneva Agreement

By mid-2009, for all the talk about 'engagement', Obama's Iran policy was getting nowhere. Shortly before the Iranian presidential election, however, the Iranian ambassador to the International

Atomic Energy Agency (IAEA) submitted a request to buy fuel pads for the Tehran Research Reactor (TRR). The Iranians estimated that the current fuel supply would run out in 2010, and with it their ability to produce vital medical isotopes. Mohamed ElBaradei forwarded the letter to Washington where the Obama administration saw in it an opportunity to finally move negotiations forward. They decided to offer Iran a 'swap': Tehran would get fuel for the TRR but that fuel would be produced from its own stockpile of low enriched uranium (LEU), which would be shipped out of Iran to another country where it would be turned into fuel.[33]

Whilst not addressing the fundamental issues between the two sides, the plan was seen as a useful confidence-building measure that could facilitate progress while having a number of other advantages. In the first place, it addressed the problem of Iran's ever-growing stockpile of LEU. In its June 2009 report, the IAEA said that Iran now had 7,200 centrifuges in operation and had amassed some 1,339 kg of LEU.[34] As one State Department official put it, 'getting 1,200 kilograms [of LEU] out would get you six months of time and a lot of political space' for negotiations. Obama himself told ElBaradei that if the proposal was accepted, 'it will change the dynamics here for me'.[35] In addition, the plan offered an opportunity to improve relations with Moscow – by offering it the role of transforming the LEU into fuel – and could help to secure its backing for future sanctions if necessary. Thirdly, in offering to exchange fuel for LEU the administration was making an implicit acknowledgement of Iran's right to enrich, something which might persuade the Iranians to accept the deal. It was also, of course, a source of potential trouble for the administration, both domestically and with some of its allies, but it was not a formal acknowledgement of the right to enrich and this was not a final deal. And if the administration did not do something to break the deadlock, Iran would simply continue to amass more LEU because neither Russia nor China was prepared to support further sanctions.[36]

The Russians accepted Washington's offer to join them in the plan and ElBaradei outlined the offer to the Iranians in mid-September. Just days after the proposal was communicated, however, a new problem emerged. On 21 September the Iranians informed the IAEA that they were constructing a second enrichment facility at Fordow, near Qom.[37] Washington had been aware of the facility for some time and had significant concerns about it. Intelligence officials estimated that the site was big enough to house approximately 3,000 centrifuges, which was, they argued, too small a capacity for civilian use and thus likely to be for the production of weapons-grade material.[38] Whether that was correct or not, the revelation ratcheted up the domestic pressure on Obama. Democrat Howard Berman, Chair of the House Foreign Affairs Committee, having previously indicated his willingness to hold back new sanctions legislation in order to give Obama time to employ diplomacy, announced that he would now allow the legislation to go forward.[39]

For Obama, nevertheless, the revelations served as a double-edged sword. Whilst they reduced his domestic leeway they also increased the pressure on Iran. Accordingly, he continued to pursue the swap proposal. On 1 October, the same day that the House of Representatives passed its version of the new sanctions legislation, representatives of the P5+1 met an Iranian delegation in Geneva. During the course of the discussions the Iranians said that they agreed in principle to the proposal and to holding another meeting by the end of the month to finalise the deal. They also agreed to allow the IAEA to inspect the site at Fordow in the next two weeks.[40] Further talks were held in Vienna from 19–21 October, at the end of which a draft agreement was drawn up by ElBaradei. Iran would ship 1,200 kg of LEU to Russia, which would enrich it further and send it to France to be turned into fuel. Within twelve months the first batch of fuel pads would be returned to Iran. Both sides were expected to confirm their formal agreement to the proposal within a couple of days.[41]

Instead, the agreement soon unravelled. During the meetings from 19–21 October the Iranians had pushed for an arrangement in which the LEU was shipped out in batches in return for provision of fuel, and over the following weeks their demands became even greater. In response to ElBaradei's draft they insisted that they must receive the fuel for the TRR before shipping out any LEU. The fuel would be stored on the Iranian island of Khish under IAEA supervision until the LEU was shipped to Russia.

The Obama administration responded that they would accept a deal in which the fuel was held in a third country in which Iran had trust (such as Turkey) but Tehran refused to budge, insisting that the fuel had to arrive on Iranian soil before the LEU was shipped.[42]

The Iranian retreat from the Geneva Agreement was a vivid demonstration of the ongoing impact of some of the factors which made resolving the Iranian nuclear crisis so difficult. In the first place, it demonstrated the profound distrust that continued to characterise relations between Iran and the West. Even with an international agreement in place, the Iranians clearly believed that Washington might prevent the delivery of fuel once the LEU had been shipped out of Iran. Secondly, and more importantly, it demonstrated the powerful constraints on agreement posed by Iranian domestic politics. It is probable that Ahmadinejad's (and Khamenei's) initial decision to accept the Geneva Agreement was shaped by a calculation that it could be presented domestically as a diplomatic coup (given the implicit acknowledgement of Iran's right to enrich), which would help to silence their domestic critics and stabilise the regime.[43] In practice, however, the effect was precisely the opposite. Rather than seeing the deal as an acknowledgement of Iran's right to enrich, many Iranians apparently regarded the transferring out of the country of a significant proportion of Iran's LEU as the surrender of a key bargaining chip.[44] Many also saw the requirement that the fuel be manufactured abroad as likely to prefigure a demand that enrichment also take place abroad in future.[45]

Such perceptions were fuelled by the vigorous criticism of the proposed agreement which was mounted from across the political spectrum in Iran. While some of that criticism came from fellow hardliners who honestly believed that Ahmadinejad was sacrificing too much,[46] a great deal of it came from pragmatic conservatives and reformists who might have been expected to welcome the terms of a deal that was broadly in line with the approach that they had previously advocated.[47] Mousavi accused Ahmadinejad of 'not even safeguarding the undeniable rights of our people', while Rouhani described the terms of the deal as 'illegal'.[48] Larijani, now Speaker of the Majlis, said that 'my assumption is that, behind the scene, there is some collusion with the Americans and they want to take our LEU and offer nothing in exchange'.[49] Given the terms of the proposed agreement, it is hard to identify any explanation for this criticism other than pure politics and the desire to undermine Ahmadinejad by playing him at his own game and exploiting 'nuclear nationalism' against him.[50]

The efficacy of these attacks, no doubt aided by the widespread loathing of Ahmadinejad amongst much of the Iranian population, helps to account for the escalation of Tehran's demands, as the regime sought to defuse accusations that it was surrendering Iran's nuclear rights. There was, however, a further factor involved, and one which emphasises the almost paranoid nature of the worldview of some in the Iranian leadership. That factor was the extent to which the proposed agreement was welcomed outside Iran, and especially in Western countries. Western policy-makers, seeking to sell the deal to a sceptical public (especially in the USA), sought to emphasise the extent to which the agreement would constrain the Iranian nuclear programme. Such claims, however, only served to provide fuel for the attacks on Ahmadinejad while also, it seems, inducing fear in the minds of Khamenei and others that the Iranian negotiators had somehow been duped into agreeing to a deal that was heavily weighted against Iran.[51]

Distrust and domestic political infighting thus undermined the Geneva Agreement. In the context of the political crisis following the 2009 presidential election, there was no possibility of securing a consensus in support of the deal, which instead became a domestic political football. Ahmadinejad and Khamenei, having initially backed an agreement they thought would enhance their political position, went into headlong retreat once they realised how it was being turned against them by their political opponents.

The Tehran Declaration

Although seemingly killed off in November 2009, the swap proposal continued to be revived periodically for another six months before being interred for good in the summer of 2010 by the P5+1's brusque rejection of the 'Tehran Declaration'. Throughout this period it was Iran which kept reviving the idea of a swap and the Obama administration which kept rejecting Iran's new variations on a theme.[52]

Those rejections indicated that Obama had given up on diplomacy in the short term and was now turning to the second track of his dual-track policy. During a visit to Israel in early December 2009, Under Secretary for Arms Control and International Security Ellen Tauscher 'reiterated the two track strategy of persuasion and pressure' but said that 'the time for persuasion is "waning"'. She told the Israelis that Russia and China were the 'lynch pins' of the strategy and that the administration was seeking to secure their support for new coercive measures.[53] The administration had been working on getting that support since it came to office, and Obama had pursued an improvement in US–Russian relations – the so-called 'reset'[54] – with some success. As well as inviting Russia to be a key player in the swap proposal, Obama also cancelled the Bush administration's plans to build a National Missile Defense (NMD) base in the Czech Republic, a plan that Putin had seen as directed against Russia. Subsequently, the administration would sign a new Strategic Arms Reduction Treaty (START) with Moscow and drop US sanctions imposed on Russian firms and state-owned enterprises for aiding the Iranian nuclear programme.[55] Under Secretary Tauscher indicated to the Israelis that the administration believed that if Russia could be persuaded to support new sanctions then China would follow, but the administration also made direct efforts to persuade Beijing that the time was ripe for tougher action.[56] In addition to direct bilateral diplomacy, including by the president himself, the administration encouraged the Saudi regime in its efforts to displace Iran as China's main source of Gulf oil and to reassure the Chinese that any shortfall in oil caused by new sanctions would be replaced.[57]

These efforts were aided and abetted by Iran's actions. The revelation of the enrichment plant at Fordow had been another example of Iran's continued dissembling, but the Iranian retreat from the Geneva Agreement was a particular irritant to the Russians, who had stood to benefit from what they regarded as a fair and sensible proposal. In January 2010 they informed the Obama administration that they would support a new sanctions resolution because they were 'fed up' with Iranian behaviour.[58] The Russians were therefore on board even before Ahmadinejad announced, in February 2010, that since the international community had refused to accept its modified version of the swap proposal, Iran would begin enriching some of its existing LEU to 20 per cent to provide fuel for the TRR.[59] In so doing Tehran once again blatantly disregarded existing United Nations Security Council resolutions (UNSCRs) and moved another step closer to producing highly enriched uranium (HEU). Unsurprisingly, the announcement further solidified support for a new round of sanctions.[60] Concerns were further heightened when, in the same month, the IAEA's latest report criticised Iran for failing to explain purchases of sensitive technology and for conducting secret tests of high-precision detonators and modified designs of missile warheads.[61] Consequently, while the Russians and Chinese were unenthusiastic about further sanctions, they were running out of reasons not to endorse them. The Iranian regime appeared to be moving closer to weapons status, was continuing to refuse to cooperate with the IAEA, and had rejected a 'reasonable' proposal to provide it with fuel for the TRR and help build confidence for future negotiations.

The change in Obama's approach was clearly demonstrated by his 2010 *Nowruz* message to the Iranian people, which made clear what his next move was going to be:

> Faced with an extended hand, Iran's leaders have shown only a clenched fist . . . let me be clear: we are working with the international community to hold the Iranian government accountable because they refuse to live up to their international obligations.[62]

In his statement Obama reiterated that 'our offer of comprehensive diplomatic contacts and dialogue stands', but there was no real expectation that Iran would respond, with the administration putting all of its efforts into securing 'meaningful sanctions that clarify for the Iranian leadership the stark choice: follow international rules or face harsh penalties and further isolation'.[63]

Not only was there little expectation of Iran responding to the offer of dialogue, by this point there was also little desire that it do so. Obama had told Netanyahu that he would give Iran until the end of 2009 before shifting to the 'pressure track'. Given the administration's continued concerns about possible unilateral Israeli action, there was good reason for it to keep its word.[64] Moreover, Netanyahu's allies in the USA were doing their utmost to make sure that it did so. The American Israel Public Affairs Committee (AIPAC) had never supported Obama's engagement strategy and had kept up a steady drumbeat of criticism, calling for the imposition of 'crippling sanctions' instead.[65] Those calls were not directed at the administration, however, but at Congress, where sentiment was much more uncritically pro-Israeli than in the White House and members were ever eager to punish Iran. By early 2010 the momentum behind the sanctions legislation introduced in the aftermath of the Fordow revelations was unstoppable. Despite the Obama administration expressing its opposition to the form of the sanctions being proposed, by the end of January bills had been approved in both chambers of Congress by veto-proof majorities.[66]

By spring 2010, therefore, all considerations pointed to pursuit of the pressure track. Most of the major powers were prepared to back that course of action, it would appease Israel, and Obama was faced with the inevitable passage of new US sanctions which would kill negotiations even if they were recommenced. Moreover, imposing new sanctions might serve to secure a future agreement in at least two ways. Firstly, if successful, they would increase the pressure on Iran to make concessions. Secondly, they would demonstrate to American domestic constituencies, and Israel, that the administration had done everything it reasonably could to compel Iran to abandon enrichment, creating room for a concession on that issue in future. Indeed, such was the level of domestic antipathy to Iran that the administration had concluded that it would be impossible to ratify an agreement domestically if it did not first demonstrate its willingness to impose 'crippling' sanctions.[67]

When the Tehran Declaration was announced in May 2010, therefore, it was too little, too late, as far as the Obama administration was concerned. After months of work, Iran, Brazil and Turkey signed an agreement according to which Iran would send 1,200 kg of LEU to Turkey in return for 120 kg of fuel for the

TRR. The fuel would be delivered within one year and Iran would retain ownership of the LEU in Turkey until such time as the fuel was delivered.[68] The Tehran Declaration was not identical to the Geneva Agreement – 1,200 kg was now just over half of Iran's stockpile of LEU given continued production since October 2009 – and there was no commitment by Iran to halt enrichment to 20 per cent.[69] Nevertheless, whilst those differences gave the administration a plausible reason to reject the proposal, the precise terms being offered were not the key factor in that decision.

New Sanctions and Covert Action

The day after the Tehran Declaration was issued, the United States announced a 'draft accord' among the P5+1 on a new sanctions resolution.[70] When formalised this became UNSCR 1929. Approved by the Security Council on 9 June 2010, it imposed a complete arms embargo on Iran, required states not to transfer any ballistic missile related technology to it, and extended the list of prohibited items related to the nuclear and missile programmes. More importantly, it called on states to deny any financial services to Iran that could contribute to those programmes and to block Iran from establishing any new banking services on their territories. It also froze the assets of the IRGC and Iran's national shipping line. In all, forty-one new individuals and entities were added to the list of those black-listed.[71]

One of the measures taken to secure Chinese and Russian support for the new resolution was the exclusion of the Iranian energy sector from those targeted by the sanctions. The US Congress, however, did not feel constrained to follow suit. The Comprehensive Iran Sanctions, Accountability and Divestment Act of 2010 (CISADA), signed into law by Obama on 1 July, sought to exploit the fact that Iran imported some 40 per cent of the refined petroleum products it consumed. The act mandated the imposition of secondary sanctions on firms that sold Iran such products or equipment or services which would enable it to expand its own production of them. It also required the imposition of sanctions on firms which made an investment of $20 million or more in the Iranian energy sector. In addition, it imposed further second-ary sanctions (denying access to US markets and trade) on for-eign banks doing business with Iran and foreign firms supplying it with dual-use technology with applications to weapons of mass destruction.[72] These measures were similar to a series of sanctions imposed by the EU on 26 July which prohibited investment by European states or private entities in the Iranian energy sector as well as the supply of equipment and technology. They also banned the opening of new Iranian bank branches in the EU and barred EU financial institutions from dealing with Iranian government and bank bonds.[73] In addition to new UN, US and EU sanctions, the Obama administration successfully pressed its main Asian allies, Japan and South Korea, to comply with its strategy of disengaging from doing business with Iran.[74]

Sanctions were the overt face of the Obama administration's 'pressure track', but the administration was also engaged in a campaign of covert action to damage and delay the progress of the Iranian nuclear programme. Starting in late 2009, centrifuges at Natanz mysteriously started to self-destruct. This, it would subsequently be revealed, was the successful outcome of a cam-paign of cyber-warfare, conducted jointly by the USA and Israel, code-named Olympic Games. Research on ways to damage the Iranian nuclear programme had begun in 2006, and implemen-tation of the policy had been approved by Bush in 2008. Accel-erated by Obama after his inauguration, the main focus of this effort was on the introduction of a computer virus, known as Stuxnet, into the control systems for the centrifuges at Natanz. When this was achieved the virus caused the centrifuges to run at both excessive speeds and unusually slow ones, eventually leading the delicate machines to disintegrate, apparently as the result of a malfunction or incorrect assembly. Just as the virus was achiev-ing success, however, it was discovered infecting computer sys-tems outside Iran. This led to efforts to identify its source and the exposure of the US–Israeli efforts. In addition to Stuxnet, the operation against Iran also involved a virus called Flame which, when successfully introduced into Iranian computer systems, recorded information by activating computer microphones and cameras, logging keyboard strokes and taking screen shots. Other cyber-warfare attacks which have not yet been exposed were also undoubtedly developed and deployed.[75]

The Obama administration confined itself to non-lethal forms of covert action, but its Israeli ally did not feel so constrained. Whilst there is, inevitably, a significant degree of ambiguity surrounding such events, four Iranian nuclear scientists were assassinated between November 2010 and January 2012. In addition, the head of the country's ballistic missile programme was killed in an unexplained explosion at a missile testing site and the commander of Iran's Cyber War Headquarters were also killed. There was a further unexplained explosion at the Parchin military complex, where Iran was alleged to have conducted weapons experiments, in October 2014.[76] Iran sought to retaliate against Israeli targets, but with limited success.[77]

Intermission

Despite the new round of sanctions and covert action, the period from mid-2010 to the end of 2012 was one in which, on the surface, nothing really changed. Negotiations were resumed periodically but without any meaningful progress being achieved, with neither side offering the kind of concessions that were necessary to secure an agreement. The Obama administration was seemingly waiting for the pressure track to bring Tehran to its senses (and for Obama to be successfully re-elected) whilst the Iranians continued to hold out for a formal acknowledgement of their right to enrich. Despite a lack of concrete progress, nevertheless, there were signs on both sides of developments that would, eventually, facilitate a deal.

The response of the Iranian government to Obama's resort to sanctions was, once again, to harden its own position. In the first place, the decision was taken to accelerate the nuclear programme by installing new centrifuges and enriching to 20 per cent. According to Mohammad Nahavandian, later President Rouhani's chief of staff, the objective was 'to break the mentality of the other side by showing them that pressure wouldn't work'.[78] This was accompanied by an utterly inflexible stance in negotiations. Having firstly responded to UNSCR 1929 by refusing to resume negotiations, in order to teach the P5+1 'the protocol of talking to other nations', it was late October before a letter was sent from the Iranian Supreme National Security Council to Catherine Ashton, the High Representative of the EU for Foreign Affairs, expressing Iran's willingness to engage in a new round of negotiations. The letter made clear, however, that the talks must not focus exclusively on nuclear issues.[79] The P5+1, for their part, were not interested in anything except the nuclear question, advancing, as a precursor to talks, a modified version of the swap proposal in which the amount of LEU Iran was required to export was increased to 1,995 kg.[80]

Unsurprisingly, when negotiators from both sides met in Geneva in December, the talks were wholly unproductive. The Obama administration was insistent that the nuclear issue had to be dealt with first, while the Iranians proposed the establishment of a series of working groups to discuss all of the issues dividing the two sides. A further round of talks in Istanbul in January 2011 saw more of the same. The P5+1 presented the Iranian delegation with a list of steps Iran needed to take to establish international confidence in the peaceful nature of its nuclear programme, including a further version of the fuel swap proposal. The Iranians, however, refused to consider the proposal and insisted that recognition of Iran's right to enrich and a lifting of sanctions were a precondition to talks.[81]

By 2011, therefore, the gap between the two sides seemed to be as wide and entrenched as it had ever been. Nevertheless, in developments that went largely unnoticed at the time, there were indications of significant changes on both sides. In December 2010 Hillary Clinton, in an unusually unambiguous statement, acknowledged that Iran would be allowed to have enrichment on its own soil at some point in the future, providing that it had 'restored the confidence of the international community'. She reiterated this position in testimony to the House Foreign Affairs Committee in March 2011. Whilst this was simply a confirmation of the position the Bush administration had established in 2006, it was a much more explicit acknowledgement than had hitherto been made by the Obama administration that Iran would be allowed to enrich at some point in the future.[82] While the administration was still insisting on an indefinite suspension of enrichment that Iran would not accept, this was, nevertheless, an indication of flexibility in the American position.

On the Iranian side, meanwhile, 2011 saw further signs of domestic instability. While the 'Arab Spring' did not extend to Iran, its events only served further to highlight the widespread demand for democratisation and the regime's legitimacy problem. The administration's recognition of this fact was emphasised by the redoubling of its clampdown on communications.[83] Whilst Iranian hardliners continued to successfully repress the opposition, however, they were falling out amongst themselves. More specifically, there was an increasingly serious power struggle, which had been developing since the 2009 election, as Ahmadinejad sought to strengthen his own position at the expense of Khamenei and the wider clerical establishment. The first public indication of this came when Ahmadinejad sought to appoint a relative by marriage, Esfandiar Mashaie, as a vice-president. When Khamenei demanded that Mashaie be removed from the post Ahmadinejad complied, only to appoint him as his chief of staff.

That episode was followed by a sustained attempt by Ahmadinejad to gain more control over foreign policy, culminating in his removal of Foreign Minister Manouchehr Mottaki in December 2010. Khamenei did nothing in that instance, but when Ahmadinejad sought to remove Intelligence Minister Heydar Moslehi in March 2011, the Supreme Leader publicly reinstated him.[84] Ahmadinejad refused to acknowledge this until Larijani engineered a vote in the Majlis referring the president to the judiciary for going beyond his constitutional authority. Larijani subsequently used his position as Speaker to have Ahmadinejad called before the Majlis for formal questioning. In retaliation, Ahmadinejad had corruption charges filed against one of Larijani's brothers and accused another of bribery. Despite demands from Khamenei that these public displays cease, they continued until Ahmadinejad left the presidency.[85] These divisions amongst conservatives would play a significant role in the 2013 presidential election.

While negotiations continued to be stalemated, the Iranian nuclear programme continued to progress, despite US–Israeli sabotage. By the end of November 2010, according to the IAEA, Iran had produced 33 kg of 20 per cent enriched uranium. The following month Iran announced that it had successfully produced yellowcake and had consequently mastered all the stages of the fuel cycle. In April 2011 the Atomic Energy Organization of Iran announced the successful testing of second and third generation centrifuges. IAEA experts estimated that, if functioning correctly, these could produce LEU at up to six times the rate of Iran's existing centrifuges.[86] Meanwhile, the IAEA continued to document Iran's non-compliance with the various UNSCRs and with the agency itself, as well as expressing increasing concerns about possible military dimensions of its programme. In successive reports the agency noted that it had received new evidence of possible military dimensions to Iran's programme, and in its November 2011 report stated for the first time that it had concluded that the evidence of weapons experiments was 'credible' and that 'some activities may still be ongoing'.[87] All of this evidence necessarily increased concerns about Iran approaching 'breakout capacity' (being in a position to build and deploy a nuclear weapon within a given period of time).

In February 2012, after a year's hiatus, Saeed Jalili sent a letter to Catherine Ashton informing her of Iran's readiness to resume negotiations without preconditions.[88] This led to three sets of talks, held in April, May and June in Istanbul, Baghdad and Moscow respectively. In Istanbul the two sides agreed that the best way forward was to pursue a 'staged' approach based on reciprocal actions at each stage of the process. Further progress proved to be impossible, however, with the two sides submitting incompatible versions of the steps that needed to be taken. The Iranians proposed a five-stage programme in which the P5+1 would recognise Iran's right to enrich at stage one and lift all sanctions at stage two in return for Iran committing itself to the Treaty on the Non-Proliferation of Nuclear Weapons (NPT) and cooperating with the IAEA. Only at stage three would Iran halt enrichment to 20 per cent. The P5+1, in contrast, required Iran to halt enrichment to 20 per cent, ship all its existing 20 per cent uranium out of the country and close the plant at Fordow. In return Iran would receive fuel for the TRR, medical isotopes and an LWR in which it could produce further isotopes. Sanctions relief was not on the table. Most of the P5+1 had wanted to take a more flexible approach to the negotiations but the Obama administration insisted on the position taken.[89]

With the P5+1 process deadlocked, Obama sought to open an alternative channel of communication. Since early in his presidency the government of Oman had been offering to act as a go-between and in late 2011 Obama decided to see whether they could actually deliver. After sending Senator John Kerry to sound out the Omanis, Obama agreed to let them approach the Iranians. After several attempts this led to Khamenei authorising secret bilateral talks on the nuclear issue. A US delegation, led by Puneet Talwar of the NSC staff and Clinton's Deputy Chief of Staff Jake Sullivan, subsequently met an Iranian delegation led by Deputy Foreign Minister Ali Asgar Khaji in Oman on 7 July 2012. The talks did not, however, go any better than those being conducted by the P5+1. The Iranians continued to demand acceptance of Iran's right to enrich as a precondition and showed no interest in considering constraints on their programme as a *quid pro quo*. Sullivan's conclusion was that 'it didn't seem the Iranians were all that serious' about negotiating.[90]

Despite small hints of change, therefore, by the end of 2012 the outlook continued to appear bleak. The Iranians showed no sign of compromising on their demand to be allowed to continue enriching and had become, if anything, even more inflexible in negotiations while accelerating the nuclear programme. Obama, for his part, was hoping for sanctions to alter Tehran's calculations and was not about to make any significant concessions in a year in which he was running for re-election.

The Effect of Sanctions

By the end of 2012 sanctions were certainly beginning to have an impact. Since 2010 the US and the EU had imposed further sanctions on Iran, for the most part extending the reach of existing provisions designed to deny Iran access to credit and investment. Through a series of executive orders and new pieces of legislation, the United States black-listed further Iranian entities including the Bank of Industry and Mines, the Bank of Iran and a range of institutions and companies associated with the Iranian nuclear programme. Secondary sanctions targeting foreign banks and companies which did business with these entities and with the Iranian energy, shipping and shipbuilding sectors were tightened by a number of further executive orders as well as the Iran Threat Reduction and Syria Human Rights Act of 2012, Section 1245 of the National Defense Authorization Act for Fiscal Year (FY) 2012 and Section D of the National Defense Authorization Act for FY2013.[91] The Obama administration also sought to put pressure on the main (non-Russian/Chinese) consumers of Iranian oil – Japan, South Korea and India – by establishing a range of punishments for companies continuing to buy, including a ban on receiving US Export-Import Bank credits or US export licences and loans of over $10 million from US banks.[92]

The new European sanctions were, if anything, more significant than those imposed by the US. In January 2012 Brussels announced a complete ban on oil and gas imports from Iran from 1 July, as well as freezing the assets of Iran's Central Bank and those of eight other entities. Then, in March, the Belgian-based Society for Worldwide Interbank Financial Transactions (SWIFT) announced that it would bar Iranian banks from its network with immediate effect. In so doing it made it virtually impossible for Iran to transfer funds either into or out of the country through normal channels, effectively isolating the Iranian financial system from the rest of the world.[93]

By 2012 the various sanctions imposed over the previous two years were having a demonstrable effect on the Iranian economy. Oil exports, the source of the vast majority of Iran's export revenue, fell from an average of 2.2 million barrels per day (bpd) in 2011 to 930,000 bpd in July 2012. The SWIFT ban, moreover, meant that three-quarters of Iran's foreign reserves were not available to offset the fall in revenue because they were in foreign accounts the Iranian government could not access.[94] The various secondary sanctions imposed by the USA were also effective in deterring companies from doing business with Iran. Munich Re and Allianz announced they would stop insuring cargo shipped to and from Iran while Vitol, Trafigura, Total, BP and Shell all stopped supplying refined petroleum products.[95] This increasing isolation of its economy showed up clearly in Iran's economic data. The currency crashed, with the rial losing some 80 per cent of its value between the end of 2011 and October 2012.[96] Inflation, in turn, accelerated, with Iran having the highest official inflation rate in the world in early 2013, at 40 per cent. Unofficial estimates suggested the real inflation rate was somewhere between 50 and 70 per cent.[97] Iran's economy also went into recession, with GDP shrinking by 6.6 per cent in 2012–13 and by a further 2 per cent in 2013–14.[98] Unemployment rose to approximately 20 per cent by 2014 while many others went unpaid for long periods or were only partially paid.[99]

Obama's Second-Term Calculations

While the sanctions were damaging the Iranian economy, however, they had had no decisive impact on the Iranian negotiating position, or on the progress of the Iranian nuclear programme, by the end of Obama's first term in office. The November 2012 IAEA report on the Iranian nuclear programme could have been a photocopy of any from the last four years bar a change in the numbers. Iran had increased production of 20 per cent enriched uranium and had added new centrifuges at Fordow and Natanz, as well as continuing to work on the HWR at Arak. It also continued to fail to cooperate with IAEA investigations of possible military programmes.[100]

That same month Obama narrowly won re-election to the presidency, freeing him from the need to worry about his future electoral prospects. A clear indication of what this presaged was provided by his appointment of Senator Kerry to replace Hillary Clinton as Secretary of State. As far back as 2009, Kerry had been quite open about what he saw as the failings of the US negotiating position. The insistence that Iran be denied the right to enrich was, according to him, ridiculous, on its face, because Iran is a signatory to the Non-Proliferation Treaty. . . . They have a right to peaceful nuclear power and to enrichment in that purpose. But they don't have a right, obviously, to be outside of the other restraints of the IAEA and of the non-proliferation agreement.[101]

Obama's appointment of Kerry was a clear indication that he was now moving toward acceptance of Iran's right to enrich, providing only that he could secure the concessions from Iran necessary to guarantee the peaceful nature of its programme.

As was noted at the start of this chapter, many in the Obama administration had always felt that acceptance of Iran's right to enrich would have to be part of any final agreement. By the start of Obama's second term, however, the need to act on that recognition was becoming compelling. Extensive, effective sanctions had been put in place but Tehran remained unmoved. Nor was it coming under significant pressure to change its position from its own population. Despite their suffering, Iranians continued to back the demand that Iran be allowed to enrich and to oppose the surrender of that right in return for sanctions relief.[102] It was thus becoming irrefutably clear that, as Obama put it,

even the so-called moderates or reformers inside of Iran would not be able to simply say, we will cave and do exactly what the US and Israelis say. They are going to have to have a path in which they feel that there is a dignified resolution to this issue. That's a political requirement of theirs, and that, I suspect, runs across the political spectrum.[103]

There was also a growing concern within the administration that, rather than increasing pressure on Iran, the sanctions regime might have reached peak effectiveness. By early 2013 there was already evidence that international support for them was weakening. Iranian oil exports were increasing again and support for sanctions would only further decline as the costs grew without any discernible impact on Iranian behaviour.[104]

Given that reality, the Obama administration found itself running out of options. Obama would later outline the choices when defending his decision to accept Iran's right to enrich: 'the choice we face is ultimately between diplomacy or some form of war – maybe not tomorrow, maybe not three months from now, but soon'.[105] It might, of course, be argued that that was a convenient way for a man trying to sell an unpopular agreement to frame the options, but it was also true. Going down the route of tougher sanctions may, as the administration believed, have been necessary to demonstrate to the American public that there was no choice but to cut a deal, but it only achieved that end by deliberately limiting the options available and making the choice as stark as possible. Once Obama had gone down the road of escalating the coercive effort without success, the only further step left, apart from compromise, was the military option. As Obama's Coordinator for Arms Control Gary Samore put it,

> if we continued to intensify the sanctions, at some point they [the Iranians] would have said, 'Now we need to start producing 60 percent [HEU]. Now we need to produce 90 percent' . . . At some point that would have ended in war. . . . That was certainly Obama's view.[106]

While Obama was never likely to have taken that option, there was genuine concern in the administration that the Israelis might. According to Dennis Ross, the possibility of an Israeli attack on Iran 'was taken very seriously, starting in 2010 but especially in the summer of 2012'.[107] In February of that year Defense Secretary Leon Panetta publicly expressed his fears that Israel might launch a strike at some point in the next few months. As if to confirm this, the following month Netanyahu told the AIPAC conference that 'we've waited for diplomacy to work. We've waited for sanctions to work. None of us can afford to wait much longer.'[108] The administration was concerned enough by such rhetoric to alter its defence posture in the Persian Gulf, sending a second carrier task force to the region.[109] Nor were the administration's fears unjustified. Subsequent leaks from inside the Israeli government demonstrated that discussions about attacking Iran were conducted at a cabinet level, and that an Israeli attack on Iran was only deterred by the opposition of key figures within the Israeli security establishment.[110] The more time that passed without a resolution that imposed constraints on the Iranian programme, the greater the risk of Israeli action became.

Were Israel to attack, the outcome was potentially disastrous. In the first place, however well planned and executed, it would almost certainly fail to destroy all elements of the Iranian programme. Nor would it destroy the knowledge and scientific capability to restart the programme. At best, therefore, the use of force would slow the Iranians down.[111] Moreover, it was an all-or-nothing choice. No Iranian government of whatever stripe would be prepared (or able) to negotiate in the aftermath of such an attack, and the pressure to develop nuclear weapons would become almost irresistible. Attacking Iran 'would guarantee that which we are trying to prevent – an Iran that will spare nothing to build a nuclear weapon'.[112] Meanwhile, the international consensus supporting the effort to prevent Iran from getting nuclear weapons would collapse, as states withdrew their support in protest. The USA would thus end up with a situation in which repeated military strikes were the only option left to it to try and control the Iranian nuclear programme.[113]

Military action would thus fail to achieve its objective whilst simultaneously leading to a range of other dangerous outcomes. The most predictable of these would be Iranian retaliation, most likely through its non-conventional proxies in Lebanon, Iraq and Afghanistan. The inevitable backlash against the United States (which would be held responsible for Israeli actions) amongst Muslims and Arabs would also have undercut all of Obama's efforts to repair the image of the United States amongst those audiences, while fuelling the propaganda of violent Islamists.[114] American policy throughout the wider Middle East would have been comprehensively undermined. On top of that, at a time when the world economy had still not recovered from the impact of the 2008 financial crisis, the impact on the global economy of further violence in the Middle East, while unpredictable, was unlikely to be anything but harmful.[115] In sum, if Obama did not compromise on enrichment, there would be no negotiated agreement, in which case Iran's nuclear programme would continue and pressure to take military action would increase. If the Obama administration refused to use force, then Israel was likely to act unilaterally. In either event, the consequences were highly unpredictable and potentially disastrous. Obama thus chose to accept Iranian enrichment because it was, in his mind, the only way to head off a much worse outcome.

In March 2013 another secret bilateral meeting was held in Oman. This time the US delegation was led by Under Secretary of State William Burns. During the course of the negotiations he indicated that the Obama administration was now prepared to consider the possibility of Iran continuing to enrich on its own soil, subject to it accepting constraints on its nuclear programme.[116] This was a momentous change that would, eventually, bring about a dramatic breakthrough, but its immediate effect was much less dramatic. The Iranians demanded that the offer be put in writing, and when the Americans refused no further progress was made. A further round of talks scheduled for May was subsequently cancelled as it became clear, according to one of the US officials involved, that 'real progress wasn't going to be possible' before the Iranian presidential election.[117]

The Iranian Presidential Election and the Joint Plan of Action

It thus transpired that it needed an Iranian presidential election, as well as an American one, before the diplomatic logjam would finally be broken, not that that was what most outside observers expected to happen. The general consensus, given the events of 2009, was that the election of another hard-line conservative would be engineered, a perception only reinforced when the Guardian Council barred Rafsanjani from standing. The election campaign certainly looked very much like its predecessor, with the opponents of the hardliners, in this case primarily Hassan Rouhani, again making the economy, Ahmadinejad's foreign policy and the connection between the two a key focus of their attacks. Rouhani's most memorable, and much-reported, assertion was that 'it is good for centrifuges to operate, but it is also important that the country operates as well and the wheels of industry are turning'.[118]

Whilst the campaign was a repeat of 2009, however, the result was not. Rouhani won 50.7 per cent of the first-round vote and was elected without the need for a run-off.[119] His victory can be explained by a number of factors, the first of which was his success in persuading enough moderate and reformist Iranians to actually vote after their experience in 2009. He certainly worked hard to cultivate the moderate/reformist vote and was aided by the lack of any alternative candidate from that side of the political spectrum, once Khatami's former Vice-President, Mohammad Reza Aref, withdrew. He also received the endorsement of Aref and of Khatami himself. Given the state of the Iranian economy, his willingness to compromise on the nuclear issue in return for sanctions relief could also hardly fail to resonate with the Iranian populace, clear majorities of which supported that position.[120] Whatever the reason, large numbers of reformist and moderate Iranians did vote, as was shown by a turnout of just over 70 per cent.[121] A further important factor in Rouhani's success was that his political opponents were still internally divided. The infighting amongst Iran's hard-line conservatives continued into the election campaign and was clearly evidenced by the creation of new conservative parties and the proliferation of hard-line candidates for the presidency. As a result, in the first round Rouhani faced five conservative opponents who split the hard-line vote between them.[122] A final factor ensuring that Rouhani won was that Khamenei and his allies in the regime chose not to try and steal the election on this occasion, a fact that will be considered in more detail below.

Once in power Rouhani was quite clear about what his priorities were going to be: 'your government ... will follow up national goals ... in the path of saving the country's economy, revive ethics and constructive interaction with the world through moderation'.[123] He further emphasised that 'we have to enhance mutual trust between Iran and other countries' and that this would require showing 'greater transparency'.[124] A greatly encouraged Obama wrote to Rouhani reiterating the offer that Burns had made in Oman in March.[125] Rouhani seized on the offer and the secret negotiations in Oman resumed with renewed vigour, with seven more meetings between August and November 2013.[126] In a speech to the UN General Assembly on 24 September, Rouhani reiterated the need for 'acceptance of and respect for the implementation of the right to enrichment inside Iran and enjoyment of other related nuclear rights', but he also expressed a desire, in measured tones, to achieve a mutually satisfactory solution and to 'engage immediately in time-bound and result-oriented talks to build mutual confidence and removal of [sic] mutual uncertainties with full transparency'.[127] Even more significantly, a week before Rouhani's address, Khamenei made a speech in which he implicitly endorsed a compromise with the West by emphasising his belief in the concept of 'heroic flexibility', albeit while also emphasising that such flexibility was to be engaged in for 'technical reasons' and without ever forgetting 'who [the] opponent is and what he is doing'.[128]

The P5+1 talks resumed in Geneva in mid-October and on 24 November 2013 the two sides announced that they had reached an interim agreement – the Joint Plan of Action (JPA). Under the terms of this agreement Iran pledged to eliminate its stockpile of 20 per cent enriched uranium by either diluting it or converting it to uranium oxide. It would also stop operating 50 per cent of the centrifuges at Natanz and three-quarters of those at Fordow while not building any more enrichment or reprocessing facilities nor adding any more LEU to its stock. Most activities at Arak would also be halted. The IAEA was to be allowed unfettered access to all facilities and the regime was to cooperate with its inquiries into the 'military dimensions' of its programme. In return no new sanctions would be imposed on Iran, which would also receive sanctions relief worth approximately $7 billion. Under the terms of any final deal, Iran would 'fully enjoy its right to nuclear energy for peaceful purposes under the relevant articles of the NPT'.[129] Several further meetings followed in December, and on 12 January 2014 it was announced that implementation of the JPA would begin on 20 January.

Iranian Calculations

Explaining how the USA came to make the concessions necessary to reach an agreement required us to explain why the president changed his mind and decided that he had to forego the demand that Iran halt enrichment. In the case of Iran the president did not change his mind. The JPA (and the final deal to which it would lead) was the kind of compromise Rouhani had been arguing for for a decade. What requires explaining in the Iranian case, therefore, is why Rouhani was finally able to secure the domestic backing to make that compromise.

The first factor, clearly, was Obama's decision to accept continued enrichment in Iran. By putting that concession on the table the Americans changed the dynamic of the negotiations. The right to enrich had been the one consistent demand that Iranians of all political persuasions were agreed on.[130] No Iranian leader, whether reformist or conservative hardliner, could take home an agreement that gave up the right to enrich. By conceding that right, therefore, Obama made an agreement possible.

However, while the JCPOA would allow Iran to continue enriching, it also contained significant restrictions on the Iranian nuclear programme, and ones that many Iranian hardliners opposed. General Ali Jafari of the IRGC accused the negotiators of betraying the IRI and of being 'infected by Western doctrine', while media outlets associated with the IRGC kept up a steady stream of criticism of the Rouhani government's conduct of the negotiations. Hard-line deputies in the Majlis were similarly critical, and the constraints that were ultimately accepted also went comfortably beyond anything that Khamenei had previously indicated he was willing to accept.[131] In order to explain why Rouhani was nevertheless able to secure domestic acceptance of the terms of the JCPOA, two key variables need to be taken into account, namely sanctions and Iranian domestic politics.

For some observers sanctions were clearly the key factor in explaining the change in the Iranian negotiating position and compelling Tehran's acceptance of major constraints on its nuclear programme.[132] However, whilst there is no question that the sanctions did have a serious impact on the Iranian economy, establishing their relationship to Iranian acceptance of the terms of the JPA is a much more complicated problem. Indeed, it is always difficult to establish the impact of sanctions – their interdependence with other variables and the impossibility of controlling for those other variables means that their effects are necessarily over-determined. In this particular case the most confounding of those other variables is the Obama administration's concession on enrichment. Had that change in policy not occurred, and had Iran accepted a deal that did not include the right to enrich, the argument that sanctions had forced Iran into compliance with the demands of the international community would be compelling. Acceptance of Iran's right to enrich, however, meant that the international community had conceded Iran's principal demand, making the JPA much less of an Iranian surrender.

Moreover, had the change in American policy not occurred, it seems likely that sanctions would not have been enough to compel Iran to accept the constraints it eventually did – that was certainly the conclusion that the Obama administration reached. Whilst such a claim is necessarily counter-factual and unprovable, Iran's absolute refusal to compromise on enrichment at any stage between 2003 and 2015, even in their 2003 'Grand Bargain' offer, when they feared that the Bush administration was targeting them for military attack, strongly supports it. Certainly, there is little evidence that sanctions caused any fundamental change of mind amongst the Iranian elite. Whilst there was evidence of concern about their effects, even amongst conservatives, most Iranian hardliners remained unmoved and opposed to the concessions made in the JCPOA.[133] Reformists and pragmatic conservatives, for their part, had been arguing for a compromise in which the right to enrich was traded for guarantees that the Iranian nuclear programme was peaceful since well before the sanctions had begun to bite.

However, while sanctions may not have changed many minds, and would not have forced Iran into compliance on their own, it does not follow that they were insignificant. Where they may have had an important role was in their contribution to the changing balance of power inside Iran. The critical development leading to the acceptance of the JPA by Iran was the decline in the power of the Iranian hardliners. The 2012 Majlis elections had seen the heavy defeat of Ahmadinejad's faction and a majority of the vote shared between factions led by Larijani and Mohsen Rezaei, both of whom, whilst conservatives, had previously indicated their support for a compromise on the nuclear issue.[134] When this was followed by Rouhani's victory in 2013, the hardliners, having effectively controlled all the main institutions of government from 2005 to 2012, found their power greatly attenuated.[135]

Given that one of the most important factors in the declining popularity of the Ahmadinejad government was economics, there is an argument to be made that sanctions contributed to the resolution of the nuclear conflict by influencing the change in the Iranian factional balance of power. Whilst it is impossible to determine with absolute confidence why Iranians voted the way that they did in 2012 and 2013, Rouhani's campaign was conducted almost entirely on the issue of the economy and the need to restore it. Moreover, as we have seen, polls made clear that most Iranians supported concessions on the nuclear issue in order to secure the lifting of sanctions. To the extent that sanctions contributed to Rouhani's election and declining support for Iran's hardliners, they also contributed to the resolution of the conflict.[136]

There would have been a similar shift in the factional balance of power in 2009, had the election not been stolen. Given the narrowness of Rouhani's winning margin in the first round in 2013, it would have been relatively easy to manipulate the results to ensure that there was a run-off against a single hard-line candidate who went on to win, had Khamenei chosen to support such a plan. He did not do so, however, and despite considerable hedging and prevarication, he also lent his support to the nuclear negotiations that followed Rouhani's election and to the JPA. That support, therefore, and the reasons for it, is the final factor underpinning Iran's signing of the deal.[137]

Doubtless, Khamenei's support for the JPA, as with that of most other Iranians, was shaped by the acknowledgement of Iran's right to enrich. Nevertheless, the deal contained constraints he would hardly have accepted had he not felt compelled to do so. The impact of sanctions may have been part of that compulsion, but another key factor was the regime's, and his own, ongoing legitimacy problem. Four years after the 2009 presidential election and the crisis that succeeded it, regime legitimacy had not evidently recovered. The opposition had certainly been successfully repressed, but there was no evidence that reformist voters had reconciled themselves to what had happened in 2009, or to the regime itself. Reformist refusal to engage with the 2012 election had been a clear indication of the ongoing problem.[138] A second stolen election would have been potentially disastrous for regime legitimacy. Once Rouhani had managed to mobilise reformist voters, refusal to acknowledge their votes would have confirmed in the minds of many the fact that the regime was beyond redemption. The 2013 presidential election was thus an opportunity for Khamenei to restore some degree of legitimacy by allowing democracy to take its course and redistribute power away from the hard-line conservative factions.[139] Having made that decision for those reasons, Khamenei then had little choice but to support Rouhani in his negotiation of the JPA. Had he opposed the compromise Rouhani pursued, he would have undone everything achieved in accepting Rouhani's election victory.

US Ratification

Whilst a major breakthrough in its own right, the JPA was only a confidence-building measure designed to facilitate trust and the creation of a space in which to negotiate a final deal. That deal was supposed to be reached within six months of the JPA being implemented. In the event, however, the negotiations would take eighteen months and multiple rounds of negotiations, starting in Vienna in February 2014 and concluding in that city on 14 July 2015.[140] Nevertheless, agreement was finally reached. Under the terms of the JCPOA Iran would be allowed to continue enrichment but would have to cut the number of operating centrifuges to 5,060 for ten years. No enrichment would be permitted at Fordow for fifteen years, and Iran would not be allowed to enrich uranium to more than 3.67 per cent or to have a stockpile of more than 300 kg of LEU for the same period. The HWR at Arak would be reconfigured so that it was unable to produce weapons grade plutonium, and Iran would sign the AP and allow the IAEA unfettered access to all of its nuclear infrastructure. In the face of any Iranian non-compliance a simple majority vote in the newly established Joint Commission (composed of the members of the P5+1 and Iran) could require it to conform. Failure to do so would lead to the automatic reimposition of sanctions. As that point implies, in addition to acknowledgement of Iran's right to enrich, the JCPOA also mandated the lifting of all UNSCR, US and EU sanctions directly related to the nuclear issue. Sanctions related to missile technologies would remain in place for eight years and the ban on conventional weapons sales for five years. Unilateral American sanctions imposed on the grounds of human rights violations, terrorism and missile development were not affected by the agreement.[141]

The JCPOA was welcomed by the vast majority of Iranians.[142] Its reception in the USA, however, was much more ambivalent. Whilst Obama and his advisers had reached the conclusion that conceding the right to enrich was necessary to avoid a much worse outcome, that was not the view of most Republicans, of AIPAC, or of Israel. The final step in resolving the conflict over the Iranian nuclear programme would therefore be securing ratification of the JCPOA in the United States.

Lobbying against the JCPOA was led by AIPAC and its domestic allies, who formed 'Citizens for a Nuclear Free Iran' to campaign against it and raised some $30 million to fund their efforts. The headline on AIPAC's home-page on 7 August 2015 was 'Urge Congress to oppose the bad deal with Iran'. This was accompanied by a series of fact sheets, a video attacking the JCPOA, and a button to click to lobby your member of Congress.[143] These efforts were reinforced by those of the Israeli government. Having previously described the JPA as a mistake of 'historic proportions' and called on Jewish Americans to 'do something about it', in March 2015 Netanyahu accepted an invitation from House Speaker John Boehner to give an address to Congress in which he savaged the proposed agreement.[144] He claimed that it 'will not prevent Iran from developing nuclear weapons. It would all but guarantee that Iran gets those weapons, lots of them', and asserted that continued pressure could force Iran to abandon its nuclear programme.[145] When the deal was eventually signed Israel's Deputy Foreign Minister, Tzipi Hotovely, tweeted that Israel would 'act with all means to try and stop the agreement being ratified', and the Israeli ambassador to the United States subsequently seemed to spend most of his waking hours campaigning against the JCPOA.[146] Surveillance of his activities by US intelligence found him directly lobbying members of Congress and asking them, 'how can we get your vote?'[147]

The target of all these efforts was Congress which, since the 2010 mid-term elections, had been controlled by the Republican Party, the vast majority of whose members were deeply opposed to allowing Iran to continue enrichment. From the announcement of the JPA until the signing of the JCPOA, Republican criticism of the Obama administration was unrelenting, and when the latter was signed Boehner, echoing Netanyahu, claimed that it would simply 'embolden' Iran, while Senator Lindsey Graham declared it to be a 'terrible' agreement.[148] But Republican efforts to derail the agreement went beyond mere rhetoric. In March 2015 forty-seven Senators sent an open letter to the Iranian leadership warning them that Congress would have to approve any agreement (and, they implied, would not do so). Under those circumstances, any agreement would be

> nothing more than an executive agreement between President Obama and Ayatollah Khamenei. The next president could revoke such an executive agreement with the stroke of a pen and future Congresses could modify the terms of the agreement at any time.[149]

In order to back up that threat, various members of Congress introduced bills requiring a congressional vote on any agreement and, after initially resisting, the administration decided it had no choice but to accept such a vote given the support for it in Congress. Even some Democrats who supported the nuclear deal felt that Congress had a constitutional right to a say. The Iran Nuclear Agreement Review Act (INARA) of 2015, providing for a congressional vote on the JCPOA, was subsequently passed on 14 May 2015.[150] Unlike a normal treaty ratification, however, the bill required a two-thirds vote to reject the agreement rather than to approve it, a fact which would ultimately ensure the JCPOA's ratification.

Obama worked extremely hard to ensure ratification would succeed. During the review period for the deal he held personal meetings with 125 members of Congress and made phone calls to a further thirty.[151] He was also careful to frame the issue in a way calculated to maximise the pressure on Congress. In a series of comments throughout 2015 Obama repeatedly sought to refute the claim of congressional opponents that rejecting the deal would pave the way for a better deal at some time in the future when Iran cracked under the pressure of sanctions. Rather, he insisted, the choice was between this and war, and if it came to the latter, the American public would know who to blame: 'Congress should be aware that if this diplomatic solution fails, then the risks and likelihood that this ends up being at some point a military confrontation is heightened – and Congress will have to own that as well.'[152]

While Obama's message was effectively crafted, however, the most crucial factor in the ratification of the JCPOA was partisan polarisation. This phenomenon had become a fact of life in US politics by 2015.[153] Typically, it represented a major hindrance to a president facing a Congress controlled by the opposition, but on this occasion it helped Obama. Polls showed that whilst Republican voters were overwhelmingly opposed to the JCPOA, clear majorities of Democrats supported it.[154] Polls also showed that a large majority of American Jews (who typically voted Democrat) supported the agreement.[155] Furthermore, there was clear evidence that the typical Democrat voter had become increasingly disenchanted with Israel – or at least the Israeli right – and was consequently far less susceptible the kind of lobbying being conducted in 2015.[156] Most Democrats in Congress thus had little reason to fear that voting against the Israeli government's preferences would hurt them electorally.

If Democrats were thus predisposed not to align with the Republicans and Israel over the JCPOA, the manner in which the latter went about opposing the agreement unquestionably cemented their opposition. Boehner's unilateral invitation to Netanyahu to address Congress and the open letter from Republican Senators to the leadership of the IRI were viewed by most Democrats as nakedly partisan actions. In an unprecedented response to the former, fifty-eight Democratic members of Congress boycotted Netanyahu's speech, which House Minority Leader Nancy Pelosi described as an 'insult to the intelligence of the United States'.[157] Netanyahu's attempts to derail the agreement and his close cooperation with the Republicans thus undermined his efforts. According to Senator Dick Durbin, 'it really caused many Democrats to step back and question the message he delivered about the threat of Iran'.[158]

If any further reason was required for Democrats to vote to ratify the JCPOA, it was provided by the members of the P5+1. On so many occasions over the previous forty years the inability of Washington to gain multilateral support for its policies toward Iran had been their undoing. On this occasion, in contrast, the unanimous support of the rest of the P5+1 was crucial. The Republican leadership, the Israeli government and AIPAC all asserted that the concession on enrichment was unnecessary and that Obama's claim that the only alternative was war was untrue. Rather, they asserted, a further tightening of sanctions could be used to force Iran to abandon enrichment. Obama, however, was able decisively to refute that assertion and he did so. The ambassadors of the rest of the P5+1 nations to the United States were invited to a meeting with Senate Democrats in which they all, as one, stated that if the JCPOA was rejected by Congress they would go ahead with it independently and there would be no new sanctions.[159] A similar meeting was held with House Democrats and the effect of the meeting was described by House Minority Leader Nancy Pelosi as 'stunning'.[160]

In the end, therefore, partisan polarisation and the inept tactics of the opponents of the JCPOA doomed their efforts to kill it to failure. The very fact that they required a two-thirds majority vote to defeat it (rather than Obama requiring a two-thirds vote to approve it) was itself a product of partisanship. The Republicans simply could not garner the necessary Democrat votes for the latter option.[161] That inability to win over sufficient Democrat votes to create veto-proof two-thirds majorities in support of rejection of the JCPOA persisted throughout the period allocated to Congress to review the deal and vote on it. The Republicans had 247 seats in the House and fifty-four in the Senate, meaning that even if every Republican voted to disapprove of the JCPOA, they still required forty-four House Democratic votes, and thirteen in the Senate, to secure two-thirds majorities. They received only twenty-five and four respectively. Indeed, not only did they not have veto-proof majorities, but in the Senate they did not even have enough votes to force the legislation to the floor for a vote, meaning Obama would not even be forced into the symbolic defeat of having to use his veto to ensure ratification.[162]

Notes

1. 'Obama's speech in Sderot, Israel', *The New York Times*, 23 July 2008, available at <http://www.nytimes.com/2008/07/23/us/politics/23text-obama.html> (last accessed 10 May 2016).
2. Ibid.
3. Ibid.
4. 'The first presidential debate', Oxford, Mississippi, 26 September 2008, *The New York Times*, 23 May 2012, <http://elections.nytimes.com/2008/president/debates/transcripts/first-presidential-debate.html> (last accessed 10 October 2015).
5. Parsi, *Single Roll of the Dice*, p. 59. The administration's position was made explicit by State Department spokesman Robert Wood, who said that the administration's position was that 'Iran does not need to develop . . . an indigenous uranium enrichment capacity'; 'Department of State daily press briefing', 25 February 2009, available at <https://2009-2017.state.gov/r/pa/prs/dpb/2009/02/119782.htm> (last accessed 3 August 2017). Secretary of State Hillary Clinton was even more explicit, saying that Iran did 'not have the right to have the full enrichment and reprocessing cycle'; David E. Sanger, 'Clinton says nuclear aim of Iran is fruitless', *The New York Times*, 26 July 2009.
6. Barack Obama, 'Videotaped remarks by the President in celebration of Nowruz', The White House, Office of the Press Secretary, 20 March 2009, US President, *Public Papers of the Presidents of the United States* (*PPPUS*).
7. 'Department of State daily press briefing', 8 April 2009, available at <https://2009-2017.state.gov/r/pa/prs/dpb/2009/04/121499.htm> (last accessed 3 August 2017); Crail, 'World powers invite Iran to nuclear talks'.
8. 'Obama envisions new Iran approach', *The New York Times*, 2 November 2007, available at <http://www.nytimes.com/2007/11/02/us/politics/02obama.html?_r=0> (last accessed 6 October 2015).
9. 'Clinton doubts Iran will respond to overtures', *Reuters*, 2 March 2009; Nicholas Kralev, '"Crippling sanctions" for Iran an option; talks preferable, Clinton says', *The Washington Times*, 23 April 2009.
10. Bob Dreyfuss, 'Dennis Ross's Iran plan: Is Obama's dialogue with Iran already doomed?', *The Nation*, 8 April 2009, available at <https://www.thenation.com/article/dennis-rosss-iran-plan/> (last accessed 12 December 2017).

11. 'Obama renews US sanctions on Iran', *BBC News*, 13 March 2009, available at <http://news.bbc.co.uk/1/hi/7941031.stm> (last accessed 4 April 2015); US Mission to the EU, Brussels, 'Iran sanctions: AA/S Glaser briefs EU on priority targets', 8 April 2009, available at <http://cables.mrkva.eu/cable.php?id=201397> (last accessed 3 August 2017).

12. Khamenei, 'OSC Khamenei's speech replying to Obama'.

13. WorldPublicOpinion.org, 'Iranian public on current issues'.

14. Crist, *Twilight War*, p. 544.

15. Barbara Slavin, 'U.S. contacted Iran's ayatollah before election', *The Washington Times*, 24 June 2009.

16. 'Obama's speech in Sderot, Israel'; 'Remarks by the President at Cairo University', 4 June 2009, *PPPUS*; Saltzman, 'Not so "special relationship"?'.

17. 'US embassy cables: Ehud Barak sets deadline to resolve Iran nuclear ambition, 1 June 2009', *The Guardian*, 28 December 2010, available at <http://www.theguardian.com/world/us-embassy-cables-documents/209599> (last accessed 6 May 2015); 'Iran talks should last twelve weeks max', *The Jerusalem Post*, 18 December 2008; 'Israel calls for time limit on Iran talks', *United Press International*, 7 May 2009, available at <http://www.upi.com/Top_News/2009/05/07/Israel-calls-for-time-limit-on-Iran-talks/UPI-11331241695592/> (last accessed 24 September 2015).

18. Steve Linde, 'U.S. to Israel: Tone down rhetoric on Iran', *The Jerusalem Post*, 17 May 2009; Anne Gearan, 'Mullen: Strike on Iran an option, but a bad one', *Associated Press*, 7 July 2009.

19. Jon Ward, 'Obama, Netanyahu at odds over Iran talks: U.S. wants progress on curbing nukes', *The Washington Times*, 19 May 2009; Scott Wilson, 'Emphasis differs for Obama, Netanyahu: For Israel, Iran supersedes peace effort', *The Washington Post*, 19 May 2009; US Embassy Tel Aviv to Department of State, 'Codels Ackerman and Casey meeting with Prime Minister Netanyahu', 2 June 2009, available at <https://archive.org/stream/09TELAVIV1184/09TELAVIV1184_djvu.txt> (last accessed 3 August 2017).

20. 'Mohsen Rezaei: Ahamdinejad ma ra be samte Partgah Mibarad' ['Mohsen Rezaei: Ahmadinejad leading us to a fall'], *Fararu*, 4 May 2009, available at <http://www.fararu.com/fa/news/24284/>, quoted in Rezaei, *Iran's Nuclear Program*, p. 165.

21. Joe Klein and Nihad Siamdoust, 'The man who could beat Ahmadinejad: Mousavi talks to TIME', *Time Magazine*, 12 June 2009; see

also Parisa Hafezi, 'Iran candidate backs nuclear talks with the West', *Reuters*, 29 May 2009.

22. Terror Free Tomorrow, 'Ahmadinejad front runner in upcoming presidential elections'; WorldPublicOpinion.org, 'Two thirds of Iranians ready to preclude developing nuclear weapons'; see also Farhi, 'Ahmadinejad's nuclear folly'. Opinion polls taken in a country without full freedom of speech and democratic rights obviously need to be treated with appropriate scepticism, but responses to questions about the nuclear programme are very consistent across time and different polling organisations.

23. Ansari, *Crisis of Authority*, pp. 48–55; Zaccara, '2009 Iranian presidential election'; Axworthy, *Revolutionary Iran*, pp. 402–4.

24. Khamenei, 'Leader's Friday prayer address'; on the accusations of foreign interference, see, for example, Hossein Shariatmadari, 'Green organization or a red carpet for America?', *Keyhan*, 17 August 2009, *BBC Monitoring*, 18 August 2009.

25. 'Iran's parliament speaker criticizes Guardian Council', *Trend News Agency*, 21 June 2009, available at <http://en.trend.az/iran/1491618. html> (last accessed 4 August 2017); 'Iran leader Rafsanjani rallies opposition', *The Washington Times*, 19 July 2009.

26. Khosrokhavar, 'Green Movement'.

27. 'Montazeri condemns Iranian regime', *Iran Press Watch*, 27 August 2009, available at <http://iranpresswatch.org/post/4932/montazeri-condemns-iranian-regime/> (last accessed 12 December 2017)

28. For more extensive analyses of the impact of the 2009 elections on the regime's legitimacy, see Ansari, *Crisis of Authority*; Jahanbegloo, 'Two sovereignties'; Abulof, 'Nuclear diversion theory'; Ghobazadeh and Zubadaih, 'Islamic reformation discourses'. To some readers the importance of legitimacy for an authoritarian regime might not seem obvious, but it is important to understand that authoritarian regimes do seek to maintain legitimacy, by whatever means, since it is a far less costly and dangerous method of retaining power than simple repression; see Albrecht and Schlumberger, '"Waiting for Godot"', p. 373; Heydemann and Leenders, *Middle East Authoritarianism*; Warnaar, *Iranian Foreign Policy*, pp. 35–40.

29. 'Transcript of the President's answer to Harry Smith's question on Iran', 19 June 2009, *PPPUS*.

30. 'The President's press conference', 23 June 2009, *PPPUS*.

31. David Weigel, 'Neocons, House GOPers demand Obama take Mousavi's side', *The Washington Independent*, 16 June 2009; Scott

Wilson, 'Muted response reflects US diplomatic dilemma', *The Washington Post*, 15 June 2009.

32. Parsi, *Single Roll of the Dice*, p. 108.
33. ElBaradei, *Age of Deception*, pp. 293–4.
34. IAEA, 'Implementation of the NPT safeguards agreement and relevant provisions of Security Council resolutions 1737 (2006), 1747 (2007), 1803 (2008) and 1835 (2008)', GOV/2009/35.
35. Parsi, *Single Roll of the Dice*, p. 116; ElBaradei, *Age of Deception*, p. 309.
36. Parsi, *Single Roll of the Dice*, pp. 118–19; Flynt Leverett and Hillary Mann Leverett, 'Obama's Iran sanctions delusion', *The Race for Iran*, 16 October 2009, available at <http://www.raceforiran.com/obamas-iran-sanctions-delusion> (last accessed 6 June 2015); Mary Beth Sheridan, 'Russia not budging on Iran sanctions', *The Washington Post*, 14 October 2009.
37. IAEA, 'Implementation of the NPT safeguards agreement and relevant provisions of Security Council resolutions 1737 (2006), 1747 (2007), 1803 (2008) and 1835 (2008) in the Islamic Republic of Iran', GOV/2009/74.
38. US President, 'Background briefing'; David Sanger and Helen Cooper, 'Iran is warned over nuclear "deception"', *The New York Times*, 25 September 2009. The Iranians would subsequently argue that the Fordow plant was simply designed to allow them to retain enrichment capacity if Natanz was subject to a military strike.
39. 'Berman calls new nuclear plant news disturbing, says it reinforces his determination to have committee consider sanctions legislation', US House of Representatives, Committee on Foreign Affairs Democrats, 25 September 2009, available at <http://democrats.hcfa.house.gov/press_display.asp?id=653> (last accessed 6 June 2015).
40. US Department of State, 'Background briefing on P5+1 talks in Geneva'.
41. IAEA, 'Transcript of Director General's remarks to media'; ElBaradei, *Age of Deception*, p. 307.
42. ElBaradei, *Age of Deception*, pp. 307–11; Parsi, *Single Roll of the Dice*, pp. 138–48; David Sanger, Steven Erlanger and Robert Worth, 'Iran rejects proposal for enrichment of uranium', *International Herald Tribune*, 31 October 2009; Ali Akbar Dareini, 'Iran brushes aside UN nuclear deal', *Associated Press*, 18 November 2009; Thomas Erdbrink, 'Iran says fuel swap must occur on its soil', *The Washington Post*, 25 November 2009.

43. Jay Solomon, 'Offers, doubts greet Iran talks', *The Wall Street Journal*, 2 December 2010.

44. The evidence is far from indisputable. There is no polling data on Iranian opinions of the agreement, for example, making any analysis of popular Iranian responses to the deal impressionistic, but see Gareth Porter, 'Obama's Iranian discontent', *Agence Global*, 9 December 2009; Kaussler, *Iran's Nuclear Diplomacy*, p. 83.

45. Barzegar, 'Middle way'. Again, this demonstrates the perception gap between the two sides. What was to American hardliners a dangerous concession (Alan J. Kuperman, 'There's only one way to stop Iran', *The New York Times*, 23 December 2009) was to many in Iran a plot to deny them their nuclear 'right'.

46. Crail, 'Iranian response to LEU fuel deal unclear'.

47. Hossein Mousavian argues that the agreement was a step toward acknowledgement of Iran's right to enrich, that it would have strengthened Obama's hand against his own hardliners, and that it would have helped head off further sanctions; Mousavian, *Iranian Nuclear Crisis*, p. 358.

48. Mir Hosein Mousavi statement, 30 October 2009, quoted in Parsi, *Single Roll of the Dice*, p. 148; *E'temad*, 5 November 2009, *BBC Monitoring*, 6 November 2009.

49. 'The big NO of conservatives on Ahmadinejad's table', *Alborz News*, 5 November 2009, available at <http://www.alborznews.net/fa/news/12001/>, quoted in Rezaei, *Iran's Nuclear Program*, p. 170.

50. Michael Slackman, 'Iran's politics stand in the way of a nuclear deal', *The New York Times*, 2 November 2009.

51. 'US embassy cables: US fails to dissuade Turkey from Iran "meddling"', *The Guardian*, 17 November 2010, available at <http://www.theguardian.com/world/us-embassy-cables-documents/235183> (last accessed 7 July 2015); US Embassy Dubai, 'Tehran nuclear fuel deal drawing domestic political fire', 26 October 2009, available at <https://cablegatesearch.wikileaks.org/cable.php?id=09RPODUBAI459> (last accessed 7 May 2015); Solomon, 'Offers, doubts greet Iran talks'.

52. 'Iran: Counter offer pulls in Turkey', *Times Wire Reports*, 26 December 2009; Mark Landler and Alan Cowell, 'Clinton issues another warning to Iran', *The New York Times*, 17 February 2010.

53. US Embassy, Tel Aviv, 'U/S Tauscher's December 1–2 visit to Israel', available at <http://www.telegraph.co.uk/news/wikileaks-files/8314526/US-TAUSCHERS-DECEMBER-1-2-VISIT-TO-ISRAEL.html> (last accessed 7 August 2017).

54. Glen Kessler, 'Clinton "resets" Russian ties – and language', *The Washington Post*, 6 March 2009.

55. David Sanger, 'US makes concessions to Russia for Iran sanctions', *The New York Times*, 21 May 2010.

56. US Embassy, Beijing, 'Under Secretary Burns' December 2009 conversation with Chinese Foreign Minister Yang Jiechi', 11 December 2009, available at <https://wikileaks.org/plusd/cables/09BEIJING3312_a. html> (last accessed 11 August 2017).

57. Steve Holland and Jeff Mason, 'Obama presses Iran, gains nuclear summit pledges', *Reuters*, 13 April 2010; US Embassy, Riyadh, 'Scenesetter for Secretary Clinton's Feb 15–16 visit to Saudi Arabia', 11 February 2010, available at <http://cables.mrkva.eu/ cable.php?id=248348> (last accessed 7 August 2017); Mattis, 'Oil sheik-down'; Elizabeth Bumiller, 'US defense chief visits Saudi Arabia to bolster effort against Iran', *The New York Times*, 11 March 2010.

58. US Embassy, Moscow, 'U/S Burns' Moscow meetings', 22 January 2010, available at <https://archive.org/stream/10MOSCOW144/ 10MOSCOW144_djvu.txt> (last accessed 9 August 2017).

59. Borzou Daragahi, 'Iran to boost enrichment: Ahmedinejad tells atomic agency to process uranium to a higher purity', *The Los Angeles Times*, 8 February 2010.

60. US Mission, IAEA, Vienna, 'Iran ups its nuclear ante to 20 percent', 8 February 2010, available at <http://wikileaks.1wise.es/ cable/2010/02/10UNVIEVIENNA43.html> (last accessed 9 August 2017).

61. IAEA, 'Implementation of the NPT safeguards agreement and relevant provisions of Security Council resolutions 1737 (2006), 1747 (2007), 1803 (2008) and 1835 (2008) in the Islamic Republic of Iran', GOV/2010/10.

62. 'Remarks of President Obama marking Nowruz', 20 March 2010, *PPPUS*.

63. 'Remarks by Vice-President Biden: The enduring partnership between the United States and Israel', 11 March 2010, available at <http://www.whitehouse.gov/the-press-office/remarks-vice-president-biden-enduring-partnership-between-united-states-and-israel> (last accessed 6 May 2014).

64. 'Mullen worried about "unintended consequences" of Iran strike', *Newsmax*, 14 February 2010, available at <http://www.newsmax.com/InsideCover/mullen-iran-nuclear-obama/2010/02/14/ id/349856/> (last accessed 9 August 2017).

65. US Embassy, Tel Aviv, 'Codels Ackerman and Casey meeting'; 'Getting a yes on Iran advocacy day', *Jewish Telegraphic Agency*, 11 September 2009, available at <http://www.jta.org/2009/09/11/news-opinion/politics/getting-a-yes-on-iran-advocacy-day> (last accessed 7 July 2015); AIPAC, 'Back crippling sanctions on Iran', *Talking Points*, March 2010, available at <http://www.politico.com/static/PPM145_new_032010.html> (last accessed 12 October 2014); Thouin, 'Under a cloud of uncertainty'.

66. US Congress, Senate Committee on Banking, 'Minimizing potential threats from Iran', Testimony of James B. Steinberg; Josh Rogin, 'Exclusive: State Department letter to Kerry outlines "serious concerns" with Iran sanctions bill', *Foreign Policy*, 11 December 2009, available at <http://foreignpolicy.com/2009/12/11/exclusive-state-department-letter-to-kerry-outlines-serious-substantive-concerns-with-iran-sanctions-bill/> (last accessed 20 February 2015); Laura Rozen, 'House Iran petroleum sanctions bill passes', *Politico*, 15 December 2009, available at <http://www.politico.com/blogs/laurarozen/1209/House_Iran_sanctions_debate.html?showall> (last accessed 7 July 2015); Laura Rozen, 'Senate passes Iran sanctions bill', *Politico*, 28 January 2010, available at <http://www.politico.com/blogs/laurarozen/0110/Senate_passes_Iran_sanctions_bill.html> (last accessed 7 July 2015).

67. Parsi, *Single Roll of the Dice*, p. 209.

68. 'Nuclear fuel declaration by Iran, Turkey and Brazil', 17 May 2010, *BBC News*, available at <http://news.bbc.co.uk/1/hi/world/middle_east/8686728.stm> (last accessed 10 August 2017).

69. Laura Rozen, 'Obama admin. dismisses leak of letter on Iran fuel deal', *Politico*, 28 May 2010, available at <http://www.politico.com/blogs/laurarozen/0510/Obama_admin_dismisses_leak_of_Obama_letter_on_Iran_fuel_deal.html> (last accessed 10 August 2017).

70. 'Clinton says Russia, China, U.S. back Iran sanctions (update4)', *Businessweek*, 18 May 2010, available at <http://www.business-wekk.com/news/2010-05-18/clinton-says-russia-china-u-s-back-iran-sanctions-update4-.html> (last accessed 20 May 2012).

71. United Nations, UN Security Council Resolution 1929.

72. US Department of the Treasury, *Comprehensive Iran Sanctions, Accountability and Divestment Act of 2010*; Katzman, 'Iran sanctions' (2017), pp. 11, 13, 29.

73. Council of the European Union, 'Council decision of 26 July 2010'; Patterson, 'EU sanctions on Iran'.

74. Parsi, *Losing an Enemy*, p. 121; Jonathan Soble, 'Japanese energy group to quit Iran oilfield', *Financial Times*, 30 September 2010; Katzman, 'Iran sanctions' (2011), p. 32.

75. Thomas Erdbrink and Allen Nakashima, 'Iran struggling to contain "foreign-made" "Stuxnet" computer virus', *The Washington Post*, 27 September 2010; David E. Sanger, 'Obama order sped up wave of cyberattacks against Iran', *The New York Times*, 1 June 2012; Collins and McCombie, 'Stuxnet', p. 88; Ellen Nakashima, Greg Miller and Julie Tate, 'U.S., Israel developed Flame computer virus to slow Iranian nuclear efforts, officials say', *The Washington Post*, 19 June 2012.

76. Yossi Melman, 'The war against Iran's nuclear program has already begun', *Haaretz*, 2 December 2011; Yaakov Katz, 'Mystery surrounds assassination of Iranian nuclear scientist', *The Jerusalem Post*, 13 January 2010; Borzou Daragahi and Ramin Mostaghim, 'Iran physicist killed in blast outside of his home: Officials blame the West, but friends say he was government critic assassinated by hard liners', *Los Angeles Times*, 13 January 2010; 'Mossad hit-squads behind Iran scientists' murders – US official', *RT*, 9 February 2012, available at <http://rt.com/news/iranian-scientists-assassinations-israel-923/> (last accessed 10 August 2017); Julian Borger and Saeed Kamali Dehghan, 'Iranian missile architect dies in blast: But was explosion a Mossad mission?', *The Guardian*, 14 November 2011; Jonathan Marcus '"Blast" deepens mystery of Iran's Parchin military complex', *BBC News*, 9 October 2014, available at <http://www.bbc.co.uk/news/world-middle-east-29550156> (last accessed 20 April 2015).

77. Ethan Bronner, 'Israel says Iran is behind bombs', *The New York Times*, 14 February 2012; Jason Burke, 'Iran plotted to bomb Israeli diplomats', *The Guardian*, 18 June 2012.

78. Parsi, *Losing an Enemy*, p. 118.

79. Thomas Erdbrink, 'Iran's Ahmadinejad faults sanctions, delays nuclear talks until late August', *The Washington Post*, 29 June 2010; 'Iran accepts invitation to nuclear negotiations', *NTI Global Security Newswire*, 29 October 2010, available at <http://www.nti.org/gsn/article/iran-accepts-invitation-to-nuclear-negotiations/> (last accessed 10 August 2017); 'No indication of Iranian nuclear strategy shift, diplomat asserts', *NTI Global Security Newswire*, 3 November 2010, available at <http://www.nti.org/media/pdfs/iran_nuclear.pdf?_=1316542527> (last accessed 10 August 2017).

80. Arms Control Association, 'History of official proposals on the Iran nuclear issue'.
81. Hilary Leila Krieger, 'US, Iran agree to meet again in early 2011: Tuesday's talks in Geneva don't yield substantive progress on nuclear program', *The Jerusalem Post*, 8 December 2010; Julia Damianova, 'Nuclear negotiations with Iran end in failure', *Los Angeles Times*, 23 January 2011; Steven Erlanger, 'Talks on Iran's nuclear program close with no progress', *The New York Times*, 23 January 2011.
82. Kim Ghattas, 'Clinton urges Iran to fully engage in nuclear talks', *BBC News*, 3 December 2010, available at <http://www.bbc.co.uk/news/world-us-canada-11917186 8/6/150> (last accessed 10 August 2017); Clinton, 'Foreign policy priorities'.
83. Amanda Lanzillo, 'Iran and the Green Movement: Changes in media censorship capabilities', *Changing Communications*, available at <https://changingcommunications.wordpress.com/research/iran-and-the-green-movement/> (last accessed 10 August 2017).
84. Saeed Khamali Dehghan, 'Ahmadinejad allies charged with sorcery', *The Guardian*, 5 May 2011; Geneive Abdo, 'Iran's standoff: Khamenei vs. Ahmadinejad', *Al Jazeera*, 12 May 2011, available at <http://www.aljazeera.com/indepth/opinion/2011/05/2011512101644247806.html> (last accessed 4 May 2015).
85. Sherrill, 'Why Hassan Rouhani won'.
86. IAEA, 'Implementation of the NPT safeguards agreement in the Islamic Republic of Iran', GOV/2010/62; 'Iran self-sufficient in yellow cake', *Press TV*, 5 December 2010, available at <http://previous.presstv.ir/detail.aspx?id=153963&sectionid=351020104> (last accessed 11 August 2017); Joby Warrick, 'Iran touts major advances in nuclear program', *The Washington Post*, 11 April 2011
87. IAEA, 'Implementation of the NPT safeguards agreement in the Islamic Republic of Iran', GOV/2010/62; 'Implementation of the NPT safeguards agreement and relevant provisions of Security Council resolutions in the Islamic Republic of Iran', GOV/2011/29; 'Implementation of the NPT safeguards agreement and relevant provisions of Security Council resolutions in the Islamic Republic of Iran', GOV/2011/65.
88. Crail, 'Iran responds to call for talks'.
89. Arms Control Association, 'History of official proposals on the Iran nuclear issue'; Julian Borger and Chris McGreal, 'Iran raises hopes of nuclear trade-off to halt oil sanctions', *The Guardian*, 14 April 2012.

90. Parsi, *Losing an Enemy*, pp. 165–72; Mohammad Ali Shabani, 'Salehi reveals new details of secret US, Iran back channel', *Al-Monitor*, 23 December 2015, available at <http://www.al-monitor.com/pulse/originals/2015/12/salehi-interview-conveys-new-details-of-secret-back-channel.html#ixzz4wbnTh78t> (last accessed 26 October 2017).

91. Chris McGreal and Julian Borger, 'Iran faces new wave of sanctions over nuclear programme', *The Guardian*, 21 November 2011; Katzman, 'Iran sanctions' (2017), pp. 3, 11, 13–15, 20, 21–2, 30.

92. Julie Pace, 'Obama: Oil supply enough to keep squeeze on Iran', *Associated Press*, 30 March 2012, available at <http://www.deseretnews.com/article/765564532/Obama-Oil-supply-enough-to-keep-squeeze-on-Iran.html> (last accessed 11 August 2017).

93. Council of the European Union, 'Council Implementing Regulation (EU) No. 54/2012'; 'Iran's banks to be blocked from global banking system', *BBC News*, 15 March 2012, available at <http://www.bbc.co.uk/news/business-17390456> (last accessed 11 August 2017); Paterson, 'EU sanctions on Iran'.

94. Matthew M. Reed, 'Iranian oil survey: autumn update', *PBS Tehran Bureau*, 21 September 2012, available at <http://www.pbs.org/wgbh/pages/frontline/tehranbureau/2012/09/business-2012-iranian-oil-survey-autumn-update.html> (last accessed 8 May 2015); Prasenjit Bhattacharya and Biman Mukherji, 'New US sanctions hamper Iran–India oil trade', *The Wall Street Journal*, 6 February 2013.

95. Rezaei, *Iran's Nuclear Program*, p. 173.

96. 'Iran's rial hits an all-time-low against the US dollar', *BBC News*, 1 October 2012, available at <http://www.bbc.co.uk/news/business-19786662> (last accessed 11 August 2017).

97. World Bank, 'Inflation, consumer prices (annual %)'; 'Katzman, 'Iran sanctions' (2017), p. 57.

98. 'Iran: Real GDP growth from 2010 to 2020', *Statista*, available at <http://www.statista.com/statistics/294301/iran-gross-domestic-product-gdp-growth/> (last accessed 11 August 2017); 'Iran: Economy's fate hinges on outcome of negotiations', *Institute of International Finance*, 4 December 2014, available at <https://www.iif.com/press/iif-iran-s-economy-hinges-outcome-negotiations> (last accessed 11 August 2017).

99. Katzman, 'Iran sanctions' (2017), p. 55.

100. IAEA, 'Implementation of the NPT safeguards agreement and relevant provisions of Security Council resolutions in the Islamic Republic of Iran', GOV/2013/56.

101. Daniel Dombey, 'Transcript: John Kerry interview', *Financial Times*, 10 June 2009.

102. Jay Loschky and Anita Pugliese, 'Iranians split, 40% to 35%, on nuclear, military power', *Gallup*, 15 February 2012, <http://www.gallup.com/poll/152633/Iranians-Split-Nuclear-Military-Power.aspx> (last accessed 3 November 2016); Zogby Research Services, 'Iranian attitudes (2013)'.

103. 'Remarks by the President in a conversation with the SABAN Forum', Washington DC, 7 December 2013, *PPPUS*.

104. Parsi, *Losing an Enemy*, pp. 179–80.

105. 'The President speaks on the Iran nuclear deal at American University', 5 August 2015, *PPPUS*.

106. Parsi, *Losing an Enemy*, p. 182.

107. Jeffrey Goldberg, 'Explaining the toxic Obama–Netanyahu marriage', *The Atlantic*, 9 October 2015, available at <https://www.theatlantic.com/international/archive/2015/10/dennis-ross-iran-obama-netanyahu/409420/> (last accessed 10 August 2017). See also Jeffrey Goldberg, 'The point of no return?', *The Atlantic*, September 2010, available at <https://www.theatlantic.com/magazine/archive/2010/09/the-point-of-no-return/308186/> (last accessed 18 October 2017).

108. 'Israeli Prime Minister Benjamin Netanyahu addresses AIPAC in Washington DC', 6 March 2012, available at <https://israeled.org/resources/documents/israeli-prime-minister-benjamin-netanyahu-addresses-aipac/> (last accessed 18 October 2017).

109. David Ignatius, 'Is Israel preparing to attack Iran?', *The Washington Post*, 2 February 2012; Adam Entous, 'Spy vs. spy: Inside the fraying U.S.–Israel ties', *The Wall Street Journal*, 22 October 2015. See also Panetta, *Worthy Fights*, pp. 403–8; Parsi, *Losing an Enemy*, pp. 150–60.

110. 'Likud MK slams Barak for tapes discussing Israeli plans to attack Iran', *Times of Israel*, 22 August 2015, available at <http://www.timesofisrael.com/likud-mk-unsure-what-political-gain-barak-sought-with-iran-tapes/> (last accessed 15 January 2015); Amir Tibon, 'Netanyahu vs the Generals', *Politico*, 3 July 2016, available at <http://www.politico.com/magazine/story/2016/06/netanyahu-prime-minister-obama-president-foreign-policy-us-israel-israeli-relations-middle-east-iran-defense-forces-idf-214004> (last accessed 19 October 2017).

111. Gary Milhollin, 'The futility of an Israeli air strike against Iran's nuclear strikes', *The Atlantic*, 18 August 2010, available at <http://

www.theatlantic.com/international/archive/2010/08/the-futility-of-an-israeli-air-strike-against-irans-nuclear-sites/61669/> (last accessed 10 July 2011).

112. Former Director of the CIA Michael Hayden, quoted in Josh Rogin, 'Bush's CIA Director: We determined attacking Iran was a bad idea', *Foreign Policy*, 19 February 2012, available at <http://foreignpolicy.com/2012/01/19/bushs-cia-director-we-determined-attacking-iran-was-a-bad-idea/> (last accessed 19 October 2017).

113. Mattair, 'United States and Iran', p. 60; US Congress, House Committee on Oversight and Government Reform, 'Iran sanctions', Testimony of James Dobbins; Marc Lynch, 'Striking Iran is unwarranted and it would mean disaster', *The Atlantic*, 23 August 2010, available at <http://www.theatlantic.com/international/archive/2010/08/striking-iran-is-unwarranted-and-it-would-mean-disaster/61886/> (last accessed 10 July 2011).

114. Pickering et al., 'United States and Iran'; Ulrichsen, 'Internal and external security'; Kaye and Wehrey, 'Nuclear Iran', pp. 115–16.

115. George Friedman, 'Rethinking American options on Iran', *Stratfor*, 31 August 2010, available at <http://app.response.stratfor.com/e/es.aspx?s=1483&e=9381&elq=1065aa24e4dc450793d165a12f546c1f> (last accessed 10 July 2011); Jean-François Seznec, 'Why Saudi Arabia does not support a strike on Iran', *The Race for Iran*, 8 March 2010, available at <http://www.raceforiran.com/2010/03/page/3> (last accessed 10 July 2011).

116. Parsi, *Losing an Enemy*, p. 193.

117. Laura Rozen, 'Three days in March: New details on how US, Iran opened direct talks', *Al-Monitor*, 8 January 2014, available at <http://backchannel.al-monitor.com/index.php/2014/01/7484/three-days-in-march-new-details-on-the-u-s-iran-backchannel/> (last accessed 17 August 2017). See also US Congress, Senate Committee on Foreign Relations, 'Nomination hearing, Puneet Talwar'.

118. 'Rouhani, a man of the Islamic Revolution, opens Iran to west', *Associated Press*, 22 May 2017, available at <https://www.voanews.com/a/rouhani-portrait/3865027.html> (last accessed 14 August 2017).

119. 'Hassan Rouhani wins Iran presidential election', *BBC News*, 15 June 2013, available at <http://www.bbc.co.uk/news/world-middle-east-22916174> (last accessed 14 August 2017).

120. Mohseni et al., 'Iranian attitudes on nuclear negotiations'.

121. 'Hassan Rouhani wins Iran presidential election'.

122. Sherrill, 'Why Hassan Rouhani won', pp. 69–70; Keynoush, 'Iran after Ahmadinejad', pp. 136–8.
123. Saeed Kamali Dehghan, 'Iranian president-elect Rouhani promises better relations with the west', *The Guardian*, 17 June 2013.
124. Saeed Kamaali Dehghan, 'We have to build trust: Rouhani pledges return to moderation in Iranian politics', *The Guardian*, 18 June 2013.
125. Thomas Erdbrink and Mark Landler, 'Iran said to seek a nuclear accord to end sanctions', *The New York Times*, 20 September 2013.
126. Parsi, *Losing an Enemy*, p. 219.
127. Rouhani, 'Statement by H. E. Dr. Hassan Rouhani'.
128. Khamenei, 'Leader's speech in meeting with commanders of Islamic Revolutionary Guards Corps'.
129. 'Joint Plan of Action'.
130. Mohseni et al., 'Iranian public opinion on the nuclear negotiations'.
131. Blanche, 'Rouhani vs Revolutionary Guards'; Bastani, 'How powerful is Rouhani?' As late as June 2015, Khamenei was expressing concern about aspects of the proposed agreement; 'Iran's Khamenei rules out freezing sensitive nuclear work for long period', *Reuters*, 23 June 2015, available at <http://www.reuters.com/article/2015/06/23/us-iran-nuclear-freeze-idUSKBN0P32A420150623> (last accessed 9 September 2015).
132. Katzman et al., 'Iran: Interim nuclear agreement', p. 49; Rezaei, *Iran's Nuclear Program*.
133. Concern about the impact of sanctions was evident in the 2013 presidential debates; 'Presidential hopefuls clash on Iranian nuclear policy', *Reuters*, 7 June 2013, available at <http://www.reuters.com/article/2013/06/07/us-iran-election-debate-idUSB-RE9560UR20130607> (last accessed 14 July 2015).
134. Damian Pearse, 'Iran election results cause major setback for Mahmoud Ahmadinejad', *The Guardian*, 5 May 2012. The reformist parties mostly chose not to engage with the election.
135. Alfoneh, 'President Rouhani's cabinet'.
136. Two caveats should be noted here. Firstly, while most Iranians thought that sanctions had damaged the Iranian economy, they identified domestic mismanagement as being of greater importance; Mohseni et al., 'Iranian public opinion on the nuclear negotiations'. Secondly, according to Trita Parsi, a poll taken after Rouhani's victory suggested that only 9 per cent of Rouhani's supporters cited

either sanctions (2 per cent) or the economy (7 per cent) as their reasons for voting for him; Parsi, *Losing an Enemy*, p. 206.

137. On Khamenei's prevarication, see Hossein Bastani, 'Why Ayatollah Ali Khamenei could still scupper the nuclear talks', *The Guardian*,1 February 2014. For examples of his mixed messages, see 'Supreme Leader's speech in meeting with members of Supreme Council of Basij-e Mostazafin', 27 November 2014, available at <http://www. leader.ir/en/content/12704/Supreme-Leader's-Speech-in-Meeting-with-Members-of-Supreme-Council-of-Basij-e-Mostazafin> (last accessed 24 September 2016) and 'Iran's Khamenei rules out freezing sensitive nuclear work'.

138. 'Iran's looming election: Restoration or deterioration of regime legitimacy?', *Afro-Middle East Centre*, 11 June 2013, available at <http://www.amec.org.za/iran/item/1063-iran-s-looming-election-restoration-or-deterioration-of-regime-legitimacy.html#sthash. TeCTyv7z.dpuf> (last accessed 17 September 2015).

139. Axworthy, *Revolutionary Iran*, pp. 416–17, 427; Keynoush, 'Iran after Ahmadinejad', p. 133; Fayez, 'Iranian presidential elections'; Bastani, 'How powerful is Rouhani?', p. 7; Sherrill, 'Why Hassan Rouhani won', pp. 70–1; Tabatabai, 'Reading the nuclear politics in Tehran'.

140. Parsi, *Losing an Enemy*, provides a detailed account of the negotiations.

141. 'Joint Comprehensive Plan of Action'.

142. Mohseni et al., 'Iranian public opinion on the nuclear negotiations'; Saeed Kamali Dehghan and Ian Black, 'Thousands take to Iran streets to celebrate the historic nuclear deal', *The Guardian*, 14 July 2015.

143. Ron Kampeas, 'AIPAC, J Street face off over Iran deal', *Haaretz*, 23 July 2015; Catherine Ho, 'Mega-donors opposing Iran deal have upper hand in fierce lobbying battle', *The Washington Post*, 13 August 2015; AIPAC website, available at <http://ww.aipac.org> (last accessed 7 August 2015).

144. Brian Murphy and Adam Lee, 'Anatomy of Iranian nuclear deal', *Associated Press*, 24 November 2013; 'Barack, Bibi and Iran', *The Economist*, 16 November 2013.

145. 'The complete transcript of Netanyahu's address to Congress', *The Washington Post*, 3 March 2015, available at <http://www. washingtonpost.com/blogs/post-politics/wp/2015/03/03/full-text-netanyahus-address-to-congress/> (last accessed 15 July 2015).

146. 'Iran, big powers clinch nuclear deal', *Reuters*, 7 July 2015, available at <http://www.reuters.com/article/2015/07/14/us-iran-nuclear-idUSKCN0PM0CE20150714> (last accessed 14 July 2015); Lauren French, 'Israel's ambassador addresses GOP hardliners on Iran deal', *Politico*, 22 July 2015, available at <http://www.politico.com/story/2015/07/israels-ambassador-addresses-gop-hardliners-on-iran-deal-120509> (last accessed 18 September 2015); 'Israeli ambassador Ron Dermer on the Iran nuclear deal', *CNN*, 15 August 2015, available at <http://edition.cnn.com/videos/tv/2015/08/15/exp-gps-0816-dermer-netanyahu.cnn/video/playlists/iran-u-s-relations/> (last accessed 18 September 2015); Eric Roby, 'Israeli ambassador: Iran deal a powder keg', *SunSentinel*, 25 August 2015, available at <http://www.sun-sentinel.com/local/broward/fl-israeli-ambassador-20150825-story.html> (last accessed 18 September 2015).

147. Adam Entous and Danny Yadron, 'US spy net on Israel snares Congress', *The Wall Street Journal*, 29 December 2015.

148. Michael A. Memoli and Christi Parsons, 'Obama–GOP rift over Iran talks redefines partisan battles', *Los Angeles Times*, 10 March 2015; Patrick O'Connor, 'Republican White House hopefuls condemn Iran nuclear deal', *The Wall Street Journal*, 3 April 2015; 'US conservatives condemn agreement', *BBC News*, 14 July 2015, available at <http://www.bbc.co.uk/news/world-middle-east-33527844> (last accessed 15 July 2015).

149. 'An open letter to the leaders of the Islamic Republic of Iran', 9 March 2015, available at <http://www.cotton.senate.gov/sites/default/files/150309%20Cotton%20Open%20Letter%20to%20Iranian%20Leaders.pdf> (last accessed 15 July 2015).

150. 'P.L. 114–17, The Iran Nuclear Agreement Review Act of 2015', *Washingtonwatch*, available at <https://washingtonwatch.com/bills/show/114_PL_114-17.html> (last accessed 15 July 2015).

151. Parsi, *Losing an Enemy*, pp. 334–5.

152. Josh Lederman, 'Obama warns Congress on Iran sanctions effort', *The Boston Globe*, 17 January 2015, available at <https://www.bostonglobe.com/news/world/2015/01/17/obama-comes-out-swinging-against-new-iran-sanctions/izB9M1DbTezSBmNxmPPhtI/story.html> (last accessed 13 December 2017).

153. 'Partisan polarization surges in Bush, Obama ears', Pew Research Center, 4 June 2012, available at <http://www.people-press.org/2012/06/04/partisan-polarization-surges-in-bush-obama-years/> (last accessed 6 June 2013); 'The polarization of the congressional

parties', *Voteview*, 19 January 2014, available at <http://voteview.com/political_polarization.asp> (accessed 17 February 2014); Theriault, *Party Polarization in Congress*; Sinclair, *Party Wars*.

154. PollingReport, 'Iran'; WorldPublicOpinion.org, 'Iran nuclear deal backed by large majority of Americans'; Voice of the People, 'Assessing the Iran Deal'; Smelz and Kafura, 'Americans favor deal with Iran'; Jim Lobe, 'Most polls suggest Americans support the deal, especially Jews', *Lobelog*, 28 July 2015, available at <http://www.lobelog.com/most-polls-suggest-americans-support-the-deal-especially-jews/> (last accessed 18 September 2015).

155. 'The LA Jewish Journal Iran Poll, July 2015 – Iran nuclear deal survey of Jews and non-Jews', 16–20 July 2015, available at <http://www.jewishdatabank.org/Studies/details.cfm?StudyID=783> (last accessed 26 October 2017).

156. Jeffrey M. Jones, 'Americans' views of Netanyahu less positive post-visit', *Gallup*, 11 March 2015, available at <http://www.gallup.com/poll/181916/americans-views-netanyahu-less-positive-post-visit.aspx> (last accessed 10 September 2015); 'Latest Gallup poll shows young Americans overwhelmingly support Palestine', *MintPress News*, 4 August 2014, available at <http://www.mintpressnews.com/latest-gallup-poll-shows-young-americans-overwhelmingly-support-palestine/194856/> (last accessed 10 September 2015); John B. Judis, 'The breakup: The slow demise of US bipartisan support for Israel', *Foreign Affairs*, 2 March 2015, available at <https://www.foreignaffairs.com/articles/israel/2015-03-02/breakup> (last accessed 10 September 2015); Lydia Saad, 'Seven in 10 Americans continue to view Israel favorably', *Gallup*, 23 February 2015, available at <http://www.gallup.com/poll/181652/seven-americans-continue-view-israel-favorably.aspx?utm_source=Politics&utm_medium=newsfeed&utm_campaign=tiles> (last accessed 9 September 2015); Jonathan Broder, 'How the Iran nuclear deal weakened AIPAC, Washington's most powerful interest group', *Newsweek*, 1 September 2015, available at <http://www.newsweek.com/2015/09/11/whos-afraid-israel-lobby-367368.html> (last accessed 10 September 2015).

157. Alexandra Jaffe, '58 members of Congress skipped Netanyahu's speech', *CNN*, 3 March 2015, available at <http://edition.cnn.com/2015/02/26/politics/democrats-missing-netanyahu-whip-list/index.html> (last accessed 27 October 2017); 'Netanyahu denounces Obama push for Iran nuclear deal', *Associated Press*, 3 March 2015, available at <http://www.monitor.co.ug/News/

World/Netanyahu--denounces--Obama--push-Iran--nuclear-deal/688340-2642512-mic54yz/index.html> (last accessed 26 October 2017).

158. Parsi, *Losing an Enemy*, p. 325. See also 'Divided on Iran, Democrats unite against GOP letter', *National Journal*, 9 March 2015, available at <http://www.nationaljournal.com/congress/divided-on-iran-democrats-unite-against-gop-letter-20150309> (last accessed 15 July 2015); Jonathan Weisman, 'Netanyahu's visit bringing uninvited problems for Jewish Democrats', *The New York Times*, 1 March 2015; Dan Roberts, 'Netanyahu's speech to Congress snubbed by prominent Democrats', *The Guardian*, 3 March 2015; Julie Hirschfield Davis, 'Fears of lasting rift as Obama battles pro-Israel group on Iran', *The New York Times*, 7 August 2015; 'AIPAC targeting vulnerable Democrats over Iran agreement', *PressTV*, 30 July 2015, available at <http://www.presstv.ir/Detail/2015/07/30/422579/AIPAC-Democrats-Iran-agreemnet> (last accessed 10 September 2015); 'Has Israel lost the Democratic Party?', *CNN*, 27 February 2015, available at <http://edition.cnn.com/2015/02/27/politics/netanyahu-speech-alienates-democrats/> (last accessed 10 September 2015); Jones, 'Americans' views of Netanyahu less positive'; Karoun Demirijian and Carol Morello, 'How AIPAC lost the Iran deal fight', *The Washington Post*, 3 September 2015.

159. Patrick Goodenough, 'Democrats admit to being lobbied by Russia, China and Europe before backing Iran nuclear deal', *CNSNews.com*, 23 September 2015, available at <http://www.cnsnews.com/news/article/patrick-goodenough/democrat-senators-lobbied-russia-china-and-europe-deciding-back-iran> (last accessed 23 December 2015).

160. Parsi, *Losing an Enemy*, p. 333.

161. Manu Raju and Burgess Everett, 'How Cardin and Corker clinched the Iran deal', *Politico*, 14 April 2015, available at <http://www.politico.com/story/2015/04/ben-cardin-bob-corker-iran-deal-116979> (last accessed 15 April 2016). Jim Lobe, 'AIPAC's annus horribilis', *Lobelog*, 31 January 2014, available at <http://www.lobelog.com/aipacs-annus-horribilis> (last accessed 20 August 2017). An alternative explanation for the terms of the act is that the Republicans never wanted to defeat the JCPOA and take responsibility for what might follow. Instead, they crafted a bill which ensured they would lose the vote while still allowing

them vociferously to oppose the JCPOA, pleasing their constituents; Steve Inskeep, 'How the Iran vote is engineered to pass',
NPR, 2 September 2015, available at <http://www.npr.org/
sections/itsallpolitics/2015/09/02/436647276/minority-rules-
capitol-hill-vote-tactics-displayed-in-iran-deal> (last accessed 16
August 2017).

162. Amber Phillips, 'Obama's Iran deal nears a major symbolic victory',
The Washington Post, 8 September 2015; Sabrina Siddiqui, 'House
rejects Obama's nuclear accord with Iran in symbolic vote', *The
Guardian*, 11 September 2015.

Conclusion

The signing of the Joint Comprehensive Plan of Action (JCPOA) in July 2015 brought about an apparent resolution of the conflict over the Iranian nuclear programme and represented a major diplomatic achievement for all of the parties involved. It had, nevertheless, been a long time coming and arrived only after decades of ill-conceived American policies had failed to achieve their objectives.

Although formally beginning in 1957, the US–Iranian nuclear relationship only became a significant preoccupation for both states in the 1970s, following the dramatic escalation of the Shah's nuclear ambitions. His announcement of his grandiose new plan and the negotiations that followed quickly brought what would become perennial concerns to the fore. Although initially keen to help its ally, the Nixon administration soon became aware of the proliferation risks involved and the extent of congressional opposition to any agreement that would transfer reprocessing or other fuel cycle technology to Iran. For their part, the Shah and Akbar Etemad were adamant that Iran must have nuclear autonomy. It was incompatible with their nuclear ambitions, their understanding of the Treaty on the Non-Proliferation of Nuclear Weapons (NPT) and their national pride that Iran should be dependent on foreigners for the technology and material required to produce nuclear energy (and, if it became necessary, weapons). The irreconcilability of the two sides' demands produced a deadlock that was only broken when the Shah, his grip on power already crumbling, conceded American demands in 1978. By then, however, it was too late, and the proposed new US–Iranian nuclear agreement was stillborn.

The Iranian Revolution and the birth of the Islamic Republic produced a fundamental transformation of the US–Iranian relationship. The conflict over Iran's right to the fuel cycle was dramatically exacerbated by the process of mutual demonisation which followed the Revolution. The American experience of the hostage crisis and Iran's experiences during the Iran–Iraq War forged a deep loathing and fear of the 'other' on both sides that would shape the nuclear relationship for the next three decades. What the majority of Americans took from the Revolution and the hostage crisis was the perception that Iran was now in the hands of a bunch of crazed religious fanatics who were bent on overthrowing America's allies and overturning the influence of the United States throughout the Middle East. The idea of nuclear weapons under the control of such a palpably unhinged regime was unthinkable. What Iranians 'learned' from the experience of the Iran–Iraq War, building on their perceptions of the 1953 coup and Washington's support for the Shah, was that the US government would do whatever was necessary to control Iran. It might assert its support for a rule-bound international order, sovereignty and democracy but in practice it would turn a blind eye to Iraqi use of chemical weapons and ignore international laws and sovereign rights whenever it suited it to do so. Under those circumstances, it seemed to at least some of the Iranian leadership that developing the capability to build nuclear weapons might be necessary to ensure the regime's survival.

While these perceptions were held to a greater or lesser degree by many amongst the policy-making elites on both sides, their absorption at a wider societal level was equally, if not more important. By the 1990s Washington was convinced that Iran had a weapons programme, but its efforts to cripple Iran's nuclear progress were singularly ineffectual. In what would become a formula that lasted the best part of two decades, a hard-line unilateral policy built around coercion through sanctions proved utterly ineffectual. Washington's insistence on Iranian guilt, regardless of a lack of concrete evidence, and its refusal to acknowledge Iranian 'rights' under the NPT, alienated the international community whose support it needed to apply effective pressure. Meanwhile, its unilateral actions had no significant impact on either the

Iranian economy or its nuclear programme. A key reason for the pursuit of such an inadequate policy was the constraint imposed by the 'othering' process on the domestic politics of the United States. The first Bush administration's failure to follow through on its inclination to engage and Clinton's first-term imposition of 'dual containment' were both influenced by domestic political considerations. Both were concerned with re-election and the possible exploitation of any 'softness' on Iran by political opponents, while Clinton was pushed into a corner by the congressional imposition of sanctions. Clinton's inability to offer Iran any significant concessions also undermined his second-term efforts to engage Iran. Whilst he did make a genuine effort to reach out to Tehran after Khatami's election, Clinton never offered the kind of significant concession that might have handed the Iranian president the leverage he needed in his struggle with his own hardliners. Khatami's failure to respond to Clinton, despite the former's repeated efforts, also demonstrated the extent to which demonisation of the USA had come to make any discourse with Washington a politically perilous course of action in Iran.

The second Bush administration saw a return to the hard-line policies of the Clinton first term, though this time driven less by political calculation than genuine conviction. Nevertheless, this pursuit of confrontation was as fruitless as before. By the end of George W. Bush's two terms of office Iran had made dramatic strides in its efforts to master the fuel cycle and nothing the Bush administration had done had significantly hindered it. As with the Clinton administration, Bush never developed a coherent strategy for achieving his desired ends. Indeed, the administration was not even able to formulate a consistent position as to what those ends were, caught as it was between hardliners' desires for regime change and pragmatists' more modest hopes of constraining Tehran's nuclear ambitions. Whilst Bush did shift, gradually, toward the latter objective, this was less the result of considered thought than of a grudging acceptance of the impossibility of regime change. The resulting policy, such as it was, never developed a coherent relationship between the desired ends and the means employed, with the latter being wholly inadequate to the task.

In particular, the administration never achieved an appropriate mixture of incentives and punishments in the means it employed. The incentives offered were insufficient to meet Iran's minimum demand of continued enrichment while sufficient coercive force was never imposed because of Washington's continued unilateralism and inability to persuade the other major international players to join it in imposing effective sanctions.

What makes the inadequacies of Bush's policies all the more damning is the possibility that the nuclear crisis might have been resolved much earlier, with Iran at a significantly less advanced stage of its nuclear development, had he been more attuned to the realities of the situation. The exposure of Iran's violations of its agreement with the International Atomic Energy Agency had put Tehran under greater scrutiny than ever before and revealed important divisions within the regime over the nuclear programme. What became clear after 2002 was that there were those within Iran who were willing to accept a compromise which involved a commitment not to pursue weapons, and measures to guarantee that, if only the right to enrich was guaranteed in return. Several offers along those lines were made in 2003–5, all of which the Bush administration rejected. While it is necessarily unclear that Bush's acceptance of one of those offers would have led to an agreement, the refusal to even test the possibility was a significant error.

Not only did Bush's refusal to engage with those offers pass up a potential opportunity to resolve the issue, but it also played out in the domestic politics of the Iranian nuclear programme in an entirely predictable and self-defeating fashion. While certainly not a decisive factor in Ahmadinejad's 2005 presidential election victory, Bush's actions reinforced the Iranian hardliners' narrative about the impossibility of trusting the Americans and undermined those arguing for engagement and compromise. Ultimately, Bush ended up with the worst of both worlds. His pursuit of confrontation and refusal to compromise reinforced the political position of the Iranian hardliners without putting in place sufficient pressure to actually deter them from their chosen course.

Barack Obama was finally able to end the long history of American policy failure and to achieve a diplomatic breakthrough partly through skill and partly as a result of good fortune. In the first place, he had the sense to recognise the failings of existing policy and to make a concerted effort to bring the ends and means of American strategy into much closer alignment. Initially, he altered the means, putting in place a more effective sanctions regime than had previously existed (albeit building on developments made in Bush's second term). This was achieved partly through better diplomacy, notably the adoption of the policy of engagement and the swap proposal, both of which worked to make Washington appear flexible and Tehran the recalcitrant partner. Nevertheless, there was also an element of luck involved. Quite simply, by the time Obama became president, most alternatives to a tightening of the sanctions regime had been exhausted. The EU3 had played all their cards, Russia had made various proposals, and nothing had achieved the desired result. Russia, China and the EU therefore joined the USA in imposing comprehensive sanctions in part because they had run out of options.

More important than his forging of more effective punishments for Iran, however, was Obama's offering of a much improved incentive, in the form of acceptance of Iran's continued enrichment. Though the key end of policy – denying Iran nuclear weapons – remained in place, the intervening goal of denying it the fuel cycle was abandoned because of an acceptance that sanctions were not going to compel Iran to surrender it and that a refusal to abandon the goal risked war.

Obama thus reduced the ambitiousness of the policy objective whilst bringing more effective means to bear on it. The change in the objective was the critical development because it brought what was an acceptable outcome for the Obama administration into line with Iran's win set, in which continued control of the fuel cycle was the minimum demand. Obama thus put on the table an outcome which was palatable to most Iranian citizens and to a significant proportion of the Iranian elite. Whether that change would have been enough, in and of itself, to secure an agreement is doubtful, however. Obama needed some more luck in the form of developments in Iranian domestic politics. The growing dissatisfaction amongst Iranians with the policies of Ahmadinejad and the dominance of hardliners, and the legitimacy crisis that became much more significant after 2009, created the political conditions in which Rouhani won the 2013 election and was then able to secure the backing of the Supreme Leader for the JCPOA. Without the marginalisation of Iranian hardliners Obama's changes in strategy would still not have been enough to secure an agreement.

If we return then to the questions outlined in the Introduction in light of the above: with regard to Iran's nuclear ambitions we must first note a necessary caveat. There remains a degree of uncertainty in relation to this question. There is no document or unambiguous public statement that brooks no argument as to the answer. Instead we have a range of circumstantial evidence from which to draw our conclusions. Nevertheless, it has been argued here that that evidence does support certain conclusions rather than others. In the first place, it seems clear that, given the context in which it was taken, and some of the statements made at the time, the decision to restart the nuclear programme in the 1980s was driven by an aspiration to be able to develop nuclear weapons on the part of at least some of those behind the decision. The subsequent evolution of Iranian thinking on the nuclear issue through the course of the 1990s remains unclear, however, with the programme continuing (including some weapons-related development in the late 1990s) but both Rafsanjani and Khatami indicating a willingness to negotiate. No real clarity would emerge until after 2002. At that point, with the Iranian nuclear programme under the spotlight, and real choices having to be made, the divisions amongst the Iranian elite came more clearly into view. Pragmatic conservatives and reformists concluded that their political and economic vision for the future of Iran was incompatible with a weapons programme that would lead to international isolation. Iran's hardliners, in contrast, were quite happy to accept the latter as the price of maintaining the purity of the Revolution and retaining complete freedom of action with regard to the nuclear programme.

Those observers who perceived (or perceive) there to be a widespread commitment to the pursuit of nuclear weapons amongst the Iranian elite are therefore wrong on this reading. The Iranian regime was deeply divided on the question, with a large part of it prepared to provide guarantees that Iran would not seek weapons status in return for reciprocal guarantees relating to the fuel cycle, security and access to the global economy. That conclusion, in turn, has implications for the question of how the JCPOA was finally reached and whether it represents a success or a failure of coercive diplomacy. On the one hand, it undermines the more grandiose claims that the agreement was essentially a triumph of effective coercion. Rouhani and those who shared his vision were not forced to abandon a pursuit of nuclear weapons that they did not seek in the first place. They offered a similar deal between 2003 and 2005 at a point when effective sanctions were more or less non-existent, but the Bush administration refused to take it. The efficacy of sanctions is also brought into question by Obama's concession of the right to enrich, since it is clear that it was that development, more than anything else, which was critical to breaking the diplomatic logjam. Finally, the significance of sanctions is qualified by the evident importance of internal changes in Iran to the reaching of the agreement. As one National Security Council staffer put it, 'if Rouhani hadn't won we would have been up shit-creek, despite the sanctions pressure'.[1]

At best, therefore, sanctions and coercion played a more limited role in the final agreement than some of their enthusiasts believe. Most importantly, there is little reason to believe that they would have produced an agreement without Obama's concession on enrichment and the marginalisation of Iran's hardliners. Nevertheless, that is not to conclude that they were wholly irrelevant. In the first place, the expectation of sanctions and diplomatic isolation as the more or less inevitable consequence of the pursuit of nuclear weapons was clearly a factor in the calculations of Iran's pragmatic conservatives and reformists. Whether they would have supported weapons development in some hypothetical world where there were no adverse consequences to such a choice cannot be determined, but sanctions, or the anticipation of sanctions, can at last be credited with some influence on their thought process. In addition, to the extent that the economic impact of sanctions can be credited with undermining support for Iran's hardliners (which is unclear) and strengthening the political hand of the pragmatists and the reformists, they had a role in bringing about an agreement.

Finally, what the preceding analysis demonstrates is that the answer to the question of who got the better deal in 2015 is one that needs to be answered not in terms of states but rather in terms of factions within states. In simple terms the answer is that the hardliners on both sides lost. On the Iranian side those who wanted to maintain unfettered control of the nuclear programme and retain the capability to pursue weapons development were the losers. As Abbas Araghchi, a member of the Iranian negotiating team, put it, 'if we had wanted the bomb, then the JCPOA is an utter defeat. But if we are after internationally legitimate enrichment and a completely peaceful nuclear programme, then this agreement is a great victory.'[2] On the American side, those who wanted Iran to be forced to surrender enrichment and control of the fuel cycle were the losers, as Obama chose to abandon Washington's maximal demands in favour of more modest objectives.

The JCPOA thus represented a victory for moderate and pragmatic factions in both countries over their hard-line opponents. The continued existence of groups on both sides who were deeply dissatisfied with the agreement, and the inevitability of continued shifts in the balance of political power, therefore made the deal contingent and vulnerable. This was clearly demonstrated by Trump's January 2018 announcement that, if Iran and the rest of the P5+1 did not accept a rewriting of the agreement to significantly increase the constraints on Iran's nuclear programme, by both extending them to its missile programme and making them of indefinite duration, the United States would unilaterally walk away from the JCPOA.[3]

This threat to kill the agreement had nothing to do with Iranian non-compliance with its terms. Despite the long list of accusations made in this speech, and in a previous one in October 2017, at no point was Trump able to identify any Iranian violation of the terms of the JCPOA.[4] Rather, Trump was attempting to rewrite the agreement because he objected to the original terms, like those US hardliners who had opposed it from the moment that it was signed. Underlying this course of action was the assumption that Obama had made an enormous error in 2015. According to Trump, 'the nuclear deal threw Iran's dictatorship a political and economic lifeline, providing urgently needed relief from the intense domestic pressure the sanctions had created'.[5] In the opinion of American hardliners the Iranian regime had been on the brink of collapse in 2015 and, if only the international community had maintained the sanctions regime, Tehran would have conceded all of Washington's demands. The situation could still be retrieved, however, by the reimposition of sanctions which would force the Iranians to accept Trump's new demands.[6]

The findings of this study suggest that Trump's 'Iran strategy' is a fantasy resting on a series of false premises, the first of which is that a tough and effective sanctions regime can be reimposed. One of the principle reasons that Obama accepted the terms of the JCPOA was precisely that he recognised that he had achieved as effective a sanctions regime as was possible, and that if he did not accept a deal that the other members of the P5+1 regarded as satisfactory, support for a continuation of sanctions would soon start to crumble. Predictably, therefore, when Trump announced his new policy, the EU, Russia and China all made clear that they intended to continue to adhere to the terms of the JCPOA as long as Iran did, regardless of what the Trump administration chose to do.[7] The hope of American hardliners was, no doubt, that they could use the threat of secondary sanctions and denial of access to US markets as a way of forcing the other states to cut business ties to Iran. Nor was that hope without any basis, given that such a strategy had had an impact under George W. Bush and Obama. Nevertheless, the idea that a sanctions regime as effective as that engineered by Obama could be recreated was entirely unrealistic. The EU might be coerced into compliance, though even that was doubtful, but Russia and China certainly would not be. Any new sanctions regime would consequently be a pale imitation of what had existed before 2015.

The second dubious assumption upon which Trump's decision rested was that sanctions had brought Iran to its knees before 2015. While it was true that the Iranian regime was suffering from a serious legitimacy crisis, and that this contributed to the decision to sign the JCPOA, sanctions played a limited role in bringing that situation about, with the problem primarily one of the Iranian regime's own making. In truth, as we have seen, there is no evidence that sanctions were about to compel Iran to give up the fuel cycle in 2015, let alone bring down the regime. Moreover, the idea that reimposing sanctions would somehow help to destabilise the regime further demonstrated the continued tone-deafness of the American right when it came to understanding Iranian politics. In fact, the most likely consequence of Trump's attempt to rewrite the JCPOA was to bolster the regime and Iran's own hardliners. Undercutting an agreement that most Iranians felt was fair and which recognised what they saw as Iran's legitimate nuclear rights would provoke Iranian nationalist sentiment and a rally round the flag effect. It would also legitimate the argument of those who continued to insist that the 'Great Satan' could never be trusted and undermine those who were committed to compromise.

As of this writing, the fate of the JCPOA remains unclear, but the most likely outcome would appear to be the collapse of the JCPOA. It is highly unlikely that the rest of the P5+1 would agree to attempt to renegotiate the JCPOA and even more unlikely that Iran would accept the conditions that Trump has demanded. Although both the Iranian government and the rest of the P5+1 have stated that they remain committed to the agreement even if the United States withdraws from it, without American participation and the lifting of US sanctions, the incentive for Iran to continue to abide by the agreement would be hugely reduced. Those in Iran dissatisfied with the 2015 deal would be emboldened and empowered by such a turn of events and the pressure to withdraw from the deal would likely become irresistible.

If the JCPOA thus collapsed, Tehran would be free to pursue its nuclear programme without constraint. If Iranian hardliners were also to regain power and were faced with a bellicose Trump administration, they might well decide to push ahead with weapons development as fast as they possibly could in order to deter any possible American aggression. Under those circumstances the only option available to the United States to prevent such an outcome would be the use of military force. Rather than achieving a more effective nuclear agreement, therefore, Trump's brinkmanship is most likely to return Washington to the dilemma that Obama had signed the JCPOA to avoid, namely accept a nuclear-armed Iran or go to war.

Notes

1. Parsi, *Losing an Enemy*, p. 366.
2. 'Revealed; Iran's 15 deal secrets', *Iranwire*, 3 August 2015, quoted in Parsi, *Losing an Enemy*, p. 314.
3. Trump, 'Statement by the President on the Iran nuclear deal'.
4. Trump, 'Remarks by President Trump on Iran strategy'.
5. Ibid.
6. John Bolton, 'How to get out of the Iran nuclear deal', *National Review*, 28 August 2017, available at <http://www.nationalreview.com/article/450890/iran-nuclear-deal-exit-strategy-john-bolton-memo-trump> (last accessed 28 December 2017).
7. 'EU, Russia, China rally behind Iran deal ahead of Trump speech', *Press TV*, 13 October 2017, available at <http://www.presstv.com/Detail/2017/10/13/538426/Iran-EU-Russia-Mogherini-Gabriel-Lavrov-JCPOA-US-Trump> (last accessed 20 December 2017); Robin Emmott, 'European powers urge Trump to preserve Iran nuclear deal', *Reuters*, 11 January 2018, available at <https://www.reuters.com/article/us-iran-nuclear-eu/european-powers-urge-trump-to-preserve-iran-nuclear-deal-idUSKBN1F00XN> (last accessed 26 January 2018).

Bibliography

Memoirs and Primary Sources

USA

Albright, M. K., *Madam Secretary: A Memoir* (New York: Pan, 2004).

Albright, M. K., 'Remarks before the American-Iranian Council', 17 March 2000, Washington DC, <http://fas.org/news/iran/2000/000317.html> (last accessed 15 November 2015).

Albright, M. K., 'Remarks at the 1998 Asia Society Dinner', 18 June 1988, Washington DC, <http://1997-2001.state.gov/www/statements/1998/980617a.html> (last accessed 15 November 2015).

Bolton, J. R., *Surrender Is Not an Option: Defending America at the United Nations* (New York: Threshold Editions, 2007).

Bush, G. H. W., George Bush Presidential Library, *Bush Presidential Records*.

Carter, J., Jimmy Carter Presidential Library, Folder, Box 25, Carlton Neville Collection, Subject File: 'Nuclear economic through nuclear issues' (*Carter Presidential Library, Folder, Box 25*).

Christopher, W., *In the Stream of History: Shaping Foreign Policy for a New Era* (Stanford, CA: Stanford University Press, 1988).

Clinton, H., 'Foreign policy priorities', testimony of Secretary of State Hillary Clinton before the House Foreign Affairs Committee, 1 March 2011, <http://www.c-span.org/video/?298260-1/us-foreign-policy-priorities&start=6114> (last accessed 8 June 2015).

Digital National Security Archive (*DNSA*), <http://nsarchive.gwu.edu/digital-national-security-archive>.

Ford, G., Gerald Ford Presidential Library, National Security Adviser, International Economic Affairs Staff Files, Box 1 (*Ford Presidential Library, National Security Adviser, Box 1*).

Ford, G., Gerald Ford Presidential Library, National Security Adviser, Presidential material for VIP visits, Box 9 (*Ford Presidential Library, National Security Adviser, Box 9*).

Gannon, John C., 'Remarks to the World Affairs Council, Washington D.C.', 4 June 1988, <https://fas.org/irp/cia/product/ddi_speech_060598.html> (last accessed 10 October 2015).

Haass, R., *War of Necessity, War of Choice: A Memoir of Two Iraq Wars* (New York: Simon & Schuster, 2010).

Indyk, M., 'The Clinton administration's approach to the Middle East', Report No. 84, 21 May (Washington DC: Washington Institute for Near East Policy, 1993).

Indyk, M., *Innocent Abroad: An Intimate Account of American Peace Diplomacy in the Middle East* (New York: Simon & Schuster, 2014).

Keiswetter, A., Interview with author, 29 June 2015.

National Commission on Terrorism, *Countering the Changing Threat of International Terrorism*, June 2000, <http://fas.org/irp/threat/commission.html> (last accessed 20 June 2016).

National Security Archive, *The Iranian Nuclear Program, 1974–1978: Electronic Briefing Book No. 268* (*NSA: Iranian Nuclear Program*), <http://nsarchive2.gwu.edu/nukevault/ebb268/> (last accessed 20 July 2017).

National Security Archive, *Iraqgate: Saddam Hussein, US Policy and the Prelude to the Persian Gulf War, 1980–1994*, <https://nsarchive2.gwu.edu//nsa/publications/iraqgate/iraqgate.html> (last accessed 20 May 2014).

Nixon, R. M., *Nixon Presidential Library: Virtual Documents*, <http://www.nixonlibrary.gov/virtuallibrary/documents/> (last accessed 12 January 2017).

Panetta, L., *Worthy Fights: A Memoir of Leadership in War and Peace* (New York: Penguin, 2015).

Pillar, P., Interview with author, 29 June 2015.

Powell, C., 'Confirmation hearing by Secretary-designate Colin L. Powell', 17 January 2001, <https://www.c-span.org/video/?161898-1/state-nomination-hearing> (last accessed 5 December 2017).

Reagan, R., *An American Life* (New York: Simon and Schuster, 1990).

Rice, C., 'Remarks at the American University of Cairo', 20 June 2005, <https://2001-2009.state.gov/secretary/rm/2005/48328.htm> (last accessed 10 June 2016).

Rice, C., 'Remarks by Condoleezza Rice on terrorism and foreign policy', Johns Hopkins SAIS, Washington, 29 April 2002, <https://georgewbush-whitehouse.archives.gov/news/releases/2002/04/20020429-9.html> (last accessed 4 May 2017).

Riedel, B., Interview with author, 1 July 2015.

Trump, D., 'Remarks by President Trump on Iran strategy', 13 October 2017, <https://www.whitehouse.gov/the-press-office/2017/10/13/remarks-president-trump-iran-strategy> (last accessed 26 October 2017).

Trump, D., 'Statement by the President on the Iran nuclear deal', 12 January 2018, <https://www.whitehouse.gov/briefings-statements/statement-president-iran-nuclear-deal/> (last accessed 26 January 2018).

US Congress, *Congressional Record*.

US Congress, House Committee on Foreign Affairs, 'Iran: Briefing and hearing before the Committee on Foreign Affairs', 11 and 31 January 2007, 110th Cong., 1st Sess. (Washington DC: US Government Printing Office, 2007).

US Congress, House Committee on International Relations, 'US Policy toward Iran', Hearing before the House Committee on International Relations, 9 November 1995, 104th Cong., 2nd Sess. (Washington DC: US Government Printing Office, 1996).

US Congress, House Committee on Oversight and Government Reform, 'Iran sanctions: Options, opportunities and consequences', Hearing before the Subcommittee on National Security and Foreign Affairs, 15 December, 111th Cong., 1st Sess. (Washington DC: US Government Printing Office, 2009).

US Congress, House International Relations Committee, 'United States policy toward Iran', Testimony of Nicholas Burns, Under Secretary of State for Political Affairs, 8 March 2006, 109th Cong., 2nd Sess., <http://www.iranwatch.org/sites/default/files/us-hirc-burns-prepared-testimony-030806.pdf> (last accessed 8 August 2017).

US Congress, Joint Committee on Atomic Energy, 'Proliferation of nuclear weapons', Hearings before the Joint Committee on Atomic Energy, Subcommittee on Military Applications, 10 September 1974, 93rd Cong., 2nd Sess. (Washington DC: US Government Printing Office, 1974).

US Congress, Senate Committee on Banking, 'Minimizing potential threats from Iran: Administration perspectives on economic sanctions and other policy options', Testimony of James B. Steinberg, Deputy Secretary of State Hearing before the Senate Banking Committee, 6 October 2009, 111th Cong., 1st Sess., <http://www.banking.senate.gov/public/index.cfm?FuseAction=Files.View&FileStore_id=a65aeaad-61cd-4b5a-9ab2-c865f427bbde> (last accessed 10 May 2016).

US Congress, Senate Committee on Foreign Relations, 'Iran and proliferation', Hearing before the Senate Committee on Foreign Relations, Subcommittee on Near Eastern and South Asian Affairs, 17 April and

6 May 1997, 105th Cong., 1st Sess. (Washington DC: US Government Printing Office, 1998).

US Congress, Senate Committee on Foreign Relations, 'Nomination hearing, Puneet Talwar', 11 December 2013, <https://www.foreign.senate.gov/hearings/2013/12/11/nomination> (last accessed 10 January 2017).

US Congress, Senate Committee on Government Operations, 'Hearings on the Export Reorganization Act – 1975', Hearings before the Senate Committee on Government Operations, 24 and 30 April, and 1 May 1975, 94th Cong., 1st Sess. (Washington DC: US Government Printing Office, 1975).

US Congress, Senate Committee on Homeland Security and Governmental Affairs, Federal Financial Management, Government Information and International Security Subcommittee, 'Iran's nuclear recklessness and the US response: The expert's perspective', Hearings, 15 November 2005, 109th Cong., 1st Sess. (Washington DC: US Government Printing Office, 2005).

US Department of Commerce, *Foreign Broadcast Information Service, Daily Reports (FBIS-DR)*.

US Department of State, 'Background briefing on P5+1 talks in Geneva', 1 October 2009, <http://www.state.gov/p/nea/rls/rm/2009/130181.htm> (last accessed 1 April 2013).

US Department of State, *Department of State Central Policy Files 1973–1977 (Central Policy Files 1973–1977)*, <https://aad.archives.gov/aad/series-description.jsp?s=4073> (last accessed 12 November 2015).

US Department of State, *Documents on Disarmament 1945–1959: Volume 1, 1945–1956* (Washington DC: US Government Printing Office, 1960).

US Department of State, *Foreign Relations of the United States (FRUS) 1969–1976: Vol. I, Foundations of Foreign Policy 1969–1972*, <http://history.state.gov/historicaldocuments/frus1969-76v01/> (last accessed 15 September 2015).

US Department of State, *Foreign Relations of the United States (FRUS) 1969–1976: Vol. XXVII, Iran; Iraq, 1973–1976*, <https://history.state.gov/historicaldocuments/frus1969-76v27/> (last accessed 19 September 2016).

US Department of State, *Foreign Relations of the United States (FRUS) 1969–1976: Vol. XXXVIII, Part 1, Foundations of Foreign Policy, 1973–1976*, <https://history.state.gov/historicaldocuments/frus1969-76v38p1> (last accessed 10 January 2016).

US Department of State, *Foreign Relations of the United States (FRUS) 1969–1976: Vol. E-4, Documents on Iran and Iraq 1969–1972*, <https://history.state.gov/historicaldocuments/frus1969-76ve04/> (last accessed 20 October 2015).

US Department of State, *A Report on the International Control of Atomic Energy*, <http://www.nuclearfiles.org/menu/key-issues/nuclear-weapons/history/cold-war/strategy/acheson-lilienthal-report_1946-03-06.html> (last accessed 10 June 2017).

US Department of State, *Victims of Trafficking and Violence Protection Act of 2000*, <https://www.state.gov/j/tip/laws/61124.htm> (last accessed 13 May 2015).

US Department of the Treasury, *Comprehensive Iran Sanctions, Accountability and Divestment Act of 2010*, Public Law 111–195, 1 July 2010, <https://www.treasury.gov/resource-center/sanctions/documents/hr2194.pdf> (last accessed 1 July 2017).

US Director of National Intelligence, 'Iran: Nuclear intentions and capabilities', 3 December 2007, <https://www.dni.gov/files/documents/Newsroom/Press%20Releases/2007%20Press%20Releases/20071203_release.pdf> (last accessed 23 October 2015).

US Energy Research and Development Administration (ERDA), *Iran: Atomic Energy Programme* (Washington DC: US Government Printing Office, 1976).

US National Archives and Records Administration, College Park, Maryland, *Department of State General Records, Record Group 59, Central Foreign Policy Files 1973–1976 (Department of State, RG59)*.

US President, 'Background briefing by senior administration officials on Iranian nuclear facility', 25 September 2009, <http://www.whitehouse.gov/the-press-office/background-briefing-senior-administration-officials-iranian-nuclear-facility> (last accessed 7 May 2016).

US President, *Public Papers of the Presidents of the United States (PPPUS)*, <http://presidency.proxied.lsit.ucsb.edu/ws/> (last accessed 5 September 2017).

Vance, C., *Hard Choices: Critical Years in America's Foreign Policy* (New York: Simon & Schuster, 1983).

Iran

Ahmadinejad, M., 'Address by H. E. Dr. Mahmood Ahmadinejad, President of the Islamic Republic of Iran before the Sixtieth Session of the United Nations General Assembly', New York, 17 September 2005,

<http://www.un.org/webcast/ga/60/statements/iran050917eng.pdf> (last accessed 14 May 2015).

Alam, A., *The Shah and I: The Confidential Diary of Iran's Royal Court 1969–1977*, ed. and trans. Alinaghi Alikhani and Nicholas Vincent (New York: St. Martin's Press, 1991).

Constitution of the Islamic Republic of Iran, *IranOnline.com*, <http://www.iranonline.com/iran/iran-info/government/constitution.html> (last accessed 20 September 2017).

Etemad, A., 'Interview', *Foundation for Iranian Studies Oral History Collection* (*FISOHC*), November 1982, <http://fis-iran.org/en/content/etemad-akbar> (last accessed 15 November 2017).

Khamenei, A., 'Leader's address to Air Force servicemen', 7 February 2006, <http://english.khamenei.ir/news/66/Leader-s-Address-to-Air-Force-Servicemen> (last accessed 5 December 2016).

Khamenei, A., 'Leader's address to Education Ministry officials', 17 July 2002, <http://english.khamenei.ir/news/159/Leader-s-Address-to-Education-Ministry-Officials> (last accessed 12 May 2016).

Khamenei, A., 'Leader's address to students at Shahid Beheshti University', 28 May 2003, <http://english.khamenei.ir/news/125/Leader-s-Address-to-Students-at-Shahid-Beheshti-University> (last accessed 15 May 2016).

Khamenei, A., 'Leader's address to university professors and elite academics', 13 October 2005, <http://english.khamenei.ir/news/75/Leader-s-Address-to-University-Professors-and-Elite-Academics> (last accessed 17 June 2017).

Khamenei, A., 'Leader's Friday prayer address', 19 June 2009, <http://english.khamenei.ir/news/1159/Leader-s-Friday-Prayer-Address> (last accessed 5 December 2016).

Khamenei, A., 'Leader's speech in meeting with commanders of Islamic Revolutionary Guards Corps', 17 September 2013, <http://english.khamenei.ir/news/1827/Leader-s-Speech-in-Meeting-with-Commanders-of-Islamic-Revolutionary> (last accessed 20 September 2017).

Khamenei, A., 'Leader's speech in meeting with officials of University Jihad', 21 June 2004, <http://english.khamenei.ir/news/2077/Leader-s-Speech-in-Meeting-with-Officials-of-University-Jihad> (last accessed 15 May 2016).

Khamenei, A., 'Leader's speech to residents of Qom', 8 January 2005, <http://english.khamenei.ir/news/101/Leader-s-Speech-to-Residents-of-Qom-Province> (last accessed 15 May 2016).

Khamenei, A., 'OSC Khamenei's speech replying to Obama', *Informed Comment*, 23 March 2009, <http://www.juancole.com/2009/03/osc-khameneis-speech-replying-to-obama.html> (last accessed 5 December 2016).

Khamenei, A., 'Supreme Leader's speech to government officials', 24 July 2012, <http://english.khamenei.ir//index.php?option=com_content&task=view&id=1655&Itemid=4> (last accessed 5 December 2016).

Khatami, M., *Islam, Liberty and Development* (Binghamton, NY: Institute of Global Cultural Studies, 1998).

Mousavian, S. H., *The Iranian Nuclear Crisis: A Memoir* (Washington DC: Carnegie Endowment for International Peace, 2012).

Rouhani, H., 'Beyond the challenges facing Iran and the IAEA concerning the nuclear dossier', *Rahbord*, 30 September 2005, <http://lewis.armscontrolwonk.com/files/2012/08/Rahbord.pdf> (last accessed, 5 August 2017).

Rouhani, H., 'Statement by H. E. Dr. Hassan Rouhani President of the Islamic Republic of Iran at the Sixty-eight Session of the United Nations General Assembly', 24 September 2013, <https://gadebate.un.org/sites/default/files/gastatements/68/IR_en.pdf> (last accessed 5 May 2016).

Other

AIPAC, *Comprehensive US Sanctions Against Iran: A Plan for Action* (Washington DC: AIPAC, 1995).

BBC, *BBC Monitoring*.

BBC, *Summary of World Broadcasts (SWB)*.

Chrétien, J., 'Remarks by Prime Minister Jean Chrétien', G8 Summit, Halifax, 17 June 1995, <http://www.g8.utoronto.ca/summit/1995halifax/chretien.html> (last accessed 20 June 2015).

Commission of the European Communities, 'Conclusions of the Presidency', European Council in Edinburgh, 11–12 December 1992.

Council of the European Union, 'Council decision of 26 July 2010 concerning restrictive measures against Iran and repealing Common Position 2007/140/CFSP', 26 July 2010, <http://eur-lex.europa.eu/legal-content/EN/TXT/?uri=celex:32010D0413> (last accessed 12 July 2016).

Council of the European Union, 'Council Implementing Regulation (EU) No. 54/2012 of 23 January 2012 implementing Regulation (EU) No. 961/2010 on restrictive measures against Iran', <http://eur-lex.europa.

eu/legal-content/EN/TXT/?uri=uriserv:OJ.L_.2012.019.01.0001.01.
ENG&toc=OJ:L:2012:019:TOC> (last accessed 12 July 2016).

Council of the European Union, 'Protecting against the effects of the extra-territorial application of legislation adopted by a third country and actions based thereon or resulting therefrom', Council Regulation (EC) No. 2271/96, 22 November 1996, <http://eur-lex.europa.eu/legal-content/EN/TXT/?uri=CELEX%3A31996R2271> (last accessed 10 November 2015).

ElBaradei, M., *The Age of Deception: Nuclear Diplomacy in Treacherous Times* (London: Bloomsbury, 2007).

ElBaradei, M., 'Nuclear non-proliferation: Global security in a rapidly changing world', Speech delivered at the Carnegie International Non-Proliferation Conference, Washington DC, 21 June 2004, <http://www.iaea.org/newscenter/statements/2004/ebsp2004n004.html> (last accessed 20 June 2016).

IAEA, 'Agreement and relevant provisions of Security Council Resolutions 1737 (2006) and 1747 (2007) in the Islamic Republic of Iran', Report of the Director General, GOV/2008/4, 22 February 2008, <http://www.iaea.org/Publications/Documents/Board/2008/gov2008-4.pdf> (last accessed 17 June 2016).

IAEA, 'Communication dated 26 November 2004 received from the permanent representatives of France, Germany, the Islamic Republic of Iran and the United Kingdom concerning the agreement signed in Paris on 15 November 2004', INFCIRC/637, 26 November 2004, <http://www.iaea.org/Publications/Documents/Infcircs/2004/infcirc637.pdf> (last accessed 15 June 2016).

IAEA, 'Communication dated 1 August 2005 received from the Permanent Mission of the Islamic Republic of Iran to the Agency', INFCIRC/648, 1 August 2005, <https://www.iaea.org/sites/default/files/publications/documents/infcircs/2005/infcirc648.pdf> (last accessed 15 January 2017).

IAEA, 'Communication dated 8 August 2005 received from the Resident Representatives of France, Germany and the United Kingdom to the Agency', INFCIRC/651, 8 August 2005, <http://www.isisnuclearian.org/assets/pdf/infcirc651_Aug82005.pdf> (last accessed 10 November 2016).

IAEA, 'Communication dated 27 August 2007 from the Permanent Mission of the Islamic Republic of Iran to the Agency concerning the text of the "Understandings of the Islamic Republic of Iran and the IAEA on the Modalities of Resolution of the Outstanding Issues"',

INFCIRC/711, 27 August 2017, <http://www.iaea.org/Publications/Documents/Infcircs/2007/infcirc711.pdf> (last accessed 10 June 2016).

IAEA, 'Implementation of the NPT safeguards agreement in the Islamic Republic of Iran', Report by the Director General, GOV/2003/40, 6 June 2003, <http://www.iaea.org/Publications/Documents/Board/2003/gov2003-40.pdf> (last accessed 1 June 2016).

IAEA, 'Implementation of the NPT safeguards agreement in the Islamic Republic of Iran', Report by the Director General, GOV/2003/63, 26 August 2003, <https://www.iaea.org/sites/default/files/gov2003-63.pdf> (last accessed 1 June 2016).

IAEA, 'Implementation of the NPT safeguards agreement in the Islamic Republic of Iran', Report by the Director-General, GOV/2003/75, 10 November 2003, <http://www.iaea.org/Publications/Documents/Board/2003/gov2003-75.pdf> (last accessed 1 June 2016).

IAEA, 'Implementation of the NPT safeguards agreement in the Islamic Republic of Iran', Report by the Director General, GOV/2004/11, 24 February 2004, <https://www.iaea.org/sites/default/files/gov2004-11.pdf> (last accessed 5 June 2016).

IAEA, 'Implementation of the NPT safeguards agreement in the Islamic Republic of Iran', Report by the Director General, GOV/2004/83, 15 November 2004, <https://www.iaea.org/sites/default/files/gov2004-83.pdf> (last accessed 13 June 2016).

IAEA, 'Implementation of the NPT safeguards agreement in the Islamic Republic of Iran', Report by the Director General, GOV/2010/62, 23 November 2010, <https://www.iaea.org/sites/default/files/gov2010-62.pdf> (last accessed 12 August 2016).

IAEA, 'Implementation of the NPT safeguards agreement in the Islamic Republic of Iran', Resolution adopted by the Board on 12 September 2003, GOV/2003/69, <https://www.iaea.org/sites/default/files/gov2003-69.pdf> (last accessed 1 June 2016).

IAEA, 'Implementation of the NPT safeguards agreement in the Islamic Republic of Iran', Resolution adopted by the Board on 26 November 2003, GOV/2003/81, <http://www.iaea.org/Publications/Documents/Board/2003/gov2003-81.pdf> (last accessed 5 June 2016).

IAEA, 'Implementation of the NPT safeguards agreement in the Islamic Republic of Iran', Resolution adopted by the Board on 18 June 2004, GOV/2004/49, <http://www.iaea.org/Publications/Documents/Board/2004/gov2004-49.pdf> (last accessed 10 June 2016).

IAEA, 'Implementation of the NPT safeguards agreement in the Islamic Republic of Iran', Resolution adopted by the Board on 18 September

2004, GOV/2004/79, <https://www.iaea.org/sites/default/files/gov2004-79.pdf> (last accessed 10 May 2017).

IAEA, 'Implementation of the NPT safeguards agreement in the Islamic Republic of Iran', Resolution adopted on 24 September 2005, GOV/2005/77, 24 September 2005, <https://www.iaea.org/sites/default/files/gov2005-77.pdf> (last accessed 12 February 2017).

IAEA, 'Implementation of the NPT safeguards agreement in the Islamic Republic of Iran', Resolution adopted on 4 February 2006, GOV/2006/14, 4 February 2006, <http://archiv.osn.cz/soubory/gov2006-14.pdf> (last accessed 5 July 2016).

IAEA, 'Implementation of the NPT safeguards agreement and relevant provisions of Security Council resolutions 1737 (2006) and 1747 (2007) in the Islamic Republic of Iran', Report by the Director General, GOV/2007/58, 15 November 2007, <http://www.iaea.org/Publications/Documents/Board/2007/gov2007-58.pdf> (last accessed 15 June 2016).

IAEA, 'Implementation of the NPT safeguards agreement and relevant provisions of Security Council resolutions 1737 (2006), 1747 (2007), 1803 (2008) and 1835 (2008) in the Islamic Republic of Iran', Report by the Director General, GOV/2009/8, 19 February 2009, <https://www.iaea.org/sites/default/files/gov2009-8.pdf> (last accessed 20 June 2016).

IAEA, 'Implementation of the NPT safeguards agreement and relevant provisions of Security Council resolutions 1737 (2006), 1747 (2007), 1803 (2008) and 1835 (2008) in the Islamic Republic of Iran', Report by the Director General, GOV/2009/35, 5 June 2009, <https://www.iaea.org/sites/default/files/gov2009-35.pdf> (last accessed 10 July 2016).

IAEA, 'Implementation of the NPT safeguards agreement and relevant provisions of Security Council resolutions 1737 (2006), 1747 (2007), 1803 (2008) and 1835 (2008) in the Islamic Republic of Iran', Report by the Director General, GOV/2009/74, 16 November 2009, <https://www.iaea.org/sites/default/files/gov2009-74.pdf> (last accessed 10 August 2016).

IAEA, 'Implementation of the NPT safeguards agreement and relevant provisions of Security Council resolutions 1737 (2006), 1747 (2007), 1803 (2008) and 1835 (2008) in the Islamic Republic of Iran', Report by the Director General, GOV/2010/10, 18 February 2010, <https://www.iaea.org/sites/default/files/gov2010-10.pdf> (last accessed 12 August 2016).

IAEA, 'Implementation of the NPT safeguards agreement and relevant provisions of Security Council resolutions in the Islamic Republic of Iran', Report by the Director General, GOV/2011/29, 24 May 2010, <https://www.iaea.org/sites/default/files/gov2011-29.pdf> (last accessed 12 August 2016).

IAEA, 'Implementation of the NPT safeguards agreement and relevant provisions of Security Council resolutions in the Islamic Republic of Iran', Report by the Director General, GOV/2011/65, 8 November 2011, <https://www.iaea.org/sites/default/files/gov2011-65.pdf> (last accessed 12 August 2016).

IAEA, 'Implementation of the NPT safeguards agreement and relevant provisions of Security Council resolutions in the Islamic Republic of Iran', Report by the Director General, GOV/2013/56, 14 November 2012, <https://www.iaea.org/sites/default/files/gov2013-56.pdf> (last accessed 12 August 2016).

IAEA, 'The Statute of the IAEA', <https://www.iaea.org/about/statute> (last accessed 24 May 2015).

IAEA, 'The structure and content of agreements between the agency and states required in connection with the Treaty on the Non-Proliferation of Nuclear Weapons', INFCIRC/153 (corrected), <https://www.iaea.org/sites/default/files/publications/documents/infcircs/1972/infcirc153.pdf> (last accessed 24 May 2015).

IAEA, 'The text of the agreement between Iran and the agency for the application of safeguards in connection with the Treaty on the Non-Proliferation of Nuclear Weapons', INF/CIRC 214, 13 December 1974, <http://www.iaea.org/Publications/Documents/Infcircs/Others/infcirc214.pdf> (last accessed 24 May 2015).

IAEA, 'Transcript of Director General's remarks to media following talks on supplying nuclear fuel to Iran', 21 October 2009, <https://www.iaea.org/newscenter/mediaadvisories/transcript-of-director-generals-remarks-to-media-following-talks-on-supplying-nuclear-fuel-to-iran> (last accessed 10 August 2016).

'Joint Comprehensive Plan of Action', Vienna, 14 July 2015, <http://www.eeas.europa.eu/archives/docs/statements-eeas/docs/iran_agreement/iran_joint-comprehensive-plan-of-action_en.pdf> (last accessed 20 May 2017).

'Joint Plan of Action', Geneva, 24 November 2013, <https://www.armscontrol.org/files/Iran_P5_1_Nuclear_Deal_131123.pdf> (last accessed 20 May 2017).

P5+1, 'Elements of a proposal to Iran', 1 June 2006, <http://www.consilium.europa.eu/uedocs/cms_data/docs/pressdata/en/reports/90569.pdf> (last accessed 12 February 2014).

United Nations, 'Agreement for cooperation between the government of the United States of America and the government of Iran concerning civil use of atomic energy', 5 March 1957, <http://ahlambauer.files.wordpress.com/2012/04/19570305_iran-usa_nuclear-co-operation.pdf> (last accessed 10 March 2014).

United Nations, 'Letter dated 11 October 2006 from the Permanent Representative of the Islamic Republic of Iran to the United Nations addressed to the Secretary-General', 12 October 2006, <http://www.securitycouncilreport.org/atf/cf/%7B65BFCF9B-6D27-4E9C-8CD3-CF6E4FF96FF9%7D/Iran%20S2006806.pdf> (last accessed 5 March 2015).

United Nations, 'Treaty on the Non-Proliferation of Nuclear Weapons', <http://www.un.org/disarmament/WMD/Nuclear/NPTtext.shtml> (last accessed 4 September 2015).

United Nations, UN Security Council Resolution 612, 9 May 1988, <http://unscr.com/en/resolutions/doc/612> (last accessed 10 October 2016).

United Nations, UN Security Council Resolution 1696, 31 July 2006, <https://www.iaea.org/sites/default/files/unsc_res1696-2006.pdf> (last accessed 10 December 2016).

United Nations, UN Security Council Resolution 1737, 23 December 2006, <https://www.iaea.org/sites/default/files/unsc_res1737-2006.pdf> last accessed 2 April 2015).

United Nations, UN Security Council Resolution 1747, 24 March 2007, <https://www.un.org/press/en/2007/sc8980.doc.htm> (last accessed 3 November 2016).

United Nations, UN Security Council Resolution 1803, 3 March 2008, <http://www.un.org/ga/search/view_doc.asp?symbol=S/RES/1803%282008%29> (last accessed 18 October 2015).

United Nations, UN Security Council Resolution 1835, 27 September 2008, <https://www.iaea.org/sites/default/files/unsc_res1835-2008.pdf> last accessed 10 October 2015).

United Nations, UN Security Council Resolution 1929, 9 June 2010, <https://www.iaea.org/sites/default/files/unsc_res1929-2010.pdf> last accessed 10 October 2015).

United Nations Office on Drugs and Crime, *World Drug Report 2006*, <https://www.unodc.org/pdf/WDR_2006/wdr2006_volume1.pdf> (last accessed 5 May 2016).

World Bank, 'Inflation, consumer prices (annual %)', 2013, <http://data.worldbank.org/indicator/FP.CPI.TOTL.ZG?locations=IR&year_high_desc=false> (last accessed 5 May 2016).

Secondary Sources

Abbas, M., 'Decision making in Iran's foreign policy: A heuristic approach', *Journal of Social Affairs*, 19 (73) (2002), pp. 39–59.

Abdo, G., 'Iran's internal struggles: An overview', in H. D. Sokolski and P. Clawson (eds), *Checking Iran's Nuclear Ambitions* (Washington DC: Strategic Studies Institute, 2004), pp. 39–60.

Abraham, I., *The Making of the Indian Atomic Bomb: Science, Secrecy and the Postcolonial State* (New York: St. Martin's Press, 1988).

Abrahamian, E., *Iran Between Two Revolutions* (Princeton, NJ: Princeton University Press, 1982).

Abrahamian, E., *Khomeinism* (London: I.B. Tauris, 1983).

Abulof, U., 'Nuclear diversion theory and legitimacy crisis: The case of Iran', *Politics and Policy*, 41 (5) (2013), pp. 690–722.

Acronym Institute, *Disarmament Diplomacy*, 22 (January 1988), <http://www.acronym.org.uk/old/archive/22sear.htm> (last accessed 20 July 2015).

Adib-Moghaddam, A., *Iran in World Politics: The Question of the Islamic Republic* (London: Hurst, 2007).

Adib-Moghaddam, A., 'The pluralistic momentum in Iran and the future of the reform movement', *Third World Quarterly*, 27 (4) (2006), pp. 665–74.

Afkhami, G. R., *The Life and Times of the Shah* (London: University of California Press, 2009).

Albrecht, H. and O. Schlumberger, '"Waiting for Godot": Regime change without democratization in the Middle East', *International Political Science Review*, 25 (4) (2004), pp. 371–93.

Albright, D., P. Brannan, M. Gorwitz and A. Stricker, 'ISIS Analysis of IAEA Iran Safeguards Report: Part II, Iran's Work and Foreign Assistance on a Multipoint Initiation System for a Nuclear Weapon', Institute for Science and International Security, ISIS Report, 13 November 2011, <http://isisonline.org/uploads/isisreports/documents/Foreign_Assistance_Multipoint_Initiation_System_14Nov2011.pdf> (last accessed 20 September 2015).

Alfoneh, A. 'President Rouhani's cabinet: MOIS vs. IRGC?', Foundation for Defense of Democracies, 7 August 2013, available at <http://www.defenddemocracy.org/media-hit/president-rouhanis-cabinet-mois-vs-irgc/> (last accessed 5 July 2015).

Alfoneh, A., 'The war over the war', American Enterprise Institute, 30 September 2010, <http://www.aei.org/publication/the-war-over-the-war/> (last accessed 5 May 2014).

Alikhani, H., *Sanctioning Iran: Anatomy of a Failed Policy* (London: I.B. Tauris, 2000).

Alvandi, R., 'Nixon, Kissinger and the Shah: The origins of Iranian primacy in the Persian Gulf', *Diplomatic History*, 36 (2) (2012), pp. 337–45.

Alvandi, R., *Nixon, Kissinger and the Shah: The United States and Iran in the Cold War* (Oxford: Oxford University Press, 2014).

Ansari, A. M., 'Civilizational identity and foreign policy: The case of Iran', in B. Shaffer (ed.), *The Limits of Culture: Islam and Foreign Policy* (Cambridge: Belfer Center for Science and International Affairs, 2006), pp. 241–62.

Ansari, A. M., *Confronting Iran: The Failure of American Policy* (New York: Basic Books, 2007).

Ansari, A. M., *Crisis of Authority: Iran's 2009 Presidential Elections* (London: Royal Institute of International Affairs, 2009).

Ansari, A. M., *Iran, Islam and Democracy* (London: Chatham House, 2000).

Ansari, A. M., 'Iranian foreign policy under Khatami: Reform and reintegration', in A. Mohammadi and A. Ehteshami (eds), *Iran and Eurasia* (Reading: Ithaca Press, 2000), pp. 35–58.

Ansari, A. M., *Modern Iran Since 1921: The Pahlavis and After* (London: Pearson, 2003).

Arbatov, A. G., 'The inexorable momentum of escalation', in P. M. Cronin (ed.), *Double Trouble: Iran and North Korea as Challenges to International Security* (Westport, CT: Praeger, 2008), pp. 63–76.

Arms Control Association, 'History of official proposals on the Iran nuclear issue', <http://www.armscontrol.org/factsheets/Iran_Nuclear_Proposals> (last accessed 20 September 2017).

Axworthy, M., *Revolutionary Iran: A History of the Islamic Republic* (London: Penguin, 2014).

Bar, S., 'Iran: Cultural values, self images and negotiation behavior', Institute for Policy and Strategy (The Interdisciplinary Center, Herzliya Lauder School of Government, 2004), <http://www.herzliyaconference.org/_uploads/2614iranianself.pdf> (last accessed 15 October 2015).

Barzegar K., 'A middle way, best solution to nuclear crisis', *Iran Review*, 1 November 2009, <http://www.iranreview.org/content/view/4974/36/> (last accessed 10 May 2016).

Bastani, H., 'How powerful is Rouhani in the Islamic Republic?', Research Paper, Royal Institute of International Affairs, November 2014, <https://www.chathamhouse.org/sites/files/chathamhouse/field/

field_document/20141124RouhaniislamicRepublicBastani.pdf> (last accessed 10 December 2016).

Bayandor, D., *Iran and the CIA: The Fall of Mosaddeq Revisited* (New York: Palgrave, 2010).

Bechoefer, B. G., 'Negotiating the statute of the International Atomic Energy Agency', *International Organization*, 13 (1) (1959), pp. 45–6.

Beeman, W. O., *The 'Great Satan' vs the 'Mad Mullahs': How the United States and Iran Demonize Each Other* (Westport, CT: Praeger, 2005).

Behravesh, M., 'Iran's reform movement: The enduring relevance of an alternative discourse', *Digest of Middle East Studies*, 23 (2) (2014), pp. 262–78.

Behrooz, M., 'Trends in the foreign policy of the Islamic Republic of Iran, 1979–1988', in N. Keddie (ed.), *Neither East Nor West: Iran, the Soviet Union and the United States* (New Haven, CT: Yale University Press, 1990), pp. 13–35.

Betts, R. K., 'Paranoids, pygmies, pariahs and non-proliferation', *Foreign Policy*, 27 (1977), pp. 157–83.

Bill, J. A., *The Eagle and the Lion: The Tragedy of American–Iranian Relations* (New Haven, CT: Yale University Press, 1988).

Blanche, E., 'Rouhani vs Revolutionary Guards', *The Middle East*, 452 (March 2014), pp. 12–16.

Blight, J. G., j. M. Lang, H. Banai, M. Byrne and J. Tirman, *Becoming Enemies: US–Iran Relations and the Iran–Iraq War, 1979–1988* (New York: Rowman & Littlefield, 2012).

Bostock, F. and G. Jones, *Planning and Power in Iran: Ebtehaj and Economic Development Under the Shah* (London: Frank Cass, 1989).

Brady, D. and M. Fiorina, 'Congress in the era of the permanent campaign', in N. J Ornstein and T. E. Mann (eds), *The Permanent Campaign and Its Future* (Washington DC: American Enterprise Institute, 2000).

Braun, C. and C. F. Chyba, 'Proliferation rings: New challenges to the non-proliferation regime', *International Security*, 29 (2) (2004), pp. 5–49.

Brown, W. L., 'Presidential leadership and US nonproliferation policy', *Presidential Studies Quarterly*, 24 (2/3) (1994), pp. 563–75.

Brzezinski, Z., B. Scowcroft and R. W. Murphy, *Differentiated Containment, US Policy Toward Iran and Iraq: Report of an Independent Task Force* (New York: Council on Foreign Relations, 1997).

Buchta, W., *Who Rules Iran?: The Structure of Power in the Islamic Republic* (Washington DC: Washington Institute for Near East Policy/ Konrad Adenauer Stiftung, 2000).

Burr, W., 'A scheme of "control": The United States and the origins of the Nuclear Suppliers Group, 1974–1976', *International History Review*, 36 (2) (2014), pp. 252–76.

Byman, D. L., S. Chubin, A. Ehteshami and J. Green, *Iran's Security Policy in the Post-Revolutionary Era* (Santa Monica: Rand Corporation, 2001).

Cahn, A. H., 'Determinants of the nuclear option: The case of Iran', in O. Marwah and A. Schulz (eds), *Nuclear Proliferation and the Near-Nuclear Countries* (Cambridge: Ballinger, 1975), pp. 185–204.

Chubin, S., 'Iran's strategic predicament', *Middle East Journal*, 54 (1) (2000), pp. 10–24.

Chubin, S., 'Understanding Iran's nuclear ambitions', in P. M. Cronin (ed.), *Double Trouble: Iran and North Korea as Challenges to International Security* (Westport, CT: Praeger, 2002), pp. 47–62.

Chubin, S., 'Whither Iran? Reform, domestic politics and national security', Adelphi Paper 342 (London: International Institute for Strategic Studies, 2002).

Chubin, S. and C. Tripp, *Iran and Iraq at War* (London: I.B. Tauris, 1988).

Chubin, S. and S. Zabih, *The Foreign Relations of Iran: A Developing State in a Zone of Great-Power Conflict* (Berkeley: University of California Press, 1974).

Collins, S. and S. McCombie, 'Stuxnet: The emergence of a new cyber weapon and its implications', *Journal of Policing, Intelligence and Counter Terrorism*, 7 (1) (2012), pp. 80–91.

Cordesman, A. H., *Iran's Military Forces in Transition: Conventional Threats and Weapons of Mass Destruction* (London: Praeger, 1999).

Corera, G., *Shopping for Bombs: Nuclear Proliferation, Global Insecurity and the Rise and Fall of the A. Q. Khan Network* (London: Hurst, 2006).

Cottam, R. W., *Iran and the United States: A Cold War Case Study* (Pittsburgh: University of Pennsylvania Press, 1988).

Crail, P., 'Iran presented with revamped incentives', *Arms Control Today*, 7 August 2008, <https://www.armscontrol.org/act/2008_07-08/IranIncentives> (last accessed 10 January 2017).

Crail, P., 'Iran responds to call for talks', *Arms Control Today*, 2 March 2012, <https://www.armscontrol.org/print/5232> (last accessed 10 November 2016).

Crail, P., 'Iranian response to LEU fuel deal unclear', *Arms Control Today*, 5 November 2009, <http://www.armscontrol.org/act/2009_11/Iran> (last accessed 10 January 2017).

Crail, P., 'World powers invite Iran to nuclear talks', *Arms Control Today*, 8 May 2009, <https://www.armscontrol.org/act/2009_5/world_powers_invite_Iran> (last accessed 20 June 2016).

Crist, D., *The Twilight War: The Secret History of America's Thirty-Year Conflict with Iran* (London: Penguin, 2012).

Cronin, P. M. (ed.), *Double Trouble: Iran and North Korea as Challenges to International Security* (Westport, CT: Praeger, 2008).

Davenport, K., 'Iran, P5+1 hold "substantive" talks', *Arms Control Today*, 4 November 2013, <https://www.armscontrol.org/act/2013_11/Iran-P5-1-Hold-Substantive-Talks> (last accessed 27 October 2015).

Debs, A. and N. P. Monteiro, *Nuclear Politics: The Strategic Causes of Proliferation* (Cambridge: Cambridge University Press, 2016).

Diamond, H., 'US sanctions Russian entities for Iranian dealings', *Arms Control Today*, 1 January 1999, <https://www.armscontrol.org/print/445> (last accessed 5 October 2014).

Duss, M., 'Dershowitz: Iran is suicide nation', *ThinkProgress*, <http://thinkprogress.org/security/2010/03/23/175966/dershowitz-iran-is-a-suicide-nation/> (last accessed 24 October 2016).

Ehteshami, A., *After Khomeini* (London: Routledge, 1995).

Ehteshami, A., 'The foreign policy of Iran', in R. Hinnebusch and A. Ehteshami (eds), *The Foreign Policies of Middle East States* (Boulder, CO: Lynne Rienner, 2002), pp. 283–310.

Ehteshami, A., 'The politics of economic restructuring in post-Khomeini Iran', CMEIS Occasional Paper No. 50 (Durham: University of Durham, Centre for Middle Eastern and Islamic Studies, 1995).

Ellis, H. B., 'Carter would shift toward solar energy', *Christian Science Monitor*, 25 May 1976.

Elson, S. B. and A. Nader, *What Do Iranians Think? A Survey of Attitudes on the United States, the Nuclear Program, and the Economy* (Santa Monica: Rand Corporation, 2011), <http://www.rand.org/content/dam/rand/pubs/ technical_reports/2011/RAND_TR910.pdf> (last accessed 5 November 2015).

Farhi, F., 'Ahmadinejad's nuclear folly', *Middle East Report*, 252 (Fall 2009), <http://www.merip.org/mer/mer252/farhi.html> (last accessed 31 July 2015).

Farhi, F., 'To sign or not to sign? Iran's evolving domestic debate on nuclear options', in G. Kemp (ed.), *Iran's Bomb: American and Iranian Perspectives* (Washington DC: Nixon Center, 2004), pp. 32–50.

Fayez, A. Q., 'The Iranian presidential elections: Internal challenges, critical issues', Al Jazeera Center for Studies, 24 March 2013, <http://studies.aljazeera.net/ResourceGallery/media/Documents/2013/3/24/2013324103038205734Iranian%20Presidential%20Elections.pdf> (last accessed 22 June 2015).

Fisher, L., *Congressional Abdication on War and Spending* (College Station: Texas A&M University Press, 2000).

Fitzpatrick, M., 'Is Iran's nuclear capability inevitable?', in P. Cronin (ed.), *Double Trouble: Iran and North Korea as Challenges to International Security* (Westport, CT: Praeger, 2008), pp. 23–46.

Forden, G., 'Iranian warhead evolution', *Arms Control Wonk*, 9 June 2010, <http://forden.armscontrolwonk.com/archive/2763/iranian-warhead-evolution> (last accessed 5 May 2017).

Frankel, B., 'The brooding shadow: Systemic incentives and nuclear weapons proliferation', *Security Studies*, 2 (3/4) (1993), pp. 37–78.

Frey, K., 'Of nuclear myths and nuclear taboos', *Peace Review: A Journal of Social Justice*, 18 (3) (2006), pp. 341–7.

Frey, K., *Nuclear Weapons as Symbols: The Role of Norms in Nuclear Policy Making* (Barcelona: Institut Barcelona d'Estudis Internacionals, 2006).

Friedman, A., *Spider's Web: Bush, Saddam, Thatcher and the Decade of Deceit* (London: Faber & Faber, 1993).

Fuller, G. E., *The 'Center of the Universe': The Geopolitics of Iran* (Oxford: Westview Press, 1991).

Gal, Y. and Y. Minzili, 'The economic impact of international sanctions on Iran', Working Paper, Herzliya International Conference, 6–9 February 2011, <http://www.herzliyaconference.org/eng/_Uploads/dbsAttachedFiles/YitzhakGalYairMinzili.pdf> (last accessed 1 May 2015).

Ganji, A., 'The latter-day Sultan', *Foreign Affairs*, 87 (6) (2008), pp. 45–65.

Garver, J. W., *China and Iran: Ancient Partners in a Post-Imperial World* (Seattle: University of Washington Press, 2007).

Gasiorowski, M. J., 'The 1953 coup d'etat in Iran', *International Journal of Middle East Studies*, 19 (3) (1987), pp. 261–86.

Gasiorowski, M. J. and M. Byrne (eds), *Mohammad Mosaddeq and the 1953 Coup in Iran* (New York: Syracuse University Press, 2004).

Ghafouri, M., 'China's policy in the Persian Gulf', *Middle East Policy*, 16 (2) (2009), pp. 80–92.

Gheissari, A. and V. Nasr, 'The conservative consolidation in Iran', *Survival*, 47 (2) (2005), pp. 175–90.

Ghobazadeh, N. and R. L. Zubadaih, 'Islamic reformation discourses: Popular sovereignty and religious secularization in Iran', *Democratization*, 19 (2) (2011), pp. 334–51.

Hadiyan, N., 'Iran–US Cold War', *Iran Review*, 6 June 2010, <http://www.iranreview.org/content/Documents/Iran_%E2%80%93_US_Cold_War.htm> (last accessed 1 May 2015).

Haghighatjoo, F., 'Factional positions on the nuclear issue in the context of Iranian domestic politics', *Iran Analysis Quarterly*, 3 (2006), pp. 2–10.

Hamblin, J. D., 'The nuclearization of Iran in the seventies', *Diplomatic History*, 38 (5) (2014), pp. 1114–35.

Harold, S. and A. Nader, 'China and Iran: Economic, political and military relations', RAND Center for Middle East Public Policy, 2012, <http://www.rand.org/content/dam/rand/pubs/occasional_papers/2012/RAND_OP351.pdf> (last accessed 29 September 2015).

Herzog, M., 'Iranian public opinion on the nuclear programme: A potential asset for the international community', Washington Institute for Near East Policy, *Policy Focus*, 56 (June 2006), <https://www.washingtoninstitute.org/uploads/Documents/pubs/PolicyFocus56.pdf> (last accessed 27 November 2014).

Hess, G. R., 'The Iranian crisis of 1945–46 and the Cold War', *Political Science Quarterly*, 89 (1) (1974), pp. 117–46.

Heydemann, S. and R. Leenders (eds), *Middle East Authoritarianisms: Governance, Contestation and Regime Resilience in Syria and Iran* (Stanford, CA: Stanford University Press, 2012).

Hibbs, M., 'US in 1983 stopped IAEA from helping Iran make UF6', *Nuclear Fuel*, 28 (16) (4 August 2003), p. 12.

Homayounvash, M., *Iran and the Nuclear Question: History and Evolutionary Trajectory* (London: Routledge, 2017).

Hooglund, E., 'Decoding Ahmadinejad's rhetoric on Israel', in E. Hooglund and L. Steinberg (eds), *Navigating Contemporary Iran: Challenging Economic, Social and Political Perceptions* (London: Routledge, 2012), pp. 197–214.

Hossein, S., 'Iran's assertiveness in maintaining its peaceful nuclear technology', *Perceptions*, X (3) (2005), pp. 127–51.

Hunter, S. T., *Iran After Khomeini* (New York: Praeger, 1992).

Hunter, S. T., *Iran's Foreign Policy in the Post-Soviet Era: Resisting the New International Order* (New York: Praeger, 2012).

Hurst, S., 'Myths of neoconservatism: George W. Bush's "neo-conservative" foreign policy revisited', *International Politics*, 42 (1) (2005), pp. 75–96.

Husbands, J. L., 'The prestige states', in W. H. Kincade and C. Bertram (eds), *Nuclear Proliferation in the 1980s* (New York: St. Martin's Press, 1982), pp. 112–38.

Hymans, J. E. C., *The Psychology of Nuclear Proliferation: Identity, Emotions, and Foreign Policy* (Cambridge: Cambridge University Press, 2006).

Hymans, J. E. C., 'Theories of nuclear proliferation: The state of the field', *The Nonproliferation Review*, 13 (3) (2006), pp. 455–65.

Indyk, M., 'Back to the bazaar', *Foreign Affairs*, 81 (1) (2002), pp. 75–88.

Ingram, P., 'Preliminary analysis of EU-3/EU proposal to Iran', *BASIC Notes*, 11 August 2005, <http://www.basicint.org/pubs/Notes/BN050811-IranEU.htm> (last accessed 13 October 2014).

International Institute for Strategic Studies, *Nuclear Black Markets: Pakistan, A. Q. Khan and the Rise of the Proliferation Networks: A Net Assessment* (London: International Institute for Strategic Studies, 2007).

Jahanbegloo, R., 'The two sovereignties and the legitimacy crisis in Iran', *Constellations*, 17 (1) (2010), pp. 22–30.

Jentleson, B. W., *With Friends Like These: Reagan, Bush and Saddam, 1982–1990* (New York: W. W. Norton, 1994).

Kamrava, M., 'Iranian national security debates: Factionalism and lost opportunities', *Middle East Policy*, 14 (2) (2007), pp. 84–100.

Karanjia, R. K., *The Mind of a Monarch* (London: Allen & Unwin, 1977).

Katzman, K., 'Iran sanctions', *CRS Report for Congress* (Washington DC: Congressional Research Service, 2 December 2011).

Katzman, K., 'Iran sanctions', *CRS Report for Congress* (Washington DC: Congressional Research Service, 24 July 2017).

Katzman, K., 'The Iran Sanctions Act (ISA)', *CRS Report for Congress* (Washington DC: Congressional Research Service, 12 October 2007).

Katzman, K., P. K. Kerr and M. B. D. Nikitin, 'Iran: Interim nuclear agreement and talks on a comprehensive accord', *CRS Report for Congress* (Washington DC: Congressional Research Service, 26 November 2014).

Kaussler, B., *Iran's Nuclear Diplomacy: Power Politics and Conflict Resolution* (London: Routledge, 2014).

Kaye, D. D. and F. M. Wehrey, 'A nuclear Iran: The reactions of neighbours', *Survival*, 49 (2) (2007), pp. 111–28.

Kazemzadeh, M., 'Ahmadinejad's foreign policy', *Comparative Studies of South Asia, Africa and the Middle East*, 27 (2007), pp. 423–49.

Kazemzadeh, M., 'Foreign policy decision making in Iran and the nuclear program', *Comparative Strategy*, 36 (3) (2017), pp. 198–214.

Keddie, N., *Modern Iran: Roots and Results of Revolution* (New Haven, CT: Yale University Press, 2003).

Keeley, J. F., 'Legitimacy, capability, effectiveness and the future of the NPT', in D. B. Dewitt (ed.), *Nuclear Non-Proliferation and Global Security* (London: Croom Helm, 1987), pp. 25–47.

Kerr, P., 'The Atomic Energy Organization of Iran: What role?', *Arms Control Today*, 1 October 2014, <https://www.armscontrol.org/ACT/2014_10/Feature/The-Atomic-Energy-Organization-of-Iran-What-Role> (last accessed 3 November 2016).

Keynoush, B., 'Iran after Ahmadinejad', *Survival*, 54 (3) (2012), pp. 127–46.

Khalaji, M., 'Apocalyptic politics: On the rationality of Iranian policy', Washington Institute for Near East Policy, *Policy Focus*, 79 (2008), <http://www.washingtoninstitute.org/policy-analysis/view/apocalyptic-politics-on-the-rationality-of-iranian-policy> (last accessed 5 June 2016).

Khan, S., *Iran and Nuclear Weapons: Protracted Conflict and Proliferation* (London: Routledge, 2010).

Khosrokhavar, F., 'The Green Movement', in E. Hooglund and L. Steinberg (eds), *Navigating Contemporary Iran: Challenging Economic, Social and Political Perceptions* (London: Routledge, 2012), pp. 169–84.

King, A., 'The vulnerable American politician', *British Journal of Political Science*, 27 (1) (1997), pp. 1–22.

Klare, M., *Rogue States and Nuclear Outlaws: America's Search for a New Foreign Policy* (New York: Hill and Wang, 1996).

Kuniholm, B. R., *The Origins of the Cold War in the Near East: Great Power Conflict and Diplomacy in Iran, Turkey, and Greece*, 2nd edn (Princeton, NJ: Princeton University Press, 2014).

Lieberman, R. C., 'The Israel lobby and American politics', *Perspectives on Politics*, 7 (2) (2009), pp. 235–57.

Little, D., *American Orientalism: The United States and the Middle East Since 1945* (Chapel Hill: University of North Carolina Press, 2008).

Lotfian, S., 'Nuclear policy and international relations', in H. Katouzian, and H. Shahidi (eds), *Iran in the 21st Century: Politics, Economics and Conflict* (London: Routledge, 2008), pp. 158–80.

McGlinchey, S. and J. K. Choksy, 'Iran's nuclear ambitions under the Shah and ayatollahs', *Small Wars Journal*, 8 (3) (2012), <http://

smallwarsjournal.com/jrnl/art/iran%E2%80%99s-nuclear-ambi-tions-under-the-shah-and-ayatollahs> (last accessed 20 March 2014).

Mahdi, A. A., 'The student movement in the Islamic Republic of Iran', *Journal of Iranian Research and Analysis*, 15 (2) (1999), pp. 5–32.

Maloney, S., 'Why "Iran style" sanctions worked against Tehran (and why they might not succeed with Moscow)', *Markaz*, 21 March 2014, <https://www.brookings.edu/blog/markaz/2014/03/21/why-iran-style-sanctions-worked-against-tehran-and-why-they-might-not-succeed-with-moscow/> (last accessed 12 October 2017).

Matin-Asgari, A., 'Abdolkarim Sorush and the secularisation of Islamic thought in Iran', *Iranian Studies*, 30 (1/2) (1997), pp. 95–115.

Mattair, T. R., 'The United States and Iran: Diplomacy, sanctions and war', *Middle East Policy*, 17 (2) (2010), pp. 52–61.

Mattis, A., 'Oil sheik-down: Saudi Arabia's struggle to contain Iran', *Harvard International Review*, 32 (1) (Spring 2010), pp. 10–11.

Mayhew, D. R., *Congress: The Electoral Connection*, 2nd edn (New Haven, CT: Yale University Press, 2004).

Mearshimer, J. and S. Walt, *The Israel Lobby and US Foreign Policy* (New York: Penguin, 2008).

Menashri, D., 'Iran', in A. Ayalon, B. Newson and H. Shaked (eds), *Middle East Contemporary Survey (MECS)*, XIV (1992), pp. 350–78.

Milani, A., 'US policy and the future of democracy in Iran', *Washington Quarterly*, 28 (3) (2005), pp. 41–56.

Miles, A., *The United States and the Rogue State Doctrine* (London: Routledge, 2012).

Mirbagheri, F., 'Narrowing the gap or camouflaging the divide: An analysis of Mohammad Khatami's "Dialogue of Civilisations"', *British Journal of Middle Eastern Studies*, 34 (3) (2007), pp. 305–16.

Mohseni, E., N. Gallagher and C. Clay Ramsay, 'Iranian attitudes on nuclear negotiations', Center for International and Security Studies at Maryland, September 2014, <http://cissm.umd.edu/publications/ira-nian-attitudes-nuclear-negotiations> (last accessed 20 October 2016).

Mohseni, E., N. Gallagher, N. and C. Clay Ramsay, 'Iranian public opinion on the nuclear negotiations', Center for International and Security Studies at Maryland, June 2015, <http://www.cissm.umd.edu/sites/default/files/UTCPOR-CISSM-PA%20final%20report%20060221 5.pdf> (last accessed 20 October 2016).

Monthly Review Online, 'Iranian public on current issues', 28 September 2009, <https://mronline.org/2009/09/28/iranian-public-on-current-issues/> (last accessed 10 June 2015).

Moses, R. L., *Freeing the Hostages: Reexamining U.S.–Iranian Negotiations and Soviet Policy, 1979–1981* (Pittsburgh: University of Pittsburgh Press, 1996).

Moslem, M., *Factional Politics in Post-Khomeini Iran* (New York: Syracuse University Press, 2002).

Mossavar-Rahmani, B., 'Iran', in J. E. Katz and O. S. Marwah (eds), *Nuclear Power in Developing Countries* (Lexington: DC Heath, 1982), pp. 201–19.

Mossavar-Rahmani, B., 'Iran's nuclear power programme revisited', *Energy Policy*, 8 (3) (1980), pp. 189–202.

Mottaki, M., 'Iran's foreign policy under President Ahmadinejad', *Discourse: An Iranian Quarterly*, 8 (2) (2006), pp. 1–15.

Mukhatzhanova, G., 'Pride and prejudice: Understanding Iran's nuclear program', in W. C. Potter and G. Mukhatzhanova (eds), *Forecasting Nuclear Proliferation in the 21st Century: A Comparative Perspective, Volume 2* (Stanford, CA: Stanford University Press, 2010).

Nader, A., 'Influencing Iran's decisions on the nuclear program', in E. Solingen (ed.), *Sanctions, Statecraft and Nuclear Proliferation* (Cambridge: Cambridge University Press, 2012), pp. 211–31.

Nafisi, R., 'Iran's Majlis elections: The hidden dynamics', *Open Democracy*, 11 April 2008, <https://www.opendemocracy.net/article/democracy_power/democracy_iran/majlis_elections_signals_of_change> (last accessed 12 October 2015).

Ogilvie-White, T., 'Is there a theory of nuclear proliferation? An analysis of the contemporary debate', *The Nonproliferation Review*, 4 (1) (Fall 1996), pp. 43–60.

Omelicheva, M. Y., 'Russia's foreign policy toward Iran: A critical geopolitics perspective', *Journal of Balkan and Near Eastern Studies*, 14 (3) (2012), pp. 331–44.

Ornstein, N. and T. Mann, 'When Congress checks out', *Foreign Affairs*, 85 (6) (2006), pp. 67–82.

Parsi, T., *Losing an Enemy: Obama, Iran and the Triumph of Diplomacy* (New Haven, CT: Yale University Press, 2017).

Parsi, T., *A Single Roll of the Dice: Obama's Diplomacy with Iran* (New Haven, CT: Yale University Press, 2012).

Parsi, T., *Treacherous Alliance: The Secret Dealings of Israel, Iran, and the United States* (New Haven, CT: Yale University Press, 2008).

Patrikarikos, D., *Nuclear Iran: The Birth of an Atomic State* (London: I.B. Tauris, 2012).

Patterson, R., 'EU sanctions on Iran: The European political context', *Middle East Policy*, 20 (1) (2013), <http://mepc.org/eu-sanctions-iran-european-political-context> (last accessed 20 June 2017).

Peres, S., *The New Middle East* (New York: Henry Holt, 1993).

Peterson, P. E., 'The President's dominance in foreign policy-making', *Political Science Quarterly*, 109 (2) (1994), pp. 215–34.

Picco, G., *Man Without a Gun* (New York: Random House, 1999).

Pickering, T. R., T. Parsi, K. T. Katzman and T. R. Mattair, 'The United States and Iran: What are the prospects for engagement?', *Middle East Policy*, 16 (2) (2009), pp. 1–25.

Pillar, P. R., 'The role of villain: Iran and US foreign policy', *Political Science Quarterly*, 108 (2) (2013), pp. 211–31.

Pollack, K., *The Persian Puzzle: The Conflict Between Iran and America* (New York: Random House, 2005).

PollingReport, 'Iran', *PollingReport.com*, 2015, <http://www.pollingreport.com/iran.htm> (last accessed 27 November 2017).

Poneman, D., *Nuclear Power in the Developing World* (London: Allen & Unwin, 1982).

Porter, G., *Manufactured Crisis: The Untold Story of the Iran Nuclear Scare* (Charlottesville, VA: Just World Books, 2014).

Potter, W. and G. Mukhatzhanova (eds), *Forecasting Nuclear Proliferation in the 21st Century: The Role of Theory, Volume 1* (Stanford, CA: Stanford University Press, 2010).

Putnam, R. W., 'Diplomacy and domestic politics: The logic of two-level games', *International Organization*, 42 (3) (1988), pp. 427–60.

Ramazani, R. K., 'Iran's foreign policy: Both north and south', *Middle East Journal*, 46 (3) (1992), pp. 393–412.

Reiss, M., *Without the Bomb: The Politics of Nuclear Proliferation* (New York: Columbia University Press, 1988).

Rezaei, F., *Iran's Nuclear Program* (London: Palgrave, 2017).

Rice, C., 'Promoting the national interest', *Foreign Affairs*, 79 (1) (2000), pp. 45–62.

Rice, M., 'Clinton signs "Iran Nonproliferation Act"', *Arms Control Today*, 1 April 2000, <http://www.armscontrol.org/act/2000_04/irnap00> (last accessed 20 December 2015).

Rudalevige, A., 'The contemporary presidency, the decline and resurgence and decline (and resurgence?) of Congress: Charting a new imperial presidency', *Presidential Studies Quarterly*, 36 (3) (2006), pp. 506–24.

Sadjadpour, K., 'Reading Khameini: The worldview of Iran's most powerful leader', Carnegie Endowment for International Peace, 2009,

<http://carnegieendowment.org/files/sadjadpour_iran_final2.pdf> (last accessed 29 October 2016).

Saeidi, A. A., 'Iran's para-statal organizations (bonyads)', Middle East Institute, 29 January 2009, <http://www.mei.edu/content/iranian-para-governmental-organizations-bonyads> (last accessed 28 November 2017).

Sagan, S., 'Why do states build nuclear weapons? Three models in search of a bomb', *International Security*, 21 (3) (1996–7), pp. 54–86.

Saltzman, I. Z., 'Not so "special relationship"? US–Israel relations during Barack Obama's presidency', *Israel Studies*, 22 (1) (2017), pp. 50–75.

Samii, A. W., 'Afghan war without Iran almost impossible', *RFE/RL Reports*, 4 (36) (24 September 2001), <https://www.rferl.org/a/1342847.html> (last accessed 20 May 2014).

Seliktar, O., *Navigating Iran: From Carter to Obama* (London: Palgrave, 2012).

Shaker, M. I., 'The third NPT review conference: Issues and prospects', in D. B. Dewitt (ed.), *Nuclear Non-Proliferation and Global Security* (London: Croom Helm, 1987), pp. 3–12.

Sherrill, C. W., 'Why Hassan Rouhani won Iran's 2013 presidential election', *Middle East Policy*, 21 (2) (2014), <http://www.mepc.org/why-hassan-rouhani-won-irans-2013-presidential-election> (last accessed 10 February 2017).

Siddiqi, A., 'Khatami and the search for reform in Iran', *Stanford Journal of International Relations*, 6 (1) (2005), <https://web.stanford.edu/group/sjir/6.1.04_siddiqi.html> (last accessed 10 May 2016).

Sinclair, B., *Party Wars: Polarization and the Politics of National Policy-Making* (Norman: University of Oklahoma Press, 2006).

Singh, S. and C. R. Way, 'The correlates of nuclear proliferation: A quantitative test', *Journal of Conflict Resolution*, 48 (6) (2004), pp. 859–85.

Slackman, M., 'Iran rebuffs US on talks', *International Herald Tribune*, 2 June 2006, pp. 1, 8.

Slavin, B., *Bitter Friends, Bosom Enemies: Iran, the US and the Twisted Path to Confrontation* (New York: St. Martin's Press, 2007).

Smelz, D. and C. Kafura, 'Americans favor deal with Iran: Willing to back with force', Chicago Council on Global Affairs, 6 July 2015, <http://www.thechicagocouncil.org/publication/americans-favor-deal-iran-willing-back-force> (last accessed 15 August 2016).

Smith, G. C. and C. Cobban, 'A blind eye to nuclear proliferation', *Foreign Affairs*, 68 (3) (1989), pp. 53–70.

Snyder, G. H. and P. Diesing, *Conflict Among Nations: Bargaining, Decision-Making and System Structure in International Crises* (Princeton, NJ: Princeton University Press, 1978).

Solingen, E. W., *Nuclear Logics: Contrasting Paths in East Asia and the Middle East* (Princeton, NJ: Princeton University Press, 2007).

Souresrafil, B., *Khomeini and Israel* (London: Researchers, 1988).

Spear, J., 'Organizing for international counterproliferation: NATO and US nonproliferation policy', in J. E. Nolan, B. I. Finel and B. D. Finlay (eds), *Ultimate Security: Combating Weapons of Mass Destruction* (New York: Century Foundation Press, 2003), pp. 203–28.

Stein, A. M., 'Kilowatts or Kilotons: Turkey and Iran's Nuclear Choices', PhD Dissertation (King's College London, 2015).

Suchman, M. C. and D. P. Eyre, 'Military procurement as rational myth: Notes on the social construction of weapons proliferation', *Sociological Forum*, 7 (1) (1992), pp. 137–61.

Suskind, R., *The One Percent Doctrine: Deep Inside America's Pursuit of Its Enemies* (New York: Simon & Schuster, 2007).

Tabatabai, A., 'Reading the nuclear politics in Tehran', *Arms Control Today*, 2 September 2015, <https://www.armscontrol.org/ACT/2015_09/Feature/Reading-the-Nuclear-Politics-in-Tehran> (last accessed 12 September 2016).

Tahtinen, D. R., *Arms in the Persian Gulf* (Washington DC: American Enterprise Institute, 1974).

Takeyh, R., 'Iran's municipal elections: A turning point for the reform movement', Policywatch 721, Washington Institute, 6 March 2003, <http://www.washingtoninstitute.org/policy-analysis/view/irans-municipal-elections-a-turning-point-for-the-reform-movement> (last accessed 20 May 2015).

Talwar, P., 'Iran in the balance', *Foreign Affairs*, 80 (4) (2001), pp. 58–71.

Tannenwald, N., 'Stigmatizing the bomb: Origins of the nuclear taboo', *International Security*, 29 (4) (2005), pp. 5–49.

Terror Free Tomorrow, 'Ahmadinejad front runner in upcoming presidential elections; Iranians continue to back compromise and better relations with US and West. Results of a new nationwide public opinion survey of Iran before the June 12 2009 Presidential election', May 2009, <http://www.terrorfreetomorrow.org/upimagestft/TFT%20Iran%20Survey%20Report%200609.pdf> (last accessed 29 November 2017).

Theriault, S. M., *Party Polarization in Congress* (Cambridge, MA: Harvard University Press, 2008).

Thompson, S., 'The NPT regime, present and future global security: An American view', in D. B. Dewitt (ed.), *Nuclear Non-Proliferation and Global Security* (London: Croom Helm, 1987), pp. 151–64.

Thouin, C., 'Under a cloud of uncertainty: Aipac's 2010 policy conference, 21–23 March', *Journal of Palestinian Studies*, 39 (4) (2010), pp. 60–71.

Timmerman, K., *The Death Lobby: How the West Armed Iraq* (Boston: Houghton Mifflin, 1993).

Ulrichsen, K. C., 'Internal and external security in the Arab Gulf states', *Middle East Policy*, 16 (2) (2009), pp. 39–58.

Voice of the People, 'Assessing the Iran Deal', 2015, <http://vop.org/wp-content/uploads/2015/08/Assessing_the_Iran_Deal_Quaire.pdf> (last accessed 20 November 2016).

Walker, J. S., 'Nuclear power and non-proliferation: The controversy over nuclear exports, 1974–1980', *Diplomatic History*, 25 (2) (2001), pp. 215–49.

Warnaar, M., *Iranian Foreign Policy During Ahmadinejad: Ideology and Actions* (New York: Palgrave Macmillan, 2013).

Weissmann, S. R., *A Culture of Deference: Congress' Failure of Leadership in Foreign Policy* (New York: Basic Books, 1996).

Woodward, B., *Bush at War* (London: Pocket Books, 2003).

Woodward, B., *Plan of Attack* (London: Pocket Books, 2004).

WorldPublicOpinion.org, 'Iranian public on current issues', 28 September 2009, <https://mronline.org/2009/09/28/iranian-public-on-current-issues/> (last accessed 12 February 2017).

WorldPublicOpinion.org, 'Iranian public opinion on governance, nuclear weapons and relations with the United States', 27 August 2008, <http://www.worldpublicopinion.org/pipa/articles/brmiddleeastnafricara/527.php> (last accessed 12 February 2017).

WorldPublicOpinion.org, 'Iranian public ready to deal on nuclear weapons, but not uranium enrichment', 19 July 2007, <http://worldpublicopinion.net/iranian-public-ready-to-deal-on-nuclear-weapons-but-not-uranium-enrichment/> (last accessed 5 May 2017).

WorldPublicOpinion.org, 'Iran nuclear deal backed by large majority of Americans', 3 March 2015, <http://worldpublicopinion.org/pipa/articles/2015/iran_0315.php> (last accessed 10 March 2017).

WorldPublicOpinion.org, 'Two thirds of Iranians ready to preclude developing nuclear weapons in exchange for lifting sanctions', 22 September 2009, <http://www.worldpublicopinion.org/pipa/articles/brmiddleeastnafricara/640.php?lb=brme&pnt=640&nid=&id=> (last accessed 12 February 2017).

Wright, R., 'Iran's new revolution', *Foreign Affairs*, 79 (1) (2000), pp. 133–45.

Zaccara, L., 'The 2009 Iranian presidential election in comparative perspective', in A. Ehteshami and R. Molavi (eds), *Iran and the International System* (Abingdon: Routledge, 2012), pp. 192–206.

Zahedi, D., *The Iranian Revolution Then and Now: Indicators of Regime Instability* (New York: Westview Press, 2000).

Zogby Research Services, 'Iranian attitudes (2013)', September 2013, <http://www.zogbyresearchservices.com/iranian-attitudes-2013/> (last accessed 10 May 2017).

Index